Praise for *The Leader Reader*

In *The Leader Reader*, Griffiths, Lowrey and Cassar have assembled the narratives of school leaders from around the globe, who share their experiences and musings about the lived emotions and mindset of their life's work. Leadership for them is more than just a set of intellectual constructs or formal titles, it is a way of being and doing that evolves over the course of a career, or even from one day to the next. From a professor trying to explain and understand his role in mediating the construction of knowledge with his students to an educator who builds her community through end of school year cart wheels and chocolate cake, these readings position leadership as an experience that brings out our humanity and service to one another. For those entering the field or those with many years under their belt, this book is a wonderful reminder as to why we choose this path.

–Stephen L. Jacobson,
Distinguished Professor at University at Buffalo Graduate School.

Written by leaders for leaders, *The Leader Reader: Narratives of Experience* contains a wide variety of accessible essays that consistently engage and inform. Organized across 9 major domains, the book is excellent resource for practitioners to gain insight from fellow leaders. Attentive to context and individual lived experiences, the essays in the book nevertheless highlight challenges, successes, and dilemmas that are enduring and transferable. The essays in the book come across as wonderful "guest speakers", as each author offers an intimate portrait of their personal commitments and practices in ways that come to reveal practice in theory and theory in practice.

–William R. Black, University of South Florida, Co-Editor,
Journal of Cases in Educational Leadership and Co-Editor,
Research and Theory in Educational Administration Book Series.

Urgently needed in uncertain times, *The Leader Reader: Narratives of Experience* provides on-the-ground, well-rounded, compelling narratives from multiple perspectives. An essential collection addressing the vivid complexities of the profession. The Leader Reader is eloquently energizing in ways that humanizes leadership.

–Tanetha J. Grosland, University of South Florida, Co-Editor,
Feminism and Intersectionality in Academia and Associate Editor,
Journal of Cases in Educational Leadership.

Serving as an administrator for more than 25 years in public education, the investment in reading *The Leader Reader* added exceptional value and practical ideas to better navigate my role as a principal. It is through learning from others that we best define ourselves and hone our craft as effective school leaders. This book nurtures this transformation in a fashion that is not only easily accessible but also pragmatic.

–Janet Slaney, Principal, Central Okanagan Public Schools,
British Columbia, Canada.

I am one of those people who did not necessarily plan to be a leader, but through a series of opportunities, I learnt that I could lead people and have an impact on the culture of an organization. I suggest that the short and powerful stories in this book, *The Leader Reader*, provide a great resource that will inspire you to consider your own personal philosophy and model of leadership, either before you take on a leadership role or while you are in a leadership position. The stories are like having conversations with leaders in many different settings, so the reader is treated to a breadth of learning that is unusual in books about leadership. Many stories are honest and practical with key messages about listening, learning, reflecting and very importantly, sharing the daily challenges and celebrations of being a leader in different organizations. I am sure that the stories in *The Leader Reader* will motivate leaders to share their own experiences with colleagues as they see the power of mentoring and supporting aspiring and experienced leaders.

–Prof Suzanne Carrington Assistant Dean Research,
Faculty of Education, Queensland University of Technology Australia.

The Leader Reader serves as an excellent resource for both practicing school leaders (in the PreK-12 educational setting) and professors who are charged with preparing aspiring school leaders (in the Higher Education setting). The content undoubtedly helps continue to bridge the gap between theory and practice, further ensuring that our school leaders are truly scholar-practitioners.

–Dr. Denver J. Fowler, Program Coordinator and Assistant Professor of
Educational Leadership and Policy Studies, California State University,
Sacramento and author of The 21st Century School Leader:
Leading Schools in Today's World.

The Leader Reader
Narratives of Experiences

Edited by Darrin Griffiths, Scott Lowrey, and Mark Cassar
Book design by Jim Bisakowski – www.bookdesign.ca
Copy Editing: Ruth Bradley-St-Cyr (Bradley-St-Cyr & Associates, ruthbear@sympatico.ca)

ISBN 978-0-9959782-0-1

Word & Deed Publishing Incorporated
1860 Appleby Line, Suite #778
Burlington, Ontario, Canada, L7L 7H7
(Toll Free) 1-866-601-1213

Visit our website at
www.wordanddeedpublishing.com

This edited collection of vignettes from the field represents a different take on leadership – one that is novel for many of us. The narratives in The Leader Reader do not emerge with the supposedly validated and reliable truths of formal research – truths that may or may not help those educators who work in the trenches – but with wisdom acquired through the day to day struggles of educators and leaders. This wisdom will resonate with practitioners of leadership to help them not just get through the day, but to make a meaningful impact on the students, teachers and communities that they serve. This is a must read for all leaders and those who aspire to lead.

–James Ryan, Professor of Educational Leadership,
OISE/University of Toronto.

There is no holy grail in educational leadership. There is no one style or strategy that works equally well for all leaders across all contexts. Each successful leader has a holy grail of his/her own. *The Leader Reader* provides a carefully curated collection of inspiring and mesmerizing stories from education leaders about their own holy grails, making a tour de force for all who wants to create their own leadership holy grail in education.

–Yong Zhao, Foundation
Distinguished Professor, University of Kansas

A wonderful collection of insightful essays. The stories from the various authors help us truly understand how and why leadership can make a real meaningful difference.
–Denis Simon, Executive Vice Chancellor, Duke Kunshan University,
Jiangsu Province, China

Once upon a time…. the simple power of a story has entranced us through the ages. From the campfire to the classroom, stories transport us to times of yore, journey to faraway places and ignite our sense of wonder. They teach us valuable lessons and offer nuggets of wisdom for our own work and life. The "Narratives of Experience" shared in this book offer rich insights into the experiences of school leaders around the globe and powerful lessons to consider. As we read their stories, I encourage you to think about your own. Scott, Darrin and Mark- thank you for your leadership and vision with such a wonderful collection of voices and experiences
–Susan E. Murray, Senior Consultant, Clearpath Leadership

Dedication

Darrin – To my mom, Marilyn Griffiths. She has been my biggest supporter throughout my life and I appreciate her love, patience, and support. She is an amazing person who has made me a better person and given me so much.

Scott – To the memories of Sheila Lowrey and my neighbours on Fielding Crescent for their kindness towards my family in times of both extreme joy and profound sorrow. To the memory of Gary Comack for his friendship, quiet tenacity, humility, and wisdom. Good people, young hearts, kind souls, and life-long friends, even now from a distance.

Mark - To my father Joe, who introduced me to the love of reading; my mother, Melina, who always demonstrated love for her family; my brother Andy, who always looks out for his big brother; my daughters, Andreana and Victoria, who remind me of how lucky I am to be the dad of two amazing girls. And to Jennifer, my soul mate: because of you I survive all.

Table of Contents

PART I
Leadership Mindset:
Metacognition, Empathy, and Innovation—7

PART II
Content of Character: Principles of Principals—57

PART III
Children's Champions: Equity and Inclusion—97

PART IV
Practices of Community: It Takes a Village—161

PART V
Leading in a Culture of Status Quo—189

PART VIII
Journey's Beginning, Journey's End—315

PART VII
To Thine Own Self and Community Be True:
Leadership Lessons and Reflections—249

PART VI
Only the Beginning: Moving Along Transactional, Transformational, and Transformative Continuum—225

PART IX
In the Leader's Office: Do You Have a Minute?—381

Foreword

I've always loved stories and their telling. I was blessed to land a teaching fellowship at The Branson School in 1993. John Roosevelt Boettiger mentored me and I learned lots from him that year. What has stuck with me over the years is his elective course, *Tales of Wisdom*. I saw John gently guide students each day. I observed them exploring weighty topics using classic works as springboards.

By the time I relocated to Nashville to teach, I knew I wanted to create my own version of *Tales of Wisdom*. It didn't take me long to choose the name "Echoes of an Era". It was a nod to the canon of classic works I used including *The Book of Job* and *The Epic of Gilgamesh*. It was also an homage to *Echoes of an Era*, a 1982 jazz album featuring one of my favorite vocalists, Chaka Khan.

I told my students that "Echoes of an Era" was an exploration of the self, the Hero's Journey in life, and one's connectedness to others. More than anything, "Echoes" posed questions like these:

- Who am I?
- What is the meaning of this life?
- Where am I in this journey called "life"?
- When I lose my way, how do I find it again?
- How do I connect with that which is expressed in stories?
- How do others influence my journey?
- How have they responded to ordeals in life? How will I?

The stories in *The Leader Reader* explore many of the questions I asked my "Echoes" students. Each leader offers us a nuanced response. Some leaders' stories explore the intersectionality of race, gender, and socio-economic status. Other stories examine educational equity and culturally courageous leadership as coined by John Robert Browne II:

> Culturally courageous leadership in a nutshell means leadership that challenges any personal and organizational practices that are anti-democratic and discriminatory at best, and racist at worse. It is taking calculated data-based risks to confront and change norms that do not support cultural democracy.

Some stories share lessons from geese and the ways in which leaders lead leaders. Other stories envision students as change agents.

As leaders, we make and manage countless decisions each day. Our simple and complex decisions impact children and adults and may shape generations. Although educational leadership centers on students, the work itself is often lonely. *The Leader Reader* is an invaluable portable mentor overflowing with stories for just-in-time help. From global learning and gaslighting to internalized subordination and internalized dominance and from self-care and mentorship to equity and moral purpose, the stories in this nine-part book "start with the heart" to build our individual and collective capacity.

In my book, *Bought Wisdom: Tales of Living and Learning,* I make a call for stories:

> What we need now are stories; stories of people. The truth is that more stories of living and learning need to be told today:
>
> Stories of principle; principal stories.
>
> Stories of the playground, the classroom, the library.
>
> Stories of our schools, our homes, our faith communities, our courtrooms, our boardrooms.
>
> Stories of the White House. Presidential stories.
>
> Stories of courage, of death, of life.
>
> Stories of faith, hope, and love. Teaching stories.
>
> Stories of the setting sun and of the rising moon.
>
> Stories of triumph and challenge.

Stories of healing and renewal and wisdom.

Stories of the oneness and importance of all living things.

These are our stories; what are yours?

Tony Lamair Burks II, Ed.D. Atlanta, Georgia

Dr. Tony Lamair Burks II is the Chief Learning Officer of LEADright where he coaches and trains leaders for excellence. He helps leaders with thinking differently, taking different actions, and having different breakthrough results. His career is defined by his culturally courageous leadership in support of today's learners as leaders and innovators.

Dr. Burks was the founding principal of The Early College at Guilford, North Carolina's first early college high school and one of the first such schools of its type in the world. A fellow of the British-American Project, he has earned three Fulbright awards. Dr. Burks was highlighted by NU·tribe Magazine as One of Six HBCU Grads You Should Know and by the Boys and Girls Club of Hawk-Houston with its Alveta Hawk Lifetime Achievement Award.

Dr. Burks is the author of three books, a contributor to two, and he is among five educators featured in Walking the Equity Talk: A Guide for Culturally Courageous Leadership in School Communities. His newest book, Bought Wisdom: Tales of Living and Learning, is an interactive leadership memoir.

Dr. Burks earned a BA in Philosophy with Honors from Morehouse College, an MEd in Educational Leadership from Trevecca Nazarene University, and a Doctorate in Educational Leadership from The University of North Carolina Greensboro.

Introduction
Narratives, Memories, and Roads More, or Less Travelled

Our book begins with a question. What was your leadership moment? And from that leadership moment emerges a leadership narrative often followed up with an individual or collective realization that the leadership trajectory represents an ongoing, iterative process of learning leadership lessons from leadership moments. We learn leadership by engaging in leadership and by sharing our narratives. We connect leadership theories to leadership practices while becoming scholar-practitioners and, over time, we develop an extensive inventory and repertoire of leadership skills, knowledge, traits, and principles. Leadership moments become the leadership lens through which we engage with colleagues, community, and organizations; they demonstrate a deep commitment to bigger picture, longer term, and greater good goals. Leadership is a process whether we are engaging with others formally or informally. Someone very influential in my career trajectory often framed leadership as a paradoxical combination of energy, tenacity, joy, and passion. The superbly crafted insights from contributors to this volume demonstrate these attributes in abundance.

Our previous collaboration, *The Principal Reader: Narratives of Experience,* spoke directly to practicing and aspiring school leaders. Written by school leaders for school leaders, it shared lived experiences from throughout North America and how they addressed these opportunities and challenges, among others:

- Putting leadership theories into practice
- Confronting the status quo
- Improving instructional practice
- Leading through adversity
- Building relationships and developing people
- Nurturing reconciliation through education
- Fostering equity and inclusion
- Championing social justice
- Managing change and organizational improvement
- Maintaining work–life balance (heavily predicated on humour)

Our current collaboration, *The Leader Reader: Narratives of Experience,* seeks to extend this conversation to the lived experiences of school-based and system-based educational leaders, including those who serve in international settings. Contributors were asked to write a short chapter about a leadership experience based on a specific theme. Though truthfully, each narrative represents a highly nuanced, complex web of multiple themes, for the purposes of this volume, nine themes emerged.

Theme 1—Leadership Mindset: Metacognition, Empathy, and Innovation

Successful leaders, whether formal or informal, demonstrate a leadership mindset with words and actions. They empower others, either individually or collectively, to achieve more than originally thought possible. They are deeply self-aware of who they are as leaders, and eternally grateful for those who placed faith in them at all stages of their leadership trajectory. Important dimensions of the leadership mindset include metacognition, empathy, and innovation. A leadership mindset is also aligned with moral purpose, reinforcing commitment to the bigger picture, the longer term, and the greater good.

Theme 2—Content of Character: Principles of Principals

Leadership occurs in context. Leaders are judged by the content of their character. Character is a complex concept with as many operational definitions as there are individuals who have ever been asked,

"What is character?" Character defines leaders. Character represents alignment between espoused theories and theories in action, between word and deed. When asked who they admire most, leaders describe someone influential in their decision to pursue leadership. The specific definitions of character may differ, but they often have dimensions of the pursuit of the bigger picture, the longer term, and the greater good.

Theme 3—Children's Champions: Equity and Inclusion

Children need champions. Not heroic champions, but champions who exemplify a paradoxical combination of humility and tenacity. All children can succeed when someone steps forward with unconditional belief in their unlimited potential. All children have special needs; however, some children have incredibly complex special needs. All children have a voice, including the quite ones. Principles of equity and inclusion underpin our leadership narratives. Culturally responsive pedagogy is an expectation, not a wish or a look-for. Not all challenges to equity and inclusion are visible so leaders must remain vigilant in making the invisible visible. The wisdom of a small child is sometimes greater than that of our biggest thinkers. Good leaders listen to children and to community.

Theme 4—Practices of Community: It Takes a Village

Leaders cultivate and establish relational trust with the communities that they serve. Trust cannot be assumed; it must be earned, never taken for granted. Communities have voice, agency, legacy, and stories that must be respected and honoured. It takes a whole village to raise a whole child. Multidisciplinary teams are mobilized to meet the needs of children and communities in crisis. We hear narratives of annual celebrations and of how leaders mobilize community in support of children, community, or colleagues in pain. Our school communities become our families.

Theme 5—Leading in a Culture of Status Quo

Organizational improvement planning is the work of leadership. Leaders understand that organizations exist within organizations. Leaders are frequently called upon to lead change in an organization that appears to embrace the status quo. Evidence-informed leadership requires an assessment of *cannot* versus *will not* when faced with the opportunity of leading against the status quo. When faced with several options, maintaining the status quo is typically not in the leader's repertoire, mindset, or moral purpose. By definition, maintaining the status quo does not represent change. Exemplary leaders shift the paradigm from leading in a culture of status quo to leading in a culture of change by courageously taking a road more, or less, travelled.

Theme 6—Only the Beginning: Moving Along the Transactional, Transformational, and Transformative Continuum

Leaders thrive along the scholar-practitioner continuum. Theory informs practice and practice informs theory, representing a reciprocal process. Over time, leaders develop an increasingly nuanced, integrated, sophisticated understanding of leadership theory, often combined with theories from other fields of study. The choice of leadership theory aligns with leadership context and worldview. Readers of this volume are encouraged to stop and reflect upon those leadership theories and theorists who have been most influential to their leadership thinking. Leaders recognize when the decisions of individuals and organizations are incongruent with espoused theories. The wisdom shared in narratives represents a lifetime of navigating dynamic and fluid leadership contexts.

Theme 7—To Thine Own Self and Community Be True: Leadership Lessons and Reflections

One defining characteristic of outstanding leaders is their deep commitment to ongoing learning, and their deeper commitment to the ongoing capacity-building of others. Individual and collective reflective practice and capacity-building is the work of leadership, whether formal or informal, individual or collaborative. Leadership development wisdom informs life-embedded practice and vice versa. People may not remember the content, but they will remember the level of engagement and enthusiasm within the sessions, and they will remember those who took the time to first learn about them as people first, and then as leaders in training second.

Theme 8—Journey's Beginning, Journey's End

Every leader experiences a unique career trajectory. Some careers follow a predetermined plan while others show elements of serendipity. Leaders experience multiple successes and disappointments over the course of a career. As retirement approaches, the internal dialogue shifts to the next life stage while still honouring a deep commitment to those individuals and communities who have placed their faith in your leadership. Leaders learn to lead from the front, the side, and from behind depending on the context or situation. The leadership journey never really ends; rather, it leads to life's next journey.

Theme 9—In the Leader's Office: Do You Have a Minute?

Every leader engages in leadership opportunities through a unique combination of leadership theories integrated with life experiences. At the end of the day, middle of the day, and beginning of the day, supervisors and those being supervised rely on leaders to provide guidance and direction, balancing emotional intelligence and political intelligence. Certain questions have the potential to give an adult pause. Fortunately, leaders embrace opportunities to exercise their leadership prowess. Unfortunately, there is one question that all leaders fear, especially at the end of a stressful week or when they are in a rush to call it a day and head home: "Do you have a minute?" Narratives of leadership represent all emotions. Our book ends with the types of stories that you cannot wait to share with colleagues, partners, and friends.

This volume represents the narratives and memories of highly accomplished leaders who generously share significant leadership moments encountered along roads more, or less travelled. We learn leadership by engaging in leadership. We deepen our understanding of leadership by sharing our narratives. Sharing enables us to engage in individual and collective reflective practice. One author described this volume as a leadership conference within a book. We hope that you, the reader, will join our community and add your own wisdom to the conversation.

Scott Lowrey, EdD

PART I

Leadership Mindset: Metacognition, Empathy, and Innovation

Successful leaders, whether formal or informal, demonstrate a leadership mindset with words and actions. They empower others, either individually or collectively, to achieve more than those others originally thought possible. They are deeply self-aware of who they are as leaders, and eternally grateful for those who placed faith in their leadership at each stage of their leadership trajectory. Success is an expectation. Deficit-based thinking is not an option. Challenges are framed as opportunities with innovative practices sometimes mobilized to elevate organizational collective efficacy. Commitment to children and community is unconditional. Leadership approach challenges and opportunities through a growth mindset, nuanced by political intelligence. The work of Dweck (2006) and Riel and Martin (2017) are recommended resources for those considering leadership roles. Important dimensions of leadership mindset include metacognition, empathy, and innovation. Leadership mindset is aligned with moral purpose. Leadership mindset reinforces commitment to bigger picture, longer term, and greater good.

Tailoring Leadership to Match Corporate Culture

Andrew Sutherland

Thirty years of experience in education have certainly taught me one thing: no single form of leadership will work in all situations or for all organisations. Ultimately, the most successful leaders are those who best understand—both intellectually and emotionally—the corporate culture in which they work. The term 'corporate culture', of course, comes to us from the world of business; however, the term applies to all organisations or 'bodies', which is the root of the word 'corporate' (corporeal, corpse, and so on). All of a leader's skill set, learned experience, and strategies at their disposal are often put to the test in unravelling the weaknesses and building on the strengths of the 'corporation' they lead.

Sometimes ideas fail not because they are bad, but because they are poorly led. But sometimes an idea fails simply because the societal and organisational conditions surrounding it are prejudicial to its growth. Even with a 'strong leader' in place, unless the leadership approach adapts to the cultural and organisational conditions, there is increased chance of failure.

My natural style, for example, is to lead strategically with a vison, a set of values, and a set of model behaviours that I aspire to see replicated across the organisation. I trust my colleagues, support those around me to flourish and grow, and avoid micromanagement. This style had served me well for most of my career until I landed in an organization that was used to a 'command and control' model with extensive micromanagement—in essence, the exact opposite of my approach. The organisational systems had been in place, without significant change, for over twenty years and the majority of staff—particularly the middle managers—had been in place for over a decade.

Upon my arrival, I was open about my style of leadership and my expectations for the organisation. Indeed, I hosted public sessions with over 200 staff to explain my style, my vision, my hopes, and my expectations for the organisation. The feedback from staff at all levels indicated that I was signalling the change they wanted to see. My six-month honeymoon period was very positive. So where did it all go wrong? The answer lay in their deeply ingrained corporate culture. Staff who were initially excited about being given responsibility in a more democratic structure began to realise the challenge of this in reality. Such a model of leadership demands individual accountability at all levels. This organisation, however, was trained in upward delegation; managers simply did not have the skills, experience, and confidence to take responsibility for accountable decision making.

Anxiety increased and staff reverted to the previous approach of taking no responsibility for decision making, instead deferring to those 'above.' Rather than embracing radical ideas of how to enact change, a strong cultural adherence to the way things had always been done prevailed, with no appetite to try anything new, despite the turbulence of the recession we floundered in.

I did adapt my style to compensate, but I was slow to acknowledge that radical adaptation on my part was necessary. My 'natural' skill set had to be suppressed in favour of 'command and control' while incrementally building capacity in my team over time. Honestly, another leader with a different natural style could have taken the organisation further than I was able to. My style had attracted the interview panel in theory, but a more sophisticated assessment of their own corporate culture would have resulted in the appointment of someone more appropriate to lead the incremental change required before appointing someone like me. All leaders may be able to adapt their style to work in different environments, but ultimately we perform best when our own leadership style meshes rather than clashes with the corporate culture.

When applying for a leadership role, make sure that you understand the corporate culture of the organisation. Are you confident your leadership style will bring about a successful marriage? Or will it be a battle from day one?

Andrew Sutherland is the Director of Education and Early Years for the Oldham Council. He brings thirty years of learned experience in education in a variety of roles, including secondary head teacher, Director of Education, and professional leadership coordinator working with head teachers and system leaders on how to effect system change. His previous positions include Lead Specialist (System Leadership) for the Scottish College for Educational Leadership (SCEL), Executive Director of Learning and Leisure for the North Lanarkshire Council, Director of Education for the Falkirk Council, Head of Schools for the East Ayrshire Council, and the Secondary Head Teacher of Meldrum Academy in Aberdeenshire.

Confessions of a Professor of Educational Leadership

Ira Bogotch

L et me be upfront: there are no experts in educational leadership, and that statement goes doubly, maybe triply, for university professors who teach coursework in the field of educational leadership. Of course, my saying so will not in any way reduce the amount of unsolicited advice proffered by professors. Nevertheless, I still have an abiding love for the professoriate. In the next few paragraphs, I hope to unravel the contradictions between my skepticism and my passion for the field of educational leadership, focusing on the role(s) I play as a professor.

The key to living with contradictions resides in our willingness to learn from all lived experiences within and beyond educational institutions (i.e., universities and schools). In learning, we come to understand that the journey is always incomplete, and that whatever answers we currently offer to others ought to be tentative—in the sense that we are willing to rethink and revise our responses. So how do we avoid being perceived as wishy-washy or, worse, as "weak" leaders? Our field demands countless decisions minute-by-minute. If we keep changing our minds based on new information, then why should anybody—especially other adults—follow us as leaders?

For me, the answer is twofold: first, develop a philosophy. I know that leadership is a practical field and the word "philosophy," like the word "theory," does not have great currency. Yet, without a moral and political core, you will be either too closed-minded or too wishy-washy, depending on personality and circumstances. I am not telling you, dear reader, what philosophy or core you should develop, only that you should develop one and *not* keep it hidden from others. There is a reason why articulating a vision is important to leadership. My own core begins with assessing the consequences of my actions in terms of social justice. What I mean by social justice is that any institutional practice within schools or universities has to make a positive material difference in the lives of our colleagues and students beyond schools and universities. It is one thing to be fair while working inside schools, yet quite another to be ready to fight for fairness and equity in society as a whole. No doubt, within-school (or within-university) practices are important for character development and learning, but social justice demands that we—as educational leaders—take civic (a.k.a. political and social) action.

Second, in leadership learning it is critical to nurture relationships, especially those that allow for philosophy/theory to meet with on-the-ground practice. The key words here are "relationship" and "practice." Professors need to be willing to learn from practitioners, allowing them to become our teachers. I begin every educational relationship with profound gratitude and respect for what administrators and teachers do. Yes, I am turning conventional wisdom on its head: professors must continuously learn from their students. Practitioners interact daily with their students, and so their first-hand knowledge is critical for grounding educational theory in the real world. At the same time, my role as a professor is to question and push, trying to expand the boundaries of *status quo* thinking by challenging assumptions and the subsequently complicit actions. A professor has a critical role in learning, not as an expert, but as a medium for co-constructing and reconstructing existing knowledge into new ideas. Thus, I have, for now, tentatively resolved the contradiction between skepticism and passion.

Ira Bogotch has been a professor since 1990, first at the University of New Orleans, Louisiana (1990–2000), and now at Florida Atlantic University in Boca Raton. His primary academic interest is leadership for social justice and being an advocate for John Dewey's progressive educational (i.e., moral, political, and social) ideas. He has co-edited two handbooks, one published by Springer, the other by Wiley-Blackwell—which has allowed him to engage with top scholars from around the world. Being a professor is a privilege, not to be abused.

Moving On Up!

Tom Griffiths

I went into teaching to do one thing. Teach! No matter how long the days are and what I've faced, I do feel satisfied that I've done the best I can for my class, and my school. My Dad's mantra was 'What have you done today to make you feel proud?' and each day, I will reflect on something positive (my current headteacher suggested a reflective journal, which I think is a great idea). Gradually over the years, my time in the classroom has decreased as my leadership responsibilities have increased and it has taken me many years to adjust to this. My relationships with the children and staff have changed. I now need to know the wider school community as well as policies, curriculum, governors, data… the list is endless—as well as overwhelming!

The 23-year-old me began his career at a three-form entry school in West London in Year 2 and I was surrounded by excellent teachers, some of whom became my friends as well as my colleagues. I was influenced by the leaders around me and I have continued to develop my leadership skills from all the people I've been fortunate to work with over the last nine years (even the poor leaders or the ones who would stab you in the back to take your recognition and advance their career!). I think it's important to watch, listen, and learn from everyone—even those belligerent or negative teachers and leaders will continue to develop your problem-solving skills and make you more of a versatile leader!

But how do you tell a friend what they need to do better, as a leader? Once I had to do a lesson observation on a colleague and it did not go well. It isn't easy for anyone delivering poor feedback but make it constructive and always remain professional. If you feel something could have been done differently, suggest it; offer to team-teach or for them to observe you. You have to be respected in order to be listened to. When I arrived three years ago at my current school as the Assistant Headteacher, only the Headteacher had been to my previous school and seen me teach. I didn't have a class initially, so it took me longer to gain that respect from my colleagues. Being in this particular role has been challenging, as you must be an ear to the staff whilst supporting the Deputy and Head in their senior leadership roles. I know I've made mistakes, but I've always tried to be honest, open, and just learn from them. We tell children it is okay to make mistakes and have a growth mindset, so why are we so hard on ourselves?

This autumn, I've gone back into class (Year 5) almost full time and I couldn't be more thrilled. Of course, it is hard balancing management responsibilities, but primarily I'm here to teach, to ensure that all the children in my class make the progress so they are successful in their futures. No matter what the government policy or agenda (and goodness me, the curriculum and assessment in England has changed dramatically in the last few years), this isn't just a job. It sounds ridiculously cheesy but it's true.

Last year, I lost my Dad very suddenly and then my Nan exactly thirteen weeks later. It was the most horrific experience of my life and I still struggle today. Being a leader though, I still have to support my team and boost morale, when really I just want to curl up and hide from the world. Just remember you're an important member of a team and you are all there to help each other! So be the change you want to see. As my Dad would say, 'What have you done today to make you feel proud?'

Tom Griffiths is the Assistant Headteacher at a rural primary school in the West Midlands. Originally keen to pursue a career in the legal profession, Tom studied Law at Nottingham Trent University while working as a teaching assistant in a deprived area of Nottingham. His passion for teaching saw him change his mind and study the Primary PGCE at the University of Warwick. He taught in London but now resides in the West Midlands and is an extremely proud husband, father, son, brother, and grandson.

Shaped by Values, Experiences, and Environment

Anthony H. Normore

L eadership is oft times thought to be a skillset either somehow developed through watching great leaders at work, or by reading accounts of success and drawing conclusions about what must have transpired between the lines of the story. In most instances, this is due to a naïve belief that a single attribute—perhaps an element of character or personality—creates the formula for success. In fact, there are lessons of history and thoughts of great minds from Aristotle to Aquinas from whom we can draw insight. There are frames of mind that consider leadership as work to adapt to change, and then to lead others through that change in a structured systemic way. To this end, this chapter provides a glance at the personal and professional leadership lessons that I have learned over time.

My leadership work launches from the perspective that every interaction I have as a member of the education community must be consistent with my personal values system that supports growth, respect, integrity, compassion, competence, and responsibility. It appears in my role as teacher, leader, administrator, manager, and mentor, and in the seriousness that I give to my professional productivity as a scholar and researcher. My professional values act in sync with my personal values. I believe that human needs in life, as opposed to wants, appear to be few: food, water, shelter, and a sense of personal direction or purpose. From numerous graduate students over the years, I have learned that people do not need more, at least to start, if their sense of direction or purpose is sufficiently strong. In this context, having a sense of direction or purpose for me means having values concerned with decisions about right or wrong.

My years in education encompass leadership roles and responsibilities as a public school teacher, school site and district level leader, university professor, academic program coordinator, director of doctoral programs, and academic department chair of educational leadership, special needs, and teacher education. In those roles, it has been incumbent on me to support and encourage individual talents and strengths of my students and colleagues. Though not always as successful as I would have liked, I have been responsible for facilitating student development in the skills needed to succeed as professionals and scholars. I have also devoted time and effort to support the professional and personal development of graduate students by encouraging them to engage in the professional/academic community. I have a long-term commitment to the mentor–protégé relationship with these students. Most of all, moral character has influenced and continues to influence the manner in which those who surround us exercise integrity, courage, fortitude, honesty, respect, and kindness.

My philosophy as an educator reflects a learner-centered orientation and incorporates constructivist-developmental approaches consistent with learning theories. I think of myself as an educator who facilitates learning opportunities rather than as a teacher of a subject. I believe that effective education does more than educate students—it also acts as a working model of civil society, and thereby helps to create, sustain, and improve our communities. Accordingly, I believe it is the responsibility of all educators at all levels to focus on educating and encouraging communities of students to develop into responsible, caring, contributing citizens—building the future one student at a time at the local, regional, national, and global level.

Effective education is inclusive, from the classroom to the boardroom, because supporters of education believe than an inclusive education is best for students and for the community, and an inclusive democratic government for education is best for the community. Education must be barrier-free, values-driven, and respectful of every student, every worker, and every citizen.

Having participated in the education arena for 35+ years, I can attest an effective educational system provides a quality education by guaranteeing that every child will have a place to learn and teachers to help him. This is backed by a democratic process that is open to every member of the community regardless of disadvantage or difference. As such, it is our moral imperative to promote civil democracy in preference to any sectarian perspective as the basis for thriving communities. We must also celebrate diversity by working with communities, colleagues, and students from different backgrounds, outlooks, and experiences. Experience has taught us that we must invest in high-quality education for an ethnically and culturally diverse student population, equipping them with the capability to become productive citizens who continuously contribute to a global and rapidly changing society.

Anthony H. Normore, Ph.D., is professor of Educational Leadership, and Department Chair of Graduate Education, at California State University Dominguez Hills. His research focuses on urban educational leadership development in the context of ethics and social justice. Details of Dr. Normore's Pre-K–12 teaching and leadership experiences, his higher education experiences, scholarship, publications, and various service-orientations can be found on his LinkedIn profile: https://www.linkedin.com/in/anthony-tony-h-normore-56142521/.

Where Necessary, Use Words

Marcella McCarthy

Becoming a headteacher was something of a shock. I was appointed as a vice-principal and was planning to spend a few years tucked in behind the leaders, so to speak, learning my craft before I aspired to headship—if I ever did. Once I'd started at my new school, I realised that it was not quite the steady haven I had thought that it might be. In fact, it was a school in crisis. Within a few weeks, my headteacher resigned unexpectedly, and I found myself acting head and then head of a huge 3–19 school in a tough area of one of the loveliest cities in the world.

I knew it was a challenging school—that was why I'd wanted to work there—and I already had a lot of experience in working with schools ranging from "outstanding" to "inadequate." Having said that, nothing could have prepared me for the challenges I faced in the first months of leadership. As I got to know the school, I found that the financial records were not as they should be. The school bursar resigned. So did the central business manager of the academy trust. I found myself with a prospective deficit of almost £2 million, no one who could tell me what our accounts looked like, fearful that I would not be able to pay the staff at the end of the month.

I wanted to be a spectacularly good head, and this crippled my plans for that. The last thing I wanted to think about was finance. I had to make so many changes in those first months and years, including a huge staff review, that it took a colossal toll on staff, and I knew my regime was inevitably going to be much less comfortable than that of my free-spending predecessor. I became very good at economising, and getting a lot out of a little, but I couldn't help mourning what I had planned to do for the school. It seemed so unfair that I had to be the bad guy. But I had to be the leader that they needed, not the one I would have been under better circumstances.

Of course, I survived. Up to that point, financial management was not one of my areas of expertise, but it was clear that I couldn't do much worse than my predecessor, so I rolled up my sleeves got to work. It was a steep learning curve—but at least finance now holds no terrors for me. Being an English teacher, I used Mr. Micawber's principle as our motto: "Annual income twenty pounds, annual expenditure nineteen [pounds] nineteen [shillings] and six [pence], result happiness. Annual income twenty pounds, annual expenditure twenty pounds ought and six, result misery." All we had to do, I reasoned, was to spend less money than we took in. My other guide, pinned on my office door, was a quotation said to be from St. Francis: "Preach the Gospel at all times; where necessary, use words."

This, I thought, was all I had. I did not have cash, but I still had myself, and I could still do things rather than just talk about them. So, I continued to teach; I bought resources for the school myself; I worked all hours; I made cakes for the staff. I tried to prove my commitment to the school in every way I could think of—through actions, not words. Colleagues thought that I continued teaching a tough class because we were short of cash. One advisor even told me it was beneath my dignity—I'm so grateful I ignored that. By teaching, I never forgot what it was like to be at the sharp end of the classroom. By teaching some tough boys, I formed relationships with them that went beyond the confrontational, and I understood much more about the challenges at the heart of the school. I still treasure the thank-you letters from those students.

Paying for resources is something that many teachers do. In a better financial climate I wouldn't recommend it, but it represented something critical for me. Providing cheap pens for students or equipment for teachers out of my own pocket wasn't insignificant. I was saying (even if they never knew) "well, I think you're worth it." Buying tea and coffee for staff, getting them cakes and biscuits as a treat after a tough week, reminded me that it wasn't just a job.

I think that's what St. Francis meant. Leaders use many words, but your actions will make far more impact.

Dr. Marcella McCarthy began by teaching Old English and Medieval English to students at Oxford University, later working as an Assistant Editor for the Oxford English Dictionary. She is now principal of a 3–19 school in Oxford. Dr. McCarthy has worked with schools across the UK to support literacy and gifted education, but she still spends her happiest hours in the classroom. She is a regular conference speaker, has written books on outstanding teaching, coaching, and mentoring, and many articles about leadership and literacy. She believes that good leadership means that you never stop learning. Dr. McCarthy can be emailed at mccarthy.education@gmail.com.

Cartwheels and Chocolate Cake

Jeanne Tribuzzi

"Bus 32… the last bus of the day is now here. Please walk carefully to your bus and have a great summer."

The call of that last bus signaled that a few minutes of adult fun would soon begin before teachers packed up their classrooms for the summer. The "whoop" on the announcements meant that the students had all been dismissed and the ceremonial cartwheels down the elementary hall would soon begin. The first time I cartwheeled down the hall, the teachers and I had an enormous laugh. Our few minutes of whooping together marked the end of another successful school year. We maintained this silly tradition for my remaining years at that elementary building. The celebration became part of what fed our souls as we closed out a year of dedication to kids and the demands of teaching.

A few years later, when I moved to teach at the middle school, I established the end-of-year cartwheel ritual once again, but the middle school halls were twice as long as the elementary halls. I worked at it, and although the camaraderie wasn't quite as strong, the teachers began to relish the small celebration to mark the end of another successful year. The cartwheel laughter was good medicine for teachers who had just worked their tails off to get kids to the year-end finish line. Celebrations are important, and there aren't enough of them in education!

My next move was to an administrative curriculum post in the district office where, I believed, my cartwheel days were behind me. After all, school leaders were expected to function with a high level of professionalism and restraint, right? This move to administration took place while the No Child Left Behind Act shaped the new regulations and testing that would dominate our work for the next decade and beyond. My small celebrations were being replaced by new standards, more rigorous tests (even for five-year-olds), and an accountability system designed to make the public believe that public schools weren't working. I realized that cartwheels were even more important as teachers became scapegoats for many of society's ills. There wasn't much laughter in school halls as this new era took over. However, schools create the culture they choose, and I was determined that these new punitive external demands wouldn't define the culture of our schools... school leaders can and must still impact this culture.

Scoring English Language Arts assessments were now part of my job as an administrator, and with seven elementary buildings in the district, putting together scoring teams of teachers to go through the training and mind-numbing process of scoring 400 written student assessments in a day was less than joyful. Of the many logistical decisions necessary for those days to work, lunch was key. As a district, we had to pull teachers from classrooms, spend a fortune on substitute coverage, keep teachers engaged in a focused day of scoring student writing, and all in the service of meeting standards and testing regulations. Our budget was small, but putting pizza and salad onto a nice buffet line would signal that we did care about our teachers. And... a chocolate cake simply had to be a part of that. I also knew I could sneak a few cartwheels into the scoring process when the time was right, and I'd have to be strategic about my outfit. The amount of work would make for a long day, but there was no rule stating that we couldn't squeeze in some good food and collegial laughter. Celebrating the good work of kids and teachers needed to be my message, even in the context of highly regulated state assessments.

I had two cake pans huge enough to make a cake that could feed 25–30 adults for each scoring session. So—six sessions over two weeks—chocolate, carrot cake, cheesecake, and strawberry whipped-cream cake would be a start! The testing industry has become a beast that we now feed—literally—and I had resolved to appreciate the teachers who would make the whole process work. Bringing teachers together to "work on the work," whether that means scoring or working on new curriculum, is not simple. Working together in a school setting is challenging, yet research supports teacher collaboration when learning and implementing new work. To take kids to new levels, we also need to raise the level of our teachers, who work in isolation all day with frequent policy changes coming at them. Time, substitutes, space, and collegiality are not in strong supply in schools these days, yet these elements are necessary to continually strengthen the work that we are asking teachers to implement. Working together on high-level work is necessary to take our students to new levels of achievement.

For teachers to keep seeing the best in students, we must continually celebrate and see the best in our teachers and build their capacity to continually improve the work of our schools. Change is a constant part of our work, and the way school leaders implement and manage change makes all the difference. Appreciating and elevating the work of teachers is a must, and cartwheels and chocolate cake is one way to make that happen.

Dr. Jeanne Tribuzzi works with schools both nationally and internationally to help them articulate and align their literacy curriculum. Jeanne has held positions as District Administrator at Global Concepts Charter School and Director of English Language Arts, ESL, and Second Languages in the West Seneca Central School District in New York State. Over the past 28 years, she has been a primary teacher, a middle school English teacher, Director of Staff Development, Director of English Language Arts, a curriculum writer, and a conference presenter. She completed her doctoral work at the University of Buffalo in New York State.

The Reflective Leader

Cheryl McInnes

How do we recognize effective leadership? As a school-based leader, I have often asked myself "what am I supposed to be doing?" "Should I be directing those around me?" Is my role to problem solve, to fix the issues and concerns brought forward by the community?" This often resulted in a 'must do' mindset rather than adopting the mindset of a learner, an observer, working to serve those within the school community.

In my first principalship, I was provided the challenging opportunity of moving a program that had existed within a school for 20+ years to another school community. This move of program would result in the closure of the school and the loss of those teaching and support positions. In the beginning with a naïve, 'must do' mindset, I created extensive 'to do' lists and began what I believed was the process of effecting great change. I quickly realized that the role of an effective leader is to support those around you, provide the resources they need to be successful, and most importantly, provide opportunity for others to learn and grow in their own decision making. I recognized the importance of developing strong, positive, trusting relationships and that this would be the foundation required to ensure the future success of that program within the new school community.

I believe that the ultimate purpose of an effective school-based leader is to move people and communities closer to their full potential. Our purpose is to work with each individual whether that be staff, students or parents to help them understand their role within the larger school community. Each of us has a contribution to make and this can only be realized once relationship has been established. Positive relationship develops from listening to people, seeking to understand. This can be challenging when the underlying message is drowned out by the 'noise' of emotion; blame, accusation, anger, deflection, distraction, etc. Taking the time to understand, to have clarity around a situation comes through reflection. Taking time throughout each day to reflect on conversations, differing perspectives and decisions made have provided me with a greater sense of clarity and understanding. It is difficult to find this time with the busyness of the school day, however, your daily walks about the school and your drive to and from school can be moments for refection, time to process and gain clarity on a given situation.

Our roles and responsibility change every minute of every day which can be overwhelming. Maintaining a clear vision and direction at times can be foggy, lost among the never ending 'to do' lists and emergent issues. However, the time for reflection allows us to pause, to recalibrate or reset the direction to ensure student success is the compass from which we lead. I believe the only true measure of effective leadership rests in where we set our compass. Student success, whatever this might entail, must be our compass.

Effective leadership requires that you provide the right tools to those who follow. It may not be clear or easily identifiable what those tools are in the beginning. However, as we come to better understand our communities and those we serve, the tools required to make improvements to ensure student success become more visible. These tools change day to day and across different situations. The basic foundations, however, includes a solid understanding of the curriculum, assessment practices that are holistic, an ability to communicate effectively with parents and a genuine desire to support student success academically, social-emotionally and spiritually.

We need to take stock daily/weekly of our support networks and of those around us. Have we surrounded ourselves with those who have the same basic priorities? People who have student success as their compass? We may differ in opinions, perspectives and experiences but ultimately all those around you are working in the same direction with one shared vision. Ultimately our work should bring us joy, a joy of working alongside others in a shared purpose of improving the lives of children and our school communities. Joy does not come from the completion of a 'to do' list. Joy does not come from numbers or data on a screen. Joy comes from loving what you do and how you do it!

Throughout each of my experiences as a leader I have gathered valuable insight, increased my knowledge and further developed the skills of patience, communication and reflection. I have come to learn there is no set formula for leadership, no prescribed method, recipe or book of instructions to ensure success as a leader. However, a roadmap does exist if you take the time to read the signs.

Cheryl McInnes is currently Principal of Bishop Carroll High School, Calgary, Alberta. She is in her seventh year as a school principal, with previous appointments at both the elementary and junior high levels. Cheryl has spent the last 18 years in education working with children from Kindergarten to High School. Her experiences include classroom teacher, school counsellor, district level consultant and vice-principal. Cheryl is also a wife and mother to two young daughters who keep her busy and grounded in what truly matters and ensuring that the school experience in positive for all children.

Start with the Heart

Jeannie Anthony

I currently work at an international school well known for providing supports and programs for students with disabilities in an inclusive environment.

I recently met with a group of publicly-funded educators from a nearby country who came to learn about the school's learning support programs. The principal in the group asked me how he could start programs like ours. My first response? Start with the heart. It is important to know what your values and beliefs are because changing a school's culture and shifting people's paradigms is hard work. It can be easy to give up when you face the inevitable obstacles. Knowing what is in your heart will sustain you through the challenges ahead.

Keeping your heart at the *heart* of your work is a good start, but not enough. Here are a few more things I've learned over my lengthy career:

- *Collaborate vertically and horizontally.* Some leaders may think and operate in isolation. Let's face it; our work is based on getting things done through relationships. None of us can be truly successful by doing all the work ourselves. You won't know everything, so let others help you. By getting to know the strengths and needs of others, you will gain insight into what motivates those with whom you work. Knowing your colleagues will inform your decision making. One way to learn about the people you lead is to spend time observing the work they do—from the head of your organization to the teacher, secretary, custodian, and so on. Observation provides you with invaluable information and sends a message to others that you value the work they do, which gives you credibility. People will thank you for spending the time to learn about them as individuals and professionals. Opportunities open up for you to ask questions and learn more. When the time comes for you to lead the change, be inclusive and consider who is potentially impacted. Include them either in the work itself or by communicating to them in a timely manner. Additionally, and this is vital, let people know you appreciate and value their work. It's important to feed their souls.

- *Build for sustainability.* Most of us experience a lot of turnover in both students and staff. In fact, you will likely change jobs numerous times over your career. Ask yourself, "What will my leadership legacy be?" Once answered, consider how you build your legacy so that it lives on when you and others leave. How will you build a system that has shared knowledge and common language at its foundation? Avoid the trap of building a program that relies on specific individuals. Think of professional development in very broad terms as a systemic way to increase capacity through shared expert knowledge delivered through an ongoing and differentiated plan. Remember that schools are teaching and learning organizations that require constant feeding. How you approach professional development will have an impact on sustainability and help avoid the yo-yo effect when staff become immune to change.

- *Avoid wishful thinking.* One of my doctoral professors taught me this concept. I can get really creative in my thinking and verge into the realm of wishful thinking. Creativity is good, in the short run. I have learned to accept my wild, creative thinking as a way to generate good ideas (within the realm of possibilities) and then use questioning techniques—"What if we did such and such; how could it be implemented in our current reality?"—to weed out unworkable ideas. After all, resources are scarce and can't be wasted.

- *The art of the powerful question (or assume nothing).* As a successful school leader, it is likely that you know a thing or two. You may even be an expert. However, it is a mistake to assume that you know everything. You don't. Think about a time when either you misjudged a situation or when you were misjudged because not all the information was visible. Developing the art of wondering rather than assuming and asking powerful and open questions will help you avoid the pitfall of thinking you know everything. Start by asking open-ended questions based on low inference observations. Believe what you see and hear, not how you interpret a situation (that comes later in the process).

- ▪ ***Your through line should always be to the student.*** This is the *heart* of it all. For every idea, for every plan, for every piece of work you do, ask yourself, "How does this impact students?" Be prepared to explain how everything you do and how every part of your organization is in service to students. In most cases, this will align with the mission, vision, and core beliefs of your organization. Right?

After 30 plus years as a public school educator and leader in California and Washington, **Dr. Jeannie Anthony** *is serving as the Director of Student Support Services at the International School of Brussels, Belgium. She earned her teaching and administrative credentials at Dominican University, California, and the University of California, Berkeley. Anthony earned her Doctorate of Educational Leadership and Policy Design at the University of Washington, Seattle.*

"You Can't Get There from Here!"

Wayne Annis

I am directionally challenged. It's a lifelong issue for me. On one memorable road trip, countless hours of driving led me to finally humble myself and stop at a small roadside store to ask for directions. The clerk barely disguised her inner glee when, hearing where I wanted to go, stated, "I'm so sorry, you can't get there from here." I was deflated.

This feeling was not unlike what I felt as a new school administrator in the mid-1990s. Back then, it felt like I was expected to survive on my own, figuring out where to lead my school based only on intuition and the knowledge I had demonstrated in gaining the various certificates that hung on my office wall. Sure, as a principal I collaborated with teachers, but it basically meant meeting with others to give them "voice" while selling them on my ideas. Teachers were "consulted" about our school improvement plan and other priorities. This felt good! I had sought and received input from staff.

I eventually came to realize that it was really not about me. In fact, it wasn't about my staff either. It was about maximizing the conditions needed for effective student learning through collaborative leadership! The blinders finally came off. This was the lens we needed to look through when making decisions, setting goals, and allocating our resources.

Student learning became *the* driving force as we set school improvement goals, built positive behavioural interventions, examined our classroom practices, and spent our budgets. Rather than feeling restricted, it was liberating! We gave ourselves permission to push aside opportunities that although they looked new and shiny on the outside, did not really support our central purpose and our tighter focus. Little did we know we were taking only the first steps of our journey to more effective practices.

We needed to consider evidence of student learning, determine where students were with their grasp of outcomes, tailor our instruction to further the learning of each student, and make headway without overloading, hardworking teachers. Hours of discussion led to the setting of specific, measurable, achievable, realistic, and time bound goals (SMART goals) that directly influenced our instruction and intervention strategies. Clearly, there was greater ownership of student learning, but no collective ownership. The timing was perfect for establishing a core leadership team.

We invited teachers and support staff to an information meeting; then I held my breath. To my delight, the turnout was large, representing a true cross section of our school, both teaching and support staff. Meeting norms were established and the team went to work determining its mandate. From the start, I made it clear that I did not want or expect the team simply to endorse my decisions. This group exercised true leadership in establishing academic and social directions for the school.

As a result, ownership and authorship of the school improvement plan (academic), positive learning and working environment plan (social), as well as the coordination and facilitation of professional development for teachers shifted to the team.

There were many successes to celebrate. There was clear evidence of increased student learning, a tighter focus on school improvement goals, and an increased sense of ownership of student learning among staff members. Discussions that had centered on *the* school improvement plan now were about *our* school improvement plan. The staff also had greater input into how fiscal resources would be spent. Where could we go next to further develop collaborative leadership? What was I as principal doing to further demonstrate my commitment to growth?

After discussions with my vice-principal, we removed "principal" and "vice-principal" from our letterhead, stating both our positions as co-administrators. This directly reflected our thinking, affected our day-to-day operations, and demonstrated our trust in each other. Our final step was to turn over the budget to the core leadership team, to be used in support of our school improvement plans. This was a huge step for me—one that involved a degree of trepidation. I needed to trust my colleagues around the table, and the processes we developed to ensure fiscal responsibility and transparency.

With the help and patience of my colleagues, my perspective on school leadership had completely changed. When I transitioned to a new position in March 2017, I left with the confidence that they really did not need me. What remained was a team of committed, highly trained professionals who, with their new administrator, would continue to actively support and lead our community of learners. Authentic, collaborative leadership at its best! Through these experiences (and the patience of my colleagues), I learned that you *can* get there from here.

Wayne Annis *entered the teaching profession in 1989. Throughout the years, he has served as a classroom teacher, methods and resource teacher, inclusion facilitator, and school administrator. He currently works with 26 schools as Director of Schools for the Anglophone West School District in the greater Fredericton area, New Brunswick, Canada.*

Parent Complaints:
Filtering the Sources of Anger

Timothy C. Steele

I will never forget the first parent complaint I encountered when I began my career as a new administrator in a rural, Title I elementary school. It was a crisp fall morning, and from my office, I could hear shouting and yelling coming from the front desk. Actually, shouting and yelling is not a sufficient description. *Hysterical ranting* would be more apropos. Through the obscenity-filled lobby, a parent was shrieking that her child's teacher had said something inappropriate. The parent was demanding that the teacher be fired in front of her that morning. Dealing with parent complaints is a learning process. Nothing in my administrative credentialing classes had equipped me for encounters with a volatile parent on this level. This mother was so angry that she came to school barefoot, with wild hair, wearing only men's boxer shorts and a T-shirt. I remember wondering how angry someone would have to be to simply grab the car keys, walk out in undergarments, and drive to school for a confrontation.

Trying to assuage the mother's anger was not easy. I wanted to get her out of the front office, where she was screaming at the administrative assistant and frightening the children, and into a private office so that the vice-principal and I could begin to root out the source of her anger.

As an aside, the teacher in question had approached me previously to discuss the child's problematic behavior in class. I *knew* about the event that happened, and I *knew* that the version of events the parent was sharing was inaccurate. I recall sitting and taking notes of the events she shared with me. I tried to interject once or twice without success. Each time I tried to say something, the parent would get louder and more physically aggressive. I realized it was futile to speak, and so I took notes. Lots of notes.

In retrospect, my inability to *not* get a word in edgewise was the best thing that could have happened to a new administrator. I had practiced the most crucial part of being an effective listener—staying silent and actively listening. My first instinct had been to obviate her anger. I believed that if I could just *clearly* tell her that her child's version of the event was not accurate, she would simply say, "Oh… thank you for sharing with me. I am so embarrassed that I reacted the way I did, and will explore the facts the next time, instead of blindly trusting my eight-year-old's version of truth."

What I *thought* would happen would be a clear and concise communication between two adults. What I *thought* was that we could jointly look at the facts and come to an appropriate response to those facts. Ah, to be a young administrator again!

Experience has since taught me that a parent protecting their child while in a state of extreme frustration is not always able to see a clearly presented reality. Working with an irate parent is a skill that must be developed through practice and study. When faced with an angry parent, I listen intentionally, I make eye contact, I lean forward with interest, and I take copious notes. I repeat back the concerns of the parent, so they understand that I am listening and have really *heard* what they were trying to convey. While being on the receiving end of someone's anger is uncomfortable, I have learned to value the parent's anger as an opportunity to connect with them. It also provides the school with a way to review our practices and procedures, and it develops relationships with parents for future interactions.

Over the years, I have also come to realize that often when a parent is angry in general at the world, that anger becomes misplaced. When these parents come to complain, they vent their frustration at the school, but as I take the time to listen, I hear their *real* frustration: their marriage, their financial situation, their parenting skills, or their boss. Parents living in poverty exist in a world that offers minimal control over their circumstances. Whether their anger at the school is justified or not, they seek support for the one area of their lives where they do exercise control...their children. Despite poverty and its related problems, these parents have a need to be heard, and to know that their time and experience are valued.

Timothy C. Steele, Ed.D., has over 18 years of experience working with low-income communities both as an educator and administrator. He has a passion for educational leadership and providing service-oriented leadership. He has been a frequent keynote speaker for groups such as Pan-Hellenic and FIND Food, which offers outreach to struggling communities and families. Dr. Steele serves as an active Vestry Member of the Church of St. Paul in the Desert in Palm Springs, California. He lives in Palm Desert, California, with his husband of 27 years and their three children.

Keeping Afloat in a Sea of Change

Alan Hardie

The English education system has experienced rapid change since the election of the Conservative–Liberal Democrat collation in May 2010. Much of the change was driven by a dogmatic belief in the need for a radical overhaul of a system seen by leading conservative thinkers as falling behind other nations in PISA rankings. Consequently, school leaders have been required to deal with an unprecedented level of change to school structures, curriculum, teacher education, and examination systems alongside austerity measures significantly reducing per pupil spending.

One of the key changes was the Academies Act, which allowed 'outstanding' schools to opt out of local education authority control and in essence become 'state funded independent schools', leading the charge to the creation of a 'school-led system'. Following the premature death of my predecessor in January 2011, I found myself in the role of principal in one of the first schools in the North of England to convert to academy status. I've now spent almost seven years leading a wonderful academy community through a period of tumultuous change to almost all aspects of the education system.

Nothing in my prior experience quite prepared me for the level of challenge I've experienced in my role as principal. The change in status to academy required rapid learning in terms of human resources and finance, and one of my first lessons learned was the need to delegate appropriately. Any school leader must accept that they will never be expert in all aspects of the role, so there is a crucial need to use your leadership team to its full potential. Recognise that you are working with future headteachers who have a different skillset and will be better than you in some areas. The tricky bit is empowering colleagues while holding them professionally accountable.

Making time for people is an essential part of any school leader's role and this means staff, students, and parents/carers. For me, it's about resisting the temptation to spend all day on your computer or in meetings instead of devoting time each day to getting around the building and talking to people in their classrooms, offices, the lunchroom, and so on. Not only does this give you more opportunity to have your finger on the pulse of what's happening around the school, colleagues are often more open in discussions on their 'home turf'. It also provides the opportunity to support staff in dealing with difficulties with students or rolling up your sleeves and helping colleagues if they are struggling. There is also joy when a student waves at you to come into the classroom to show you work they are proud of. We have also prioritised the development of student voice through our Junior Leadership and Staff Forum where both groups meet to discuss the school climate and drive improvement.

Fewer and fewer school leaders in England teach and I think that this is a mistake. I completely understand that pressures on time make this difficult, especially as many headteachers are now working in executive roles across more than one school. However, for me teaching is still the best part of my job. Not only does it give me the chance to inspire students with my love of geography, it also means that I'm still visibly part of the team and dealing with the same issues as my colleagues. This has never been more important than now when teachers are tossed in a sea of constant change due to reforms to the national curriculum, assessment, and examination systems. I regard the leadership of teaching as the key part of my role as principal and I'm incredibly proud that the work of my colleagues was recognised in our designation as a Teaching School in 2014. This designation mirrors in education the traditional role of teaching hospitals in healthcare.

Finally, the most important lesson I've learned in educational leadership is that we must never stop learning. During the past three years, I've worked as a National Leader of Education, which involves being deployed to support schools deemed to be struggling. While I hope that the work I do has a positive impact on each school I support, it certainly has been a catalyst for change in my own school. Visiting another school always leads to questions about our own practice and self-reflection about how we can further improve our provision. None of us can ever consider our own school as a 'done deal' so learning lessons from others is one of the very best ways to make the 'marginal gains' (Sir David Brailsford) that lead to incremental improvements in our schools.

The sea of change over the last seven years has been turbulent at times, but I hope to keep sailing in the right direction for many years to come!

Alan Hardie is principal of Whitburn Church of England Academy in North East England. He is a graduate of the University of Edinburgh (M.A. in Geography) and postgraduate of University of Durham (M.Sc. in Ecology), completing his teacher training at the University of Newcastle. Hardie has over a decade of experience in school leadership and is a National Leader of Education.

Service Leadership

Karen Jez

As a young educator, I was always looking for ways to better engage students, finding ways to connect them with the community, and developing authentic learning opportunities. If I had an idea about how to benefit the students, I would ask my building principal if I could implement change or add some new learning experiences to my classroom. Often times these philosophies led to criticism from my peers, perhaps based on experience or jealousy, but I figured: What would it hurt to ask the question? The worst that could happen is I would be told "no."

Once I moved into an administrative role, I wanted to keep this open-mindedness to innovation in classroom practice and building leadership. I believe that my roles then as building leader and now as district superintendent include ensuring that my building leaders and teachers have the ability to be creative to best meet the learning needs of the children they serve. The core standards, both state and national, are the basis of all learning; how they are taught (how they are met, or how curriculum is taught) should use the craft of individual educators to ensure that the needs of every child are being met. Board members and administrators must ensure the resources are allocated to the buildings and the classrooms; the instructional methods employed thereafter are best left to the teacher teams at each level of instruction. An example of open-mindedness practice was supporting the 7th grade level teams in implementing a classroom/team management system in which the teachers facilitated most of the consequences for poor classroom behavior. This model lasted a couple of years and then went by the wayside, but the teachers were given the opportunity to attempt it. I would argue that if the system was implemented today, using school-wide positive behavior supports research, it would be far more successful and sustained.

A great example of teacher-led innovation in education is how our Hydetown Elementary learning facilitators are transforming learning for our 1st –5th grade learners. Heeding the research and educational vision of Chuck Schwahn and Bea McGarvie, these innovative teachers, together with the leadership of their principal, have redesigned instruction at the school. The Hydetown staff had been participating in Professional Learning Community discussions that centered around student mindsets and personalized learning. When approached, staff were intrigued and enthusiastic at the chance to make learning more meaningful for our students. The decision was made to move to Mass Customized Learning Model at Hydetown Elementary. (Read Chapter 11 of *Inevitable, Mass Customized Learning,* by Schwahn and McGarvie (2012), and you will have a great grasp of what learning looks like at Hydetown.) Knowing how much time and hard work would need to be committed to transforming the learning experience, the principal tried to talk the teachers out of jumping into the deep end, total implementation all at once. She suggested that they start with a portion of the student body, but the teachers pushed back, stating, "No, if we believe customization is good for one child, it's best for all", and so for all learners at Hydetown Elementary School, the instructional design and transformation has taken place over the past two years!

Teachers—now known as learning facilitators—met over the past two summers to prepare for the transition. Classrooms were renamed and revamped to suit learner needs, curriculum was examined to understand non-grade level continuums of instruction, and systems to keep track of students and progress were put into place.

Hydetown opened its doors to a new system of educating learners with one-to-one Chromebook implementation, and a new outlook on what school could look like for the future. While technology integration is a key part of this initiative, it's not the only consideration and it does not replace instruction as we have always known it. The audience is just determined? (determined as in selected? Should this be "served"?) differently. The facilitators will tell you that Hydetown is "radically learner-centered."

Another important component of this pilot project has been helping learners to develop intrinsic motivation and responsibility for learning. Hydetown has already seen a huge change in attitudes among our learners and they feel success in each of their courses.

While there are still many challenges in completing this transition to Mass Customized Learning and all that it entails, the staff at Hydetown is excited and committed to excellence in the tradition of the Titusville Area School District (Titusville reference is lost – is this necessary? Could end after "…the staff at Hydetown is excited and committed to excellence.". Innovation in education is essential as the digital age progresses.

In conclusion, as educational leaders, we are here to serve the needs of the children we educate and how better then to permit our teacher/facilitators utilize their creativity, innovation and craft to meet the learning needs of all children. Just say, "Yes!"

Karen Jez began her teaching career as a substitute teacher in the mid-1980s. Karen was hired as an assistant principal at TMS (spell out) in 1996 before moving on to become the Middle School Principal in 1998. After serving time as the assistant superintendent, in 2006, Karen accepted the position as Superintendent of Schools for Titusville where she has continued making her mark as a top-quality school leader, not only locally, but across the Commonwealth of Pennsylvania. In addition to her professional life, Karen is the President of the State PARSS Board (Pennsylvania Rural and Small Schools Association); a member of the FORUM for the Superintendents' of Western PA; and active on the professional development committee of PASA (Pennsylvania Association of School Administrators). She truly lives by her motto, "Educating children is the most important thing our community does."

The Magical Tarot Cards

Roseline Sultana Arnéodo

Countdown to Christmas.

Three days left before the holiday break. I must come up with an original lesson for my classes. I am fed up with myself, my French Christmas carols, the *paté de foie gras* horror story, the turkey stuffed with chestnuts…

On the shelf of my new home office lies the blue box of a pack of tarot cards bought ages ago, when I was training to become a French foreign-language teacher. An expensive purchase—a pedagogical tool with an explanatory booklet to guide the students through the various stages of a fairy tale. Why did I use it so little, and so long ago? It had been stored for years behind a pile of books…

"We are going to use these cards to create a story, a tale."

"A fairy tale?"

"Maybe. Why not? Up to you really…"

The illustrations on each card are abstract enough but also tell enough to stimulate their imagination—so the explanatory booklet guarantees.

"Is this a princess? A mermaid? Is it me?"…

"And what about this one? A fortress? A lost island?"…

"A monster? A cloud? A shadow? A ghost?"…

Groups of four; not more. We shift some chairs around.

"Don't make too much noise because of our geography neighbours! … Girls, go and sit with Zachary."

Zachary grabs the pack of cards distributed to his group and starts distributing roles. He is obviously going to be the writer. I can see the girls looking at him, looking up to him. Zachary is precious. They inherited the only boy of the class… a boy in a French class is always a treasure. And he is handsome in his own cool and discrete way, with his stretch earring…

I follow the group from across the room. Bustling activity. Suggestions. Laughter.

Zachary calls me: "Miss, comment on dit (this?) 'unknown land'?"

Cards are passing from hand to hand.

"Zachary, I suggest you stick to the present…"

"But it's a fairy tale, Miss. It has to be written in the past!"

Their hero—I forget if they picked a boy or a girl—climbs mountains, clears obstacles, falls, gets up again… and reaches the goal. "Tout est bien qui finit bien." "Non, non, tu l'as bien écrit, Zachary. C'est PARFAIT!"

The hour is soon over. A perfect hour. Every little group is busy, creative, a bit noisy but healthily noisy. A day a teacher feels proud of herself, proud of her class, proud of each of the students.

Zachary is the hero of his group, visibly blossoming, happy to be in charge. I remind him twice to let the girls express their suggestions, their ideas. But he actually does. He is PERFECT. No other word. His French is not, but his attitude is. An enlightened leader, enjoying communicating in French with his group, among giggles.

Each group delegates a reader. Zachary reads. Looks are exchanged between students… smiles… claps…

It's time to go!

"Bye Miss. Happy Christmas… Joyeux Noël…"

I rush to the lift, eager to meet a colleague, any colleague!

"Today, I witnessed a 'Christmas Miracle'!!!"

* * *

Zachary was repeating the year. He had been absent from class about 70% of the time. He would sit alone at the back of the class, never answering questions. He never handed in a single homework assignment in a year and a half. He had developed school phobia the previous year and had to be followed medically. Before that day, I had never seen him smile.

I did not design this "Tarot des mille contes" activity to interest him, nor to provide him with opportunities for leadership. After some attempts to connect with him the previous year—to no avail—I had just given up on him.

A sea change took place that day. I learned to never give up. Keep providing opportunities, keep giving chances to the student. One day they may grab them.

A teacher is the class leader. To be a leader does not mean just giving orders and making students obey—even though we must. A leader analyses a situation, assesses the individuals, their weaknesses and strengths, and deliberately chooses to trigger the best in them by providing a variety of activities for different personalities and interests.

Repeating the same type of lesson never suited Zachary (fix one way or the other for consistency – until now, Zachary; from here, Zacharie). It only led him to repeat his closed-up behaviour. Encouraging words would never suffice.

A leader does not necessarily need to be "active" in the conventional way. In this case, my taking the lead meant fading into the background in order to allow Zachary to take the lead without feeling threatened by the teacher's overwhelming presence. He obviously felt more comfortable with peers; maybe he was happy to show his back to the teacher. Perhaps Zachary needed to handle some physical object to distract him from his inner tension.

Being a leader means being able to discover and promote every student's own leadership qualities. We all need to be leaders during some circumstances of life. It is important to leave school believing that we are capable because our teachers showed us our inner leadership power. On that day, Zachary left my class empowered.

A leader also shows the way. Rather than just mentioning the "Christmas miracle" to two colleagues in the lift, it was worth discussing in the staffroom. We all take leadership into our own hands by sharing positive experiences and emulating those of colleagues. We get old, tired, or temporarily disabled by life's personal events but we all enjoy talking about the students, sharing positive events in our classrooms, to rekindle our own teaching flame.

These learning experiences can also be shared more broadly through the school magazine or newsletter, adding "happy anecdotes" to inspire all. At our school, we have an important seminar once a year where these inspiring stories can also be shared and discussed, in the same way they are shared in this very book you are holding in your hands now.

It took so little to create a better learning environment for Zachary it was a pity not to have done it before—two years of missed opportunities! But now I feel stronger as a teacher, thanks to Zachary. He gave me back trust in myself as a leader. Perhaps that was the real "Christmas miracle."

Roseline Sultana Arnéodo is a Senior Lecturer at the Junior College, University of Malta, where she teaches French to 16- and 17-year-olds. Her teaching and writing focuses on civilizations across space and time. Her recent work includes a novel (Les enchanteurs de la Terre, published by Pantheon), a memoir co-authored with her mother about the Second World War (À l'ombre de la guerre, published by Xirocco), and French language and culture textbooks for students and teachers. Her Master's degree focused on the Oregon Indians; later she had the opportunity to teach Maori Students in New Zealand. Now in Malta, her special interest is students who have psychological, gender, religious, or ethnic issues after their flight from Middle Eastern conflict zones. She uses one-on-one "contact hours" to lead them out of a dead end and back to enjoying life at school.

The Fox Takes the Prize

Sara K. Green

In my hopeful assent to leadership, I have taken on some interesting supporting roles. I am the first person to apply to a position that is "lower level," with the understanding that future advancement is possible. Before starting my Ph.D., I took a job as an Academic Affairs Assistant at a local community college. Upon my arrival, I learned that the college had recently unveiled a new mascot. Apparently, very few people were for the idea. There were many concerns, the biggest of which was that no one wanted to don the attire. The mascot was passed around from department to department, until it finally landed in Advising. As I was the newest and lowliest member of advising, I was eager to please. I unwittingly volunteered myself, thinking nothing would come of it, but it wasn't long before I was trying on the fur. Sadly, the costume fit like a glove and, before I knew it, I was promoted to "Mascot Manager."

My career goals had not accounted for mascot management. Nowhere in my objectives had I stated that I wanted to run around in a costume, high-fiving kids and photobombing high school seniors. That said, the moment I put on the costume, I became the face of the school, literally. Soon, I was atop parade floats, facing a group of onlookers who may or may not have known our college, but were sure to return home remembering the fox that stood there waving at them. To be honest, being the school mascot started out being humiliating, but I learned to smile both in and out of costume. I went to the mall during winter break, representing the college. The President of the college even paid for me to get my picture taken with Santa, which was posted on the front page of our college newsletter. I got onboard with the mascot initiative whereas other staff and administrators had not. I even began a campaign to launch a Mascot Club, getting students involved and getting paid to go to a mascot training seminar.

My enthusiasm made a positive impression on my supervisor, the Dean of Student Success. When I applied for my Ph.D., he wrote my most supportive letter of recommendation. After only three months, I was promoted to an Academic Advisor. I was also asked to be on numerous committees, which required more responsibility than I had ever been afforded. The Dean entrusted projects to me that were well "beyond my paygrade," but I took every opportunity and learned more than I ever thought possible in such a short time. Some senior members of the college seemed surprised and unnerved at my involvement in issues as serious as our accreditation, but I quelled their concerns when I proved my aptitude time and time again. In my final month there, I was nominated for Employee of the Month.

I loved working for that college. I even grew to love my mascot alter ego. I imagine—had I not moved with my husband out of state, I would still be there. I gained a world of experience, made numerous lifelong friends and references, and had only worked there a total of six months.

Moral of the story: not everyone who desires a leadership position has the degree or the experience necessary, but it is important to start somewhere. I am fully confident that had I stayed at the college, I would have continued to move up. Though I would not necessarily recommend jumping into a costume at the age of 30 to advance your career goals, it is important to be a team player. Take the jobs at your organization that no one else wants and enjoy—or at least pretend to enjoy—doing it. Learn everything you can about your organization from everyone, from the president to maintenance. And, most importantly, do not be afraid to take those entry-level jobs to get your foot in the door.

It is true, once I get that Ph.D., I will most likely be applying for upper-level positions without necessarily needing to work my way up as a mascot. My Ph.D. program affords me a great deal of textbook knowledge on leadership styles as well as that coveted terminal degree. But nowhere in my education thus far have I learned that in order to be an effective leader, you sometimes need to swallow your ego and do what is best for the organization, even if it means doing something outside of your job requirements. That task may or may not be as potentially humiliating as becoming the organization's mascot, but through the most surprising routes, you might just make your mark.

Sara K. Green has worked in academia as an Academic Advisor for three years and as an Administrative Assistant for two years for two different colleges. She was also fortunate enough to teach a semester of Introduction to Philosophy. Ms. Green received her B.A. in Philosophy from Ohio Dominican University, is nearly finished her M.A. in Philosophy from Franciscan University of Steubenville, and is currently in the Ph.D. program for Educational Leadership at the University of Kentucky. Ms. Green may be reached via email at greensa.1313@gmail.com.

What Does Trust Look Like?

Toby A. Travis

Since 1980, I have had the privilege, often the joy, and sometimes the challenge, to lead a wide variety of teams, in a wide variety of settings (e.g., an entertainment production company, several faith-based non-profit corporations, two international schools, and more). I have also had the very fortunate experience of working alongside of, and being mentored by some truly extraordinary leaders who have modeled for me close up exactly what effective organizational and school management looks like. Through their example, through my own personal experience, and validated through decades of research, I have discovered that the essential quality of effective leadership is *trust*. Can trusted leadership be developed or is it simply a soft skill that we are born with? We can see it. We can identify when it is present. But can it be cultivated in others?

I believe not only that trust can be cultivated, but that it is the #1 indicator of a successful school. Show me a school where teachers are highly motivated and engaged, where student achievement levels are consistently high, where community stakeholders are quick to support initiatives, and where programs and operations are run efficiently – and you will discover a high level of trust in the school leadership.

As educators, we know that the first step in learning and growth is to assess honestly and clearly where we are starting from. I have used the following nine behaviors to assess my own *trust level*. My friend David Horsager first introduced me to these indicators. David is the bestselling author of *The Trust Edge*, a book written for business leaders but recommended for all school leaders. The following serve me on a daily basis as practical and effective steps to practice effective and trusted school leadership every day:

1. *Listen.* An essential skill to effective leadership is being able to control the tongue. Know how to be quiet and listen to others intentionally and actively.

2. *Empathize.* Empathy does not necessarily mean agreement with positions; rather, empathy is the ability to understand and treat others' varying opinions with respect.

3. *Avoid manipulation.* The use of verbal manipulation is a guaranteed method for creating distrust in leadership. Never overstate nor understate issues or situations.

4. *Speak honestly.* Keep to the facts and do not exaggerate.

5. *Stay focused; avoid distractions.* Evaluate and reflect on every element of school operation through its central mission, vision, core values, and current priorities. Reflected this focus at all times, whether in general conversations, formal presentations, or prepared social media postings.

6. *Ask questions.* Active and intentional listeners ask both *inquiry* questions to gather information and *discovery* questions to help determine a solution.

7. *Keep an open mind; don't jump to conclusions.* Review all of the data regarding an issue before deciding. Less than fully informed decision-making fosters distrust.

8. *Do not criticize.* Criticism is not analysis. Consider ideas, concepts, and views from varying perspectives, and then provide a critique of those views without criticizing the ideas or the individuals supporting those ideas.

9. *Simplify the complicated.* Maintain a *birds-eye* view of all the issues surrounding successful school operation, and the complex factors affecting policy creation and decision-making in the best and fullest interests of the school. A gifted and skilled communicator helps others to see complex ideas through simple language.

As you consider these nine behaviors of trusted school leaders, does someone come to mind? Frequently when I share these indicators, people recall an individual who was instrumental in their decision to pursue education management as a career. That was true for me as well. I serve in school leadership today largely due to the influence of a highly trusted mentor with an authentic altruistic desire to make an impact on students, teachers, families, and communities. It is the person I wish to be.

Over the years, I have discovered that these nine qualities provide daily benchmarks of where my leadership strengths are at present, and where I yet need to develop greater consistency. As I have done so, not only do I witness the personal rewards of being trusted, but I can also see a direct correlation to increased levels of student achievement, deeper stakeholder relationships, and even stronger financial operations. That's what trust looks like.

Toby A. Travis, Ed.D., is the Headmaster of Desert Christian Schools in Tucson, Arizona, and an Executive Consultant with the Global School Consulting Group. He is the author and presenter of TrustED School Leadership Development, a research-based, professional development training program for school leaders. More information is available from www. trustEDschoolleader.com and www.GlobalSchoolConsultants.com.

Imagination Matters

Gillian Judson

I recently participated in a seminar on "student engagement" with new and experienced teachers, principals, vice-principals, and district-level educational leaders. We started with a basic icebreaker activity—to introduce ourselves by giving our name and one word to reflect a central aspect of our educational philosophy. My chosen word led to a lot of blank stares and more than a few confused looks.

"Hi, I'm Gillian Judson. My word is *perfinker.*"

Most people nodded hesitantly, taking on a quizzical look that said *...Rrrriiight. And that means?* One person I met looked at me skeptically and said, "That's not a real word, Gillian." Actually, it is.

Psychologist David Kresch coined the term "perfinker." He argues that human beings never just think. They perceive, *feel*, and think at the same time. They *perfink*. Recent research in affective neuroscience also indicates this to be true. (And, of course, many people simply know this to be true.) Emotion is—as Dr. Mary Helen Immordino-Yang (2105) describes it—the mind's rudder.

Emotion, therefore, is at the helm. What a lovely metaphor for learning. Emotion directs what is meaningful to us. Put another way, the things that we most remember, the things we understand *affect* us. We are all emotional and imaginative beings. And so, I explained to my skeptical colleague that I'm a perfinker. And, the thing is... he is, too.

A few weeks later, I had the chance for a deeper conversation with that skeptical, stickler-for-English colleague. I'm glad I ordered the *large* coffee because what started out as superficial discussion about the notion of "perfinking" and what it means for teaching, turned into a much deeper examination of how imagination supports effective leadership.

With caffeine coursing through our veins, we considered the following questions: What if educational leaders saw the people in their schools/districts/communities as *perfinkers*? How would this realization influence the ways in which they shaped their interactions with their teachers/staff? How would this realization affect the kinds of professional development experiences offered to teachers? How would this realization impact policy decisions made in the name of student success/achievement?

We agreed that while effective educational leaders may not know the term "perfinker," at some deeper level they do understand the importance of emotional and imaginative engagement for their leadership practice. They know that imagination is as important for student learning as it is for teacher learning, community-building, and educational change. We decided that effective educational leaders are storytellers.

Now, my colleague and I spent a long time talking about "story" and "storyteller"—I did say a *large* coffee. Much like the notion of "imagination" itself, "story" is often misunderstood. The ability to envision the possible—the work of the imagination—lies at the heart of all human invention and understanding. It is one of the great workhorses of learning. It is *not* a childish practice of make-believe or fantasy nor is it a capacity of great artists alone. All human beings *envision the possible*. All human beings employ "cognitive tools" to make sense of the world—cognitive tools like powerful theories, vivid mental images, metaphor, humour and, of course, the story-form (Egan & Judson, 2015).

Like imagination, we agreed that the concept of "story" is often misunderstood too. The idea that effective educational leaders are *storytellers* does not mean they make up fictions, endlessly drone on and on, or exist in a world of make-believe. As storytellers, they shape their leadership practices in ways that reveal the emotional significance of what they are doing. They engage the *perfinkers* that they work with by evoking their emotions. *This* is storytelling. There's a reason why the story-form is one of the most powerful teaching tools—it engages human emotion and ignites imagination.

We ended with the following questions and made another date to have coffee: How aware are educational leaders of the imaginative needs/interests of their teachers? How often do these tools influence *how* principals introduce new ideas to their teachers or *how* school communities welcome and engage the parent community? What role does imagination play in the "brand" of schools or districts? Is the freedom to envision the possible part of their brand? It's one thing to say "Yes! We value imagination and creativity in our students. We support it in our classrooms!"—it's another thing for school leaders to enact imaginative practices themselves.

Additional Reading:

Egan, K., & Judson, G. (2015). *Imagination and the Engaged Learner: Cognitive Tools for the Classroom.* New York: Teachers' College Press.

Immordino-Yang, M. (2015). *Emotions, Learning, and the Brain: Exploring the Educational Implications of Affective Neuroscience.* New York: W.W. Norton & Co.

Dr. Gillian Judson teaches in the Faculty of Education at Simon Fraser University, serves as a director of the Imaginative Education Research Group, and coordinator of Imaginative Education and Imaginative Ecological Education program initiatives. Her work focuses on the role of imagination in all learning contexts. As an educational consultant, she investigates imaginative and ecological teaching practices, educational program design, educational change, and educational leadership. Her latest books include Engaging Imagination in Ecological Education: Practical Strategies for Teaching (2015), and A Walking Curriculum (2018).

PART II

Content of Character:
Principles of Principals

Leadership occurs in context. The August 1963, "March on Washington" gave humanity a powerful lesson on character that transcended context. Dr. Martin Luther King Jr. stated, "*I have a dream that my four little children will one day live in a nation where they will not be judged by the color of their skin but by the content of their character.*" Leaders are also judged by the content of their character. Character is a complex concept with as many operational definitions as there are individuals who have ever been asked, "What is character?" Character defines leaders. Character represents alignment between espoused theories and theories in action, between word and deed. Character is also how you behave when no one is watching. Character reflects a leader's legacy and reputation. Character defines the leader in times of both great joy and greater adversity. When asked who they admire most, leaders describe someone who was influential in their decision to pursue leadership. The specific defining characteristics of character may differ, but they often have dimensions of the pursuit of bigger picture, the greater good, and the longer term.

Leaders Must Create Other Leaders

Carin Vijfhuizen

Sometimes life lessons require only a few words instead of 800. I love one-liners, because of the concise and impactful meaning expressed in just a few words. One-liners trigger questions, compelling you to explain yourself and make your thoughts concrete. For instance, if I were to tell you that "leaders create more leaders," you would likely ask me to explain. You might ask me to show how a leader makes others lead. I would offer three key insights that I learned from practice and that I still apply to my own leadership:

1. A leader truly sees and appreciates the potential of colleagues, staff, and students. Acknowledging and appreciating their potential will increase their self-confidence and strengthen their potential (trust and appreciation are key).

2. A leader leads the joint process of formulating clear indicators on what, for example, is a good teacher, good student, or good organisation. Those indicators resemble buoys, shaping a strategic plan and learning path, lighting the way as to how to strengthen potential to do a better job and strengthen the organization.

3. A leader inspires and creates space in order for colleagues, staff, and students to feel stimulated to ask questions and to provide solutions, creating a sense of ownership in both their own and the organisation's growth.

These perspectives are based on my experiences in different organisations, in various countries across the world. I have had several jobs: working as research coordinator, researcher, professor, programme manager, senior advisor, and even a principal. Each of these jobs provided great learning opportunities. I have been able to work in an international context with many different cultures across East, West, North, and South. Different geographical locations have unique challenges, histories, climates, and understandings that shape their people and their cultures. This experience has improved my understanding of my own culture, its values, beliefs, underlying assumptions, and "artifacts" (as Edgar H. Schein, 2010, would put it). Culture is like social glue, keeping people, societies, or organizations together and allowing them to perform.

In several countries, my colleagues would ask me, "What makes Dutch leadership different?" They tried to put a finger on it, which triggered me to operationalise how the Dutch distinguish themselves. The Dutch are shaped by wind and water, so we say. The Netherlands is a small, flat country below sea level. Every day you'll cycle against the wind (teaching you to work hard for your goals). There's the constant appreciation of keeping the water at bay (reminding you of risk management) and that when the water rises we will need to help each other (emphasising cooperation). My leadership is shaped by my Dutch upbringing and (continuing) education, and by experiencing and learning from different cultures and seeing how leadership is informed in those cultures. During my leadership learning process, the following key elements emerged:

1. Openness (to walk your talk)
2. Consultation with staff and students in order to together achieve a better product, performance, and consensus to strengthen the organization
3. Efficiency
4. Learning by doing
5. Monitoring progress and adjusting (flexibility)
6. Long term vision of sustainability in education, considering the institutional, educational, technical, and financial areas

Different leadership cultures emerged in a technical college in Saudi Arabia, where I was a principal (see Vijfhuizen & Tautan, forthcoming). One of our Saudi staff used to say, "You did not tell me to do it."

In other words, I was to blame when things were not done. So, I needed to tell her exactly what to do. One of the British department heads complained, "The staff do not listen. They don't do what I tell them to do." She considered her staff as empty vessels, dependent on her commands to exercise their own potential. Neither of these approaches fit my key perspectives of leadership.

I developed a short leadership course, called the POFS approach, to create a learning path for the Saudi staff, to strengthen their potential:

- Pro-active and implement (Do)
- Observe (See)
- Follow up (React)
- Sustain through the quality assurance system (Sustain)

During bi-weekly meetings, I encouraged my Saudi colleagues to discuss the best approaches to tackle the challenges and problems they faced in their work, systematically employing the POFS approach. They participated together and strengthened their potential in a context that stimulated them to lead and to contribute towards a more successful organization.

The art of leadership is appreciation for people's insights, knowledge, and activities. The key is designing an approach for people who want to learn and strengthen their capacities to do a greater job and lead. Across all cultures, we are leaders and learners employed in a daily challenge, trying to create a better world, together.

Carin Vijfhuizen, Ph.D., is a development sociologist and the Director of SLEE-B (Strengthening Leadership in Education and Enterprise – Balance) and senior international consultant in institutional development, leadership, rural development, agriculture, and gender. She has extensive work experience in Africa, the Middle East, the Netherlands, and Southeast Asia (see www.carinvijfhuizen.com; Pick a Pearl).

Ghost in the Machine

Linc Johnson

Being a leader means modifying your leadership at every opportunity. All great leaders know that a true leader is a facilitator who distributes leadership amongst the stakeholders and constituents. On my very first day at Centinela State Prison as Supervisor of Academic Instruction, the institution scored last in comparison to the 32 other prisons in California. We were number 33 of 33. Everyone knew it, everyone accepted it, and no one cared if it changed or not. At least that is how I felt. I was told where to sit, what paperwork to complete, and which teachers to write up for not doing their jobs. What was most evident was that the school leadership and staff seemed comfortable in last place. Aside from specifically-targeted disciplinary issues, there were no other expectations or motivations to succeed. They were complacently apathetic—able to hide behind failure as a culture instead of a transitionary stage.

I observed this for six months and told myself what I would do differently if I ever got the opportunity to lead the department. At the end of six months, I got my chance. I became the Supervisor of Correctional Education Programs at Centinela State Prison. I learned from a former superintendent that leading a school is like driving a bus. You need the right people in the right seats before you even move the bus. I also have years of experience playing and watching football, so I knew that I needed to build my staff into a strong team and convince them that we were not merely competing against other prisons in the state, but that we needed to become world class. Each of my players needed to play their positions to the best of their abilities. This was met with some hemming and hawing, and even when I visited the classrooms, teachers would say, "The principal doesn't visit classrooms." Well, here I am. How do I "supervise" you if I never supervise you? It did not take long for teachers to get used to the idea that I was fully invested and wanted to change the culture, and the results, coming from this institution. I had to sell them on my vision, and then have them create a mission from that.

What they needed to understand was that what we do in prison schools creates global citizens. We are the "R" in rehabilitation, and education is important. Yes, we could write our students off as murderers, kidnappers, pimps, and rapists, but at some point, 90% of them would be released into neighborhoods that were already disenfranchised and dilapidated. The goal was to expand the students' worldviews beyond a two-mile radius and teach them that there was a whole world out there for them to discover. This led me to creating new tools for efficacy in global consciousness, influence, impact, and immersion, including extensive multicultural contact, increased shared and combined resources, special traditions, and unique local dimensions. The teachers benefitted from this process as well, expanding their 21st century toolboxes and meaningfully interacting with students on a level unseen in prison. I solicited input from the students on how the school was run and how effective they thought the teachers were. I needed the students to know that their input mattered, and the teachers needed to know that we were all leading this school to something greater. I told anyone who would listen that effective teachers have the "Four Cs": caring, controlling, captivating, and challenging.

I grew up in Compton, California, with a healthy disdain for authority. I was not a great student and my behavior in class was even worse. I was one bad decision away from being like the students in my school—incarcerated, underdeveloped, and mis-educated. What we do as leaders is important. I knew I needed to change the existing patterns of social interaction. I needed to be an accessible leader with a vision that my staff all knew and could invest in. I knew how to converge with the system, as well as when to diverge. I became a ghost in the machine in my attempts to form and test methodologies that could be generalized across institutions. Within the first year of my tenure, Centinela shot up to number 17 in the state and now hovers around number 7 out of 35 prisons. This is not only because of something I did actively and consciously, but also because I knew how to step back and let the staff and students lead, succeed, and shine on their own.

Dr. Linc Johnson is the Supervisor of Correctional Education Programs at California City Correctional facility. He also teaches English 101 at Los Angeles Southwest College, Introduction to Shakespeare at Cerro Coso College, and Introduction to Multicultural Education for the Division of Education at San Diego State University. His research and academic interests are global competence, expanding worldviews, globalization and internationalization, social practice, and organizational change.

Mentoring Artists Today

Ann Laenen

Being an artist today involves many challenges. In our demographically, technologically, and economically evolving society, young people trained as artists must redefine their role. Years ago, artistic skills training seemed perfectly fine; nowadays this is very much in question. It is important that students receive more balanced training that prepares them for current society.

When I entered higher arts education in 2009, first as a lecturer, then head of department, and later as Dean of four art campuses that covered all aspects of art and design, we were aware that we had to prepare students for the 21st century. This meant not just training them as good artists but also providing them with other skills needed to make a career.

I was lucky myself to work at the PhD level on a practice-based topic in arts education. The School of Education at the University of Leeds already had experience in this area. This gave me the opportunity to research and reflect upon the domain I had been active in for the previous ten years as a practitioner—opera education. When I started my career, we learned by doing. In Flanders, there was no formal training in arts education at the time. This has changed vastly over the years, but back then we were all pioneers.

This background was very helpful in rethinking curricula in the arts as practice and academia came together. At the faculty, we had lengthy discussions about the future role of artists and arts education and how to combine art research, theory, and practice into our courses. Arts curricula requires a combination of hard technique combined with soft skills. Practice-based research and projects with an interdisciplinary component connected with the student's creative skills seemed crucial.

We wanted to train people in very specific artistic skills as well as skills they could use to challenge today's technological, economic, and social issues. Thus, we wanted them to be ready for jobs that might not even exist yet. When the digital media design course started in 2000, for instance, barely anyone was talking about digital strategy let alone online advertising, yet many of our students moved into those areas upon graduation.

I strongly believe that artists can make us think about and reflect on social issues, creating a certain uneasiness with the status quo. In Dutch we call this "de onmaat van de Kunst" (going against the beat). Artists today have an important role in making us aware of the unseen and showing us what needs our attention. An artist must question everything to make us question everything.

As such, artists play important roles on interdisciplinary teams working on organizational and societal issues. Their creative skills should be harnessed in domains other than the arts. In an age where technology and artificial intelligence are taking over in science and society, someone who can think in different, critical, fresh ways is of utmost value.

When looking at the 21st skills now needed in education, many of them are related to the arts: creativity and innovation, critical thinking and problem solving (although I prefer to call it "going for the best possible solution"), collaboration, social and cross-cultural interaction, communication and leadership. These could easily be integrated into the BA, MA, and PhD levels in higher arts education.

Many of these skills are implicit to the arts. What needs extra attention is creative leadership, collaboration and co-creation, interdisciplinary work, and cross-cultural interaction. I have always supported interdisciplinary projects within the faculty and have been pleased to shape courses such as Design Thinking and Active Design Processes. These courses focus on societal and human-centred issues, where collaboration, co-creation with non-designers/artists, creative leadership, and solution-based work are key. In this way, we teach future artists to look beyond their comfort zone and show them how their expertise can impact society.

Teaching them how to function in an interdisciplinary team is my new mission. The nicest complement you can get as an educator is to meet one of your students a few years later and be told how much the learned from the course. Teaching in the arts means that, for me, this happens all the time.

Dr. Ann Laenen studied Arts and Theatre Science at KU Leuven and did her PhD at the University of Leeds on audience development. She became the coordinator of the Communication Media Design programme at the Media & Design Academy in Genk in 2009, department head in 2010, and Dean of the LUCA School of Arts (KU Leuven) in 2012. Currently she teaches active design processes and design thinking at the University of Malta, combining her academic work with project coordination and consultancy in the arts, culture, creative, and education sectors.

Making Meaningful Connections

Debra Berner

A s a veteran elementary school principal, I believe that one of the most important tasks of a school leader is to be effective at establishing, maintaining, and communicating key information to the school community. I must be open to listening to what parents, staff, and students think about the school, and have in place the necessary structures and processes to promote effective communication and timely resolution of tasks and conflicts.

Over the years, I have ensured that everyone understands and implements the vision and mission of our school. In order to do this, I must begin by understanding how vital good communication is and then learn when and how to communicate effectively. Communication is actually the link to many school successes—with staff, with parents, and most importantly, with our students. It is imperative that I align my actions with my words and that I continually reflect upon them to ensure they are meaningful to all.

So, how do I make communication in my school a priority? How does one communicate effectively? When is it appropriate? Why is it necessary? Most of us are not born communicators; we must practice this learned skill frequently. Throughout my life, I have been observing how others communicate effectively and I model those who demonstrate success and earn respect. I also learned to modify how I communicate to various groups and to appreciate cultural differences. The way I communicate as a parent, as a significant other, as a colleague, as a friend, as a mentor, all differ. My job as principal is to communicate to all stakeholders that our students come first, and our focus is always on what is best for them.

My communications with staff need to be consistent and have a personal touch. It may be as simple as an informal visit to their classroom or simply a short note about something wonderful that they did that day. I have an open-door policy, so when I can, I drop what I am doing to talk with teachers. I also respond to their emails in a timely manner. Staff members want to know they are being heard and that you will follow up.

I also strive to be thoughtful and transparent. People want the facts; though they may not like the truth, they would much rather receive it straight from me and then address the situation. I also do my homework before I send anything out. Nothing is more damaging than approaching someone with the wrong information.

Although I am always working on some type of timeline, I also respect the timelines of others. The easiest way to frustrate anyone is to send out a Friday request with a Monday or Tuesday deadline. I respect their time by not inundating them with messages throughout the week and by respecting their evenings and weekends; messages need to be short, to the point, and timely.

Equally important is communicating with parents. I use a variety of methods to involve members of the school community regarding local or system-wide policies and initiatives. For example, I make personal calls regarding their children. I hold parent update meetings for their input on our School Improvement Plan. I communicate meaningful and timely information through the weekly school and PTA newsletters and send short, weekly email messages to the community. This provides the entire school community with everything from a regular Sunday night news blast for the upcoming week to a more specific request for parental support of our new recess procedures. I attend all PTA meetings and sponsored events to keep myself a visible, active partner.

Finally, I take great pride in my interactions and communications with our students. Relationship-building contributes to student achievement. Students who feel connected, who are taught by teachers who feel supported, and whose parents model that school is a positive place achieve more. I hold lunch meetings, monitor recess daily, use restorative practices to hold kids accountable, do a "Whatever Wednesday" segment on the morning announcements, and most importantly, I *always* end a disciplinary visit to my office with the statement that I believe in them and know they will make better choices next time.

I know my actions and words matter—I am not perfect at this skill but through personal reflection, I am finding my own voice as I get older. As an administrator, I must be committed to truly listening to the concerns of staff, students, and parents and regularly encourage open and reciprocal communication with all. Making meaningful connections throughout the day takes thought and practice—it is not a skill that can be learned overnight but is one of the most worthwhile ones to develop.

__Debra Berner__ began her career in 1979 as a special educator and continued working with students with all types of disabilities until 1999 when she left the classroom to begin her administrative career. She has also worked at the central office level, most recently as the Director of Student Services. She is currently in her 11th year as an elementary school principal and is the proud Principal of Lakewood Elementary School, Montgomery County Public Schools, Rockville, Maryland. Ms. Berner also is an adjunct professor for Hood College, where she teaches aspiring administrators about student services and special education.

Whose *Normal* is *Normal*?
International Mindedness in International Schools

Lana Al-Aghbar

Several years ago, while attending an international recruiting fair, I engaged in a conversation with colleagues from other schools about recruiting teachers with international experience. Their perception was that these teachers were more adept at living abroad and working with students from diverse backgrounds. I must admit that I didn't reflect much on this discussion until years later when I was fortunate enough to witness a conversation in the faculty lounge at my school. This exchange, involving several highly respected, seasoned, international educators, was about trying different foods, to which one teacher responded with the statement, "I only eat *normal* food." The word *normal* struck a chord with me. I found myself pondering the meaning of *normal*. What is *normal*, whose *normal* is *normal*, and is there a universal *normal*?

Normal, an everyday word used in this simplistic and innocuous way, led me to the realization that unless our perceptions change about what is *normal*, we can never accept others' understandings of *normal*, nor their respective affiliations as equally valid states of *normal*. Alarming were the implications of this interpretation of *normal*. I found myself questioning our thinking as educators working with culturally diverse student populations. Are our students' perceptions of *normal* not as valid as ours? How are we honoring and respecting the diverse backgrounds and beliefs of our students?

This incidental conversation proved to be most influential in my professional life. Due of this casual encounter, I have become deeply committed to promoting international mindedness. The reality of working in a school setting with a student body comprised of 74 nationalities made it all the more relevant! I began to reflect critically on how much I was doing as a leader to enhance the learning experiences of all my students, by fostering learning from and about each other, within our school setting. It became very apparent that our students' learning could be further enriched, and this would only happen if the "right" people were leading the learning. These "right" people are internationally minded educators who celebrate diversity and understand its power within the classroom.

This commitment to international mindedness has had a significant impact on my recruiting efforts. In reflecting on my previous practice, and while I pride myself on having recruited outstanding educators over the years, I recognize that a very limited portion of my attention was dedicated to ascertaining candidates' international mindedness and their suitability to working in culturally diverse settings. I found myself becoming more and more deliberate about getting to know candidates, and more genuinely invested in garnering information pertaining to their worldviews, biases, and in turn perceptions of international mindedness within a school setting.

During recruiting, my focus shifted from one that centered around suitability to attend to excellence in academics and general social/emotional student wellbeing, to one that focused on demonstrating a commitment to respecting, promoting and optimizing on student diversity.

By concentrating on international mindedness, I was in no way de-emphasizing academic importance; rather, I was attempting to determine how academic learning might be enhanced. Responses to certain questions—such as "What does international mindedness mean to you?" and "How do you take advantage of student diversity in your classroom?", proved to be most informative. I have come to the realization that in the absence of internationally minded teachers, we risk sacrificing learning potential within culturally diverse classrooms.

While we as educators communicate a shared commitment to understanding our learners, this investment has predominantly centered on academic achievement, learning behaviors, and learning styles. Other than reference to home language and nationality, there seems to be a limited focus on students' cultural identities, beliefs, and values. Omitting this vital information highlights a significant gap in our learner profiles and can inevitably hinder the process of designing meaningful learning experiences for all students. Capitalizing on diversity translates into providing all students with opportunities to learn firsthand from their peers. Is this not the authentic learning we pride ourselves on and convey to parents?

I must admit that it is no easy feat to identify shortcomings in one's work and I wonder if I would have arrived at this realization had I not been struck by the naive reference to the word *normal*. It is time to examine our practice of international mindedness through critical and clear lenses. We must implement practices that extend beyond the typical kinds of international celebrations we witness in schools, such as International Week, that merely scratch the surface of cultivating international mindedness. This is a call to move towards nurturing learning environments where diversity is a way of life and not simply a demographic composition.

Normal... a powerful word in my dictionary and definitely my game changer.

Lana Al-Aghbar has been an international educator for 24 years. She is experienced as an elementary classroom teacher, elementary curriculum coordinator, and elementary principal. Lana holds a B.Ed. in Elementary Education with a specialization in Early Childhood Education, and a Master's in Curriculum and Instruction, both from McGill University. Additionally, Lana has worked with the International Baccalaureate Primary Years Program and U.S. standards-based curricula. Lana is pursuing a Doctor of Education in Educational Leadership from the University of Western Ontario.

The Student/Teacher Binary:
A "Gift" to Consider

Natalie Davey

I have been teaching for 17 years, and in that time I have become attuned to both the nervous feeling in my stomach and the inevitably fitful sleep that signals the beginning of a new school year. I would say that I have made it this far in my career because of a few glasses of wine on Labour Day and the annual reminder of one important truth. Year after year, I coach myself through those "first day jitters" because I know that I'll be met by a group of young people who, before even meeting me, will accept me as their teacher. No questions asked. My study of educational philosophy has provided me with a word to describe this truth. I call it a "gift."

I borrow this term from philosopher Emmanuel Levinas who writes about the notion of "gift" as something deemed so solely through the act of its giving. A Levinasian perspective would point to the very real and necessary potential for that gift to be rejected, even though the giver, no doubt, hopes for a different response. Thus, to give a gift is a very vulnerable act. The giver is left with hands open as the potential receiver decides on her next move. From an educational perspective, I would suggest that year after year, the students I meet on the first day of school are gift givers. They do all the hard behind-the-scenes work of getting themselves to school—not an easy task for many. I have only to show up, write my name on the dry-erase board, and there you have it. They gift me with the title of teacher—a weighty title, loaded with meaning—and I accept that gift simply by taking my place at the front of the room.

I have written this essay because the truth is that after almost two decades of classroom teaching I have finally admitted something to myself. I am certain that I do not deserve this student gift! I am not saying I'm not a good teacher. I try hard to respond to the needs of my students, differentiating from the get-go, always aiming to listen first and respond accordingly. I avoid reading credit counseling summaries and student reports until we have had a little bit of time to get to know one another. Clean slates.

But this year, on the first day of class, when I turned from the dry-erase board to face my audience, I saw something new in front of me. As I stood there with the unearned attention of two dozen 17- and 18-year-olds, labeled "disengaged" and "at risk" by their schools, which is how they landed spots in my program, I recognized that I was being presented with a gift. It was wrapped in clear cellophane, transparent. What I saw was this: a group of almost-adults who have been in school since they were four years old. From early on, complicated systems that beget disenfranchisement in the classroom have been at play in most of their lives. And yet, living with the intertwined realities of race, class, gender, and ability—a list that must feel endless and systemically hard to tackle—there they sat, trying again, wondering if this time things would be different. I had seen similar students with similar stories over the years, but what struck me in this about-face moment of lifelong learning was the new way I was seeing myself. For a brief moment, I had to discern whether to accept their gift, knowing full well that I had not earned it. The weight of the implicit trust and beauty in its giving was almost too heavy to bear.

These days, in the early morning light, I sit with a coffee and ready myself for class by asking a difficult question: Do I want the gift they will give me today? The inexplicable magic of this student/teacher binary is that without one there is no other. As educators, we often fail, and the systems we teach within are inherently flawed—yet students continue to show up, asking to learn. I would like to believe that by seeing myself anew I am starting to earn the gift that keeps on giving. Some will beat me to class and some will straggle in after I have started. Some will email excuses and others will talk to me in person as the week wears on. Some will mumble and stare at the floor, while others will look me boldly in the eye, daring me to ask questions—begging me to be interested—simply because, as one young woman said to me this week, stating what was painfully obvious to her, clear as day: "You're my teacher."

What a gift.

Natalie Davey, Ph.D., began her career as an educator in the public secondary school environment, then moved into the realm of higher education. Today she bridges those two worlds as she works with student success and "Learning to 18" initiatives on college campuses. In each setting, she has desired to learn with, learn from, and advocate for her students. Davey's teaching and research interests include critical pedagogy, with a narrative focus on student engagement and the education of youth in detention.

Leading Through Non-Attrition

Charles Anthony

Teaching is the most important job in the world; therefore, as a society we must all strive to have the best, most qualified teachers in every classroom, in every country. I believe that teaching is indeed a calling and is therefore not suited to everyone. This, coupled with the mass exodus of teachers from the profession and shortages around the globe, leaves us all in a bit of a quandary! How do we balance the real dilemma of teacher shortages with teacher quality?

The educational community, both in my state of Arizona and nationally, are constantly struggling with the high rate of teacher attrition. Many teachers are leaving the field, mostly within the first three to five years of their careers. In my current role as a professor who works with future teachers and administrators, it is my duty to explore these challenges in order to promote awareness on the "front lines." The problem of teacher attrition is both visible and measurable; it can also be an opportunity for leaders to improve the climate of the school and the district.

A less-explored but equally pressing issue also plagues our schools—"teacher non-attrition". In non-attrition, teachers remain in the classroom after they have lost their commitment to students and their love for the profession. This often requires the hard decision of terminating a teacher who is no longer serving our students and the greater educational community.

Based on my 23-year background as a U.S. Army officer, I follow the basic tenant of always making decisions in the best interests of the organization or team. This is not always popular. Terminating employees is one of the worst aspects of our job as school leaders! Schools all have policies and protocols for evaluating teachers and helping them improve their pedagogy and content knowledge. Unfortunately, the process gets a bit murky when dealing with real people and the various laws that protect teachers despite some needing to be counseled out of our profession. This hard task is often not addressed, left for the next administrator to grapple with.

I inherited such a task during my first year as a school principal. It involved a teacher who had been working at the school for over four years and who was well liked by the faculty and staff. On my first observation, it became clear that he just was not committed to working with students. During our pre-observation meeting, he spent the majority of our time together explaining how terrible and unmanageable "these students" were. He followed this rant by proclaiming that he would fail most of them if not for the repercussions from parents and the administration. I decided to simply listen to him on this first meeting and follow through with the planned observation.

Once I entered his classroom, however, it was immediately evident that not only did he not respect his students but that they thought even less of him! The back row of the class included at least six students in a deep slumber with the vast majority of the rest of the class in idle sidebar conversation. It made no difference to them or to him that I was present. The observed lesson was on American History, specifically industrialization. After his 35th PowerPoint slide and his proclamation that "We don't have any more real thinkers in this entitled generation," the bell saved us all! I left with a sense of sadness for both his students and for him. As I was preparing my post-observation report, trying to fit into a rubric what I had just observed, it became clear that this was someone who, at the very least, needed help but possibly needed counseling out of the profession.

The specific protocol required documentation and even disciplinary action, yet no one had placed him on an improvement plan. He just barely made the "satisfactory" level of the rubric. I would need to start this multi-stage process and I wanted it to be truthful yet respectful. I also needed to get myself psychologically ready to lay out the plan.

At the onset of our post-observation meeting, he began by telling me that he thought his lesson did not fare well because it was "his terrible fifth period" class. I decided to start our discussion with a simple question: "Do you truly want to continue teaching?" What followed was not at all on my plan. His reply was, "No, I really don't, but have no back up plan and I've never been asked that question with such candor." I noticed tears forming in his eyes, so I discussed my observation notes briefly. He explained that he did not plan to return the next school year but, if allowed, would stay the remaining three months until the summer break. He actually knew that he was doing a disservice to the students, but he had never been challenged on it by an administrator or by his peers.

We came to an agreement that he would continue through the remainder of his contract but would have a co-teacher with him in order to help with the transition and allow him to explore other opportunities outside of education. I would like to say that this was the only time I had to have this chat with someone, but more did follow. Not all resulted in the teacher leaving; rather, many turned out to be opportunities for training and coaching.

As leaders, we all must make time to know and observe our classroom teachers, help those willing to improve, and help those who are not to "find their happiness elsewhere." That teacher and I met several years later, and he had found his career and happiness in another field. He actually thanked me for the chance to leave the school that had made him miserable after his first year of teaching.

Dr. Charles Anthony has had a long and diverse career serving in a multitude of leadership positions. As a U.S. Army officer, he trained and led soldiers for 23 years in such places as Korea, Egypt, and Iraq. Dr. Anthony has also been a vice president for Wells Fargo Bank, launching the Emerging Markets Division and leading many strategic initiatives. As a teacher, he earned several local and national awards, including the Veterans of Foreign Wars Teacher of the Year. Dr. Anthony has served as an administrator and principal and helped launch a STEM-based blending learning center with over 6300 students. He is currently a clinical professor for Arizona State University working with future teachers and administrators. He may be reached via email at drcharlesanthony@gmail.com.

Authentic Leadership is a Great Start

Lisa Gonzales

A uthentic leadership isn't an approach I was introduced to in my advanced studies in organizational leadership, which still surprises me. Had I heard about it earlier, and the value of this type of leadership style, I clearly would have adopted it a decade ago.

Honest relationships and promoting openness are at the center of authentic leadership: finding one's true self and leading from it. Funny though...I've been through advanced certification programs at Stanford and USC with professors who pooh-poohed the idea of being genuine, authentic, and true. Instead, they used phrases like "Fake it 'til you make it" or "Never let them see your true self." But *Harvard Business Review* and *Forbes Magazine* have penned articles in the last few years around the connections made, ability to be in tune, and the self-awareness that comes with being real, and from my experiences as a public school leader, I tend to agree.

Early on in my career, a challenging scenario came my way shortly after I accepted a job as principal. Going through the books and reviewing financial reports, I noted inconsistencies that ultimately unearthed a staff member who was embezzling funds. To say I was devastated was an understatement. Colleagues told me that no matter how I communicated what had taken place, my staff would turn on me. In a meeting with my supervisors, I teared up.

Shortly after the meeting ended, my boss approached me in the hallway. Her anger palpable, she chastised me for getting emotional: "Don't ever let me see you do that again. You are not to show your emotions like that. It's a sign of weakness for a female leader." She stormed down the hallway.

I'm a rule follower, so I took her message to heart. In the ensuing years, I kept my feelings and emotions in check, even though it didn't feel right. Fast forward five years: I was principal in another district. My superintendent sat me down for a heart to heart: "I'm concerned that perhaps you aren't connecting with enough of your staff. I want you to go into your staff meeting next week and cry. They will like you better if you do."

After five years of leading in an emotionless manner, fabricating a reason to cry in front of my staff was simply inauthentic. I couldn't do it. When he called to follow up, I leveled with him that if a situation came up that warranted emotion—such as a death in the school community or something equally difficult—the show of emotion would have that real feel. My credibility dropped in his eyes because I didn't do what he said.

Why are these examples important? They show what challenges we struggle with as leaders, especially women. Many of us have that soft motherly side that makes our leadership style a little different from men, but finding our emotional balance can be somewhat elusive. It's important to know who you are and how you feel, and go from there. When you second-guess what emotions you should share, paralysis by analysis creeps in, and then finding that true emotional north can be a struggle.

Vulnerability is a major aspect of authentic leadership. To truly connect with others, it is critically important to find your true heart and share that with others. That doesn't mean wearing it on your sleeve, but being aware that people like people who are like them. If they feel they can relate to you because you are approachable, down-to-earth, and genuine, your authenticity quotient increases. So how can you become a more authentic leader?

- **Know your people**: Really get to know your team. When you understand their interests, family situations, and challenges, you are more apt to share more in conversations that deepen connections.

- **Be optimistic**: Teams are more effective when led by a positive and optimistic leader, which reinforces the real part (which reinforces the "real" part? Which reinforces authenticity?). Find the upside and keep negativity in check so as not to distance others.
- **Bypass perfection**: It's great to have high expectations, but be realistic. If your overly- high bar is set at 100% performance and a subordinate is functioning at 90%, let it go. Praise the 90% and don't feel you always need to have everyone at 100%. Always making others feel that they can't do great work doesn't strengthen relationships, nor is it caring and compassionate.

Learn to be passionate and be real with the stories you share and the connections you make. Don't feel a need to keep buried what makes you real and human. Your success will only increase as your authentic leadership skills strengthen.

Dr. Lisa Gonzales, *Ed.D., is the eternal energizer bunny, serving as the Assistant Superintendent of Educational Services in the Dublin Unified School District, leading the Association of California School Administrators as its President, coaching marathons, and shepherding her twelve-year-old twin daughters all over the Silicon Valley to soccer games. She loves to mentor colleagues, write for publications, speak on an array of topics to education leaders, and read mystery novels. In the afterlife, her goal is to catch up on her sleep.*

Be Bold, Be Yourself, Be Candid, and Stay Humble

Dan Stepenosky

Sometimes the best leadership lessons are on what not to do. I received one such lesson in leadership was while I was an ensign in the U.S. Navy. During my 1992 transfer from the *USS Waddell* to the *USS Chancellorsville*, the captain of the ship had a sit-down with me to review my file and evaluation. He looked at me and said, "You have always been one of my favorites. I knew you always cared because when I yelled at you, you would become embarrassed, and that showed me that you cared."

At that moment, I realized he had actually admitted to using humiliation as a leadership and motivational tool. In fact, he had used this technique throughout the entire year with everyone on the ship. Morale under his leadership was the worst I had experienced on two different ships under four different commanding officers. From that moment forward, I knew I never wanted to be that kind of leader.

Leadership is all about people. As superintendent, 90% of my budget goes into people—their salaries, medical benefits, tools/supplies, etc. My ability to connect in small but meaningful ways with my staff has an unquantifiable but very, very powerful impact on our mission as a school district. They need to know that I care about them, that I know them, and that I will work hard to support them.

I remember when I first became principal at Beverly Hills High School. As a teacher, I could pass easily through the hallways, but now as principal, students and staff would stop me in the hallway, excited to talk to me or have a quick word. They were thrilled when I visited their classrooms. I thoroughly enjoyed being principal of a school with 2,400 students, but if I tried to get around the campus between classes or at lunch, I would never get anywhere.

I kept thinking, "I was just down the hallway teaching a couple of years ago, why would they treat me so differently now?" I am still the same person who cared about them, but I was now the principal, and that thirty-second conversation might be the only opportunity they have to talk to the principal during the entire year. I quickly realized the importance of each of those thirty-seconds with students or staff. I had to be present and engaged during these short periods; my response would define how they viewed me, how they viewed the school, and whether or not they felt connected.

Therefore, as a superintendent, I try to get into every nook and cranny of my 14-school district. I challenge myself to find places I have never been and get off the beaten track, to get face-to-face with students and staff.

One book that has had a strong impact on my leadership is *Radical Candor: Be a Kick-Ass Boss without Losing Your Humanity,* by Kim Scott. I am a more effective leader when I lean in and provide feedback as soon as I see areas where a staff member can improve. If you care about people, be honest and direct with them. This can lead to difficult conversations when change is needed. If you have addressed issues and improvement has not occurred, then you must have that next hard conversation: "This may not be the best place for you."

My job is to do everything I can to help my team reach their full potential. Someone not able to succeed here can often be very successful elsewhere. There are hundreds of school districts in California, each with its own unique personality, culture, and needs. Several principals who did not meet my expectations went on to be successful superintendents throughout the state. It may be counterintuitive, but if you really care, do not leave them where they are not reaching their maximum potential. Let them move on and find a better position inside or outside of education.

Finally, humility is essential. The most successful people are not only confident, proud, and bold, but humble as well, giving them the ability to reflect, listen to external input, and gather data from the outside. When I run across struggling leaders, their egos are often in their way. Those who are humble, who can stop and listen, and who are coachable can be successful in all lines of work.

So be bold, be yourself, be candid, and stay humble.

Dr. Dan Stepenosky attended Villanova University on a Naval Reserve Officer Training Corps (NROTC) scholarship and graduated in 1990 with a BSc in Physics. Dan served four and a half years in the United States Navy. He taught Physics, AP Physics, and Astronomy at Beverly Hills High School and served as Assistant Principal and Principal from 1995 to 2006. He received his doctorate from UCLA in 2003. Dr. Stepenosky joined the Las Virgenes Unified School District in 2006 and then became Superintendent of Schools in 2012. In 2016 Dr. Stepenosky was selected Superintendent of the Year by the Association of California School Administrators.

On Mentoring Principals

Catherine M. Finger

"Without a vision, the people perish."—Proverbs 29:18

What fuels you with a sense of purpose as a leader? One of the experiences I most enjoy is walking alongside developing principals as they discover their gifts and passions. My greatest joy as a leader is my ability to see in others something they have yet to recognize in themselves, and to call it forth. I believe mentoring others is essential to creating the expertise, depth, and grit that today's school principals require. Fostering relationships with aspiring and practicing principals marked by trust, honesty, vulnerability, and mutual respect equips them to lead our school communities—while taking better care of themselves and their loved ones at the same time.

Spending time with a principal is essential to getting an intuitive sense of who they are, what makes their heart sing, and how they present themselves to the world. Taking the time to learn what drives another person is a gift to them, and a gift to myself. The time I spend with colleagues of various ages and stages in learning and in life is more powerful when I take a back seat and let the emerging leader set the course. My role is to listen, to ask thoughtful questions, and to shine a light on parts of their path that they may not have recognized as significant. In doing so, I find myself propelled by the "aha" moments that occur in their lives when a new truth is illuminated or a new ability emerges.

I have found that starting from the inside out—from the heart of the leader outward to the day-to-day routines of the organizations they lead—works best. Watchman Nee said it well when he stated that there are three parts to us humans: the outermost man, or the mask that we portray to the world; the inner man, where our thoughts and personality rest; and the innermost man, or "the garden where only God Himself may tread." For those of us who mentor principals, getting behind that leader's mask is the only way I know to see the hidden beauty, fears, and hopes waiting to be called forth by a suitable challenge or a trusted mentor.

Equally important is giving these leaders permission to enjoy life. Time-strapped school principals often need a push away from the demands of their organizations and into the arms of loved ones. Modeling balance by honoring family time myself, by engaging in my hobbies and prioritizing rest, gives the leaders I mentor permission to embrace the personal side of their own lives far more effectively than does my best advice. In demonstrating my interest in their personal lives over their work-related pursuits, I build bridges that stretch beyond the workplace.

Here's where a healthy dose of personal vulnerability comes in handy. During my tenure as a high school superintendent, I re-learned that actions speak louder than words. No matter how many times I told my principal colleagues to go home and spend time with their families, they only did so once I demonstrated healthier workplace habits myself. I was open with them regarding my time management challenges, and I showed them as best I could how I handled them. My principals knew which day I left the office early for a piano lesson. They knew I had a personal life—and that I valued theirs.

So, how can *you* become a safe haven of support and sustenance, ready to offer encouragement and refreshment to the principals in your life when they need it? In a word, *relationship, relationship, relationship.* When people share their hopes and dreams, and you listen with genuine interest, you will identify meaningful ways to affirm and encourage them. You don't need to tell your own stories. You don't need to offer advice. That's not what people are typically seeking when they turn to us in confidence. What a leader's heart longs for is affirmation, a gentle-firm push in the direction they know they should take. A strong shot of encouragement and validation from a trusted advisor is more valuable than a thousand "When I was a principal..." or "I had a teacher who..." stories.

In summary, most of us learn by sharing ideas and experiences, either aloud with each other, or by writing out our thoughts and sharing them with someone we trust. Instead of offering advice and telling our own war stories, we can try to create a safe space for other principals to tell their stories and reveal the longings of their hearts. Offering the gifts of listening without judgment and encouraging without advising is a powerful way to mentor and love aspiring leaders. And the unbridled joy that courses through us as we experience growth while supporting our fellow principals is a great gift to us as well.

Catherine M. Finger, Ed.D., loves to dream, write, and tell stories. Recently retired from a wonderful career in public education, she enjoys new professional roles as an executive search consultant for the Illinois Association of School Boards, and as a business development manager for NaviGate Prepared. She spends her off-work hours serving as the Vice-Chair of the College of Lake County Board of Trustees, writing the Jo Oliver thriller novels, and riding horses. Catherine lives in Lake County, Illinois, with a warm and wonderful combination of family and friends.

Ground Rules: Lead from the Heart

Melissa D. Patschke

On any given day, we are instructional leaders, system managers, caretakers, advisors, disciplinarians, supervisors, consultants, safety specialists, and general motivators. Daily decisions are made frequently and quickly. Time is the single resource that we never have enough of and rarely know if we are truly using it well. We act and move forward, forever hoping that our support, advice, judgements, and directions are made with informed integrity, and always centered on what's best for kids. Heart-centered leadership is the foundation by which trust, respect, quality, acceptance, and ownership are spread in a school. Embedding these beliefs is not another thing to do; it's the lubricant that makes everything work at higher levels of speed and efficiency. The time dedicated to this work is paid forward in experiential gains.

There's no golden path to leading from the heart. You must reflect, react, and respond to the human capacity in your school community. It's the difference between a job and a passion. It's opportunity, not obligation. It's the feeling of empowerment verses conformity. It's a pointed belief in unconditional caring, authentic trust, and inspirational practices. Leading a heart-centered system means taking care of people. It's seeing each individual as a valuable human being. It's finding strengths and building capacity in each person. Leading with the heart is a game changer. Start strong by establishing the following seven beliefs as ground rules for everyone you influence:

1. **Acknowledge**: All human beings deserve to be acknowledged. This is one of our basic human needs—to be included. A heart-centered leader must consistently send the message to all people that they are valuable, wanted, and have something to contribute to the school. This applies to the five- or fifteen-year-old walking down the hallway, to the parent visiting a classroom, and to the technician servicing the copy machine. It means that staff members talk to each other, smile, nod, shake hands, and high five. This is done as a genuine gesture that signals to those involved and those watching, *"You are worthy of my time; you are a valuable human being."*

2. **Require School Significant Others**: Everyone in a school must find a person that they can trust, talk to, and will listen to them vent. This significant someone is a person that will advise, offer a shoulder, and not take your conversation anywhere beyond the walls where it happened. We all have bad days, difficult interactions, and frustrating situations that come up, and it is very healthy to blow off steam in an appropriate "closed-door" setting. Establish it as a requirement that staff members find their person and also be that person for another staff member. Some people will have several of these "go-to" friends, but everyone *must* have at least one person to fill this role. Ultimately, the permission to rant and rave with confidentiality solves concerns and provides just enough support that the issue doesn't need to travel further. If it does, it is more often handled with appropriate and intentional professional filters.

3. **Touch**: We all have a need for supportive feedback, positive or corrective. The expectation of touch is one of outreach. It is basic caring for each other. It's the requirement that you reach out and send a note, write an e-mail, have a conversation, express that you care. Share messages of gratitude, of pride, of support verbally, in writing, or by action. Buy a cup of coffee for someone going through a hard time. Give a needed pat on the back or a high five. Prioritize the time to touch a heart and build relationships.

4. **Assume Positive Intent**: Ninety-nine percent of people wake up each day and want to do the right thing. The majority of people we meet, work with, teach, or lead are truly trying to make good choices. Step into every situation assuming that the person on the other side of the conversation has a positive intention. Try hard to reframe your own thinking to hear the other person's perspective. It may not change your mind, but you will be better prepared to compromise, empathize, or find a common place of agreement where you can rebuild and create a new outcome.

5. **Adopt an Attitude of Gratitude**: Gratitude is the most powerful emotion in the toolkit of human emotion—the single feeling that can stamp out all other negative feelings. Try to place yourself in a pure state of appreciation and remain angry, mad, or upset. It's impossible. The general expectation you need to set is to express gratitude purposely, openly, and freely. There are never too many genuine actions of appreciation taking place. When you express gratitude, receive gratitude, witness gratitude, or even tell the story of an act of gratitude, you benefit emotionally as a human being and you affect heart-centered culture immediately.

6. **Grant Permission to be Human**: Everyone has "off" days. Everyone makes mistakes. Everyone feels down sometimes. This is human. This is normal. The expectation you need to establish here is forgiveness. It must be okay in the culture to mess up. We must learn to accept life's challenges and be able to share our feelings about them. Forgiveness can be very difficult to manage, especially when it is ourselves that we must give grace. It is critical to move past wounds and not harbor the negative. Everyone needs help, support, and time to heal. Everyone needs to be heard. We all deserve "permission to be human." We all deserve to be forgiven.

7. **Celebrate Success and Share Joy**: Since the beginning of time, people have used diverse methods of celebration to reward, unite, and express joy. It is play, it is gratitude, and it

is togetherness. As emotionally-functional beings, we connect to each other through our memories of joys. We hold on to the treasure of traditions and find comfort in the smiles generated through sharing happiness. Take photos, eat cake, host events, make announcements, break bread, deliver balloons, blow bubbles, wear hats, dress in common T-shirts, hold ceremonies, attend weddings, hold baby showers, high five, hug, smile, laugh, and most importantly, have *fun*! Create the expectation in your school of announcing, rejoicing, and enjoying positive achievements, spontaneous happenings, and long-term milestones. These times will not be forgotten and, in turn, the smallest of joys will become the fabric of happy memories for years to come.

Dr. Melissa D. Patschke (Missie) is a thirty-year veteran of public education. Dr. Patschke has taught in a variety of special and regular education programs, worked at the middle and elementary levels, and served students from both urban and suburban areas. She is the lead learner and Principal of Upper Providence Elementary School in Royersford, Pennsylvania. Her professional passions include whole child philosophies, culturally responsive teaching, service-learning projects, global educator connections, teacher leadership, principal mentoring, and collaborative school cultures. She partners with many amazing school leaders at the local, state, and national levels to advocate for what's right for children and schools. You can reach her at MDPatschke@aol.com or follow her on Twitter: @MelissaPatschke.

The Road to Change:
The Impact of Culture on Leadership

Melvin (Jai) Jackson

olleges and universities have existed for centuries as shining ivory towers of elevated thought and higher consciousness. Their traditions and history are pervasive and engrained in their mission, vision, and values. For instance, fraternities, sororities, and secret societies on college campuses publicly celebrate their history and contributions to the thriving campus culture, but higher education leaders secretly fear the liability they pose if some of their shady (semi-) ritualistic actions are made public. So, which has more influence on the campus community of colleges and universities: culture or leadership? Furthermore, which has a greater influence on the other? Or do they cancel each other out?

Culture is the glue that bonds together colleges and universities. Culture is pervasive and influences both the strategic vision of the future and present-day decision-making. Upsetting institutional culture can also swiftly end one's leadership.

Working for a highly selective university, where the larger community has deeply influenced the campus culture, I was asked to research ways in which administrators could change the campus culture to minimize perceived liabilities. No sugar coating. The administration wanted to abolish all alcohol from campus and quash partying because they were tired of the expense of covering up poor student behavior. In this situation, however, the campus culture was the city culture; therefore, it was impossible to influence the university without dividing from the community.

Most higher education institutions have a four-year cycle of institutional knowledge and culture, meaning that it typically takes four years for the changes to be recognized and accepted. You make the change and allow all the students who push back to graduate; the new students have only known the changed model.

In higher education institutions, who are the leaders? Faculty? Staff? Students? Presidents? The answer is, all of the above. I consider any individual with considerable influence as a leader in the realm of higher education. Leadership at higher education institutions will ebb and flow but s/he who controls the culture will maintain control of the leadership. Today's version of higher education is more customer service oriented and the customer is always right, right? In the "McDonaldization" of higher learning coupled with uncertain economic times, students (and parents) are paying a fortune to be educated and prepared for the future. If they want dining halls that cater to vegans, pescatarians, raw-vegans, and people on paleo diets then that is what they shall have.

True leadership exists as a facade; college presidents and chancellors understand that student happiness is paramount to a job well done. At one southern institution in the United States, the university leadership justified a $50 million expenditure on a new recreation center complete with a lazy river, sauna, and other accoutrements more reminiscent of a spa than a recreation facility for college students. Without the approval and support of students, the leadership crumbles and loses their ability to mold and influence the university culture.

Internationally, the debate about culture and leadership takes a different tone. As a professional working in the Middle East, the cultural implications to my leadership are excessively long and dubiously vague. For those wanting explore employment internationally, I suggest you think long and hard about whether you can ethically, morally, and personally accept a foreign culture with all its quirks and differences. As an administrator working in both student affairs and academic affairs, I understand and promote the value of developing rapport with my students. I find it is essential to get to know your students and for them to know who you are so you can develop trust and respect. In the society in which I currently work, the cultural norms and beliefs dictate a strictly transactional relationship. The culture is so highly influential of leadership that a leader who is not born of the culture, assimilated by the culture, or acclimated to the culture will fail. Resistance to cultural practices, either stated or assumed, is seen as a sign of disrespect not only to the culture but also to the country, the religion, and the people.

Those who embark on the journey of becoming an inspirational and successful leader in higher education must understand that the culture of an institution is imbedded. To lead successfully, you must understand the culture of the institution, respect the influence that culture has on the institution, and remember that culture is pervasive and engrained deeply in all aspects of an institutional identity.

Dr. Melvin (Jai) Jackson is a native of North Carolina though currently residing in the United Arab Emirates as an Assistant Professor and Chair of the Department of Advising & Academic Development for Zayed University in Abu Dhabi. Dr. Jackson earned his Ph.D. in Educational Leadership and Research from Louisiana State University. He can be reached by email at Mjonathan86@hotmail.com.

PART III

Children's Champions:
Equity and Inclusion

Schools and school systems exist to serve all children. Children need champions. Not heroic champions, but champions who exemplify a paradoxical combination of humility and tenacity. What is best for systems is not necessarily what is best for children and community. All children can succeed when someone steps forward with unconditional belief in their unlimited potential. All children have special needs; however, some children have incredibly complex special needs. All children have a voice including the quiet ones. It is the voice of children that informs the learning needs of educators and it is the learning needs of instructors that drive the learning needs of leaders and leadership teams. Principles of equity and inclusion underpin our leadership narratives. Culturally responsive pedagogy is an expectation, not a wish or a look-for. Not all challenges to equity and inclusion are visible, so leaders must remain vigilant in making the invisible visible. The wisdom of a small child is sometimes greater than that of our biggest thinkers. Leaders listen.

Diverse Leaders Leading Differently

Rosemary Campbell-Stephens

With some curiosity, I accepted the invitation to join other Black school leaders at a dinner at the Institute of Education, University College London, in 2003. I am an African-Caribbean woman of Jamaican origin—born, educated, and having had most of my professional experience in England. At the time, I was living in Birmingham, about 120 miles out of London, and had recently left my headship at a challenging school located just outside of the city where I lived with the goal of putting my 25 years of experience in education into leadership preparation for those aspiring to lead.

The school that I had led as principal had the unenviable reputation of having been the first high school in England to have been put into special measures—before my time I hasten to add—following an inspection by OFSTED (the then Office for Standards in Education). The previous incumbent had been knighted by the Queen for his services to education having begun the turnaround process that brought the school 'out of measures.' Anyone who has ever taken up a post in such a school, at that particular juncture in its history, will understand the difference between 'seeming' and reality. The real work was yet to begin.

When I arrived at the school during the summer holidays of July 1999, before taking up the post in September, the school was virtually empty. The head teacher and the deputy head had left an entire school term before, at Easter, and the school was being 'run' by two senior teachers, neither of whom could be found upon my arrival. The school was deep in debt, which of course was not revealed at my interview, and neighbouring head teachers were understandably unsympathetic and infuriated that their respective school budgets had been 'plundered', as they saw it, in order to pump funds into the first school in the country to have gone into special measures.

The local authority wanted this particular nightmare to go away, and fast. That meant drawing funding from the budgets of nearby schools to do all the superficial things that, at that time, passed for 'transformation' in a challenging school. This was, at least, enough of a deflection away from the real deep-set issues, to take the heat and the spotlight of government scrutiny off. The 'funding' provided to the previous white male head teacher to turn the school around—promised to be 'written off' when he left—suddenly became a 'loan' to the incoming Black female head teacher that had to be paid off, urgently.

Prior to my arrival, the school uniform had changed, as had the school crest and motto. A prospectus was developed that would have been the envy of any advertising agency, all students had logbooks (even if there was nothing in them), and a new IT infrastructure had been installed to, among other things, register students electronically (remember this was 1999). The physical environment was at least clean and tidy, if tired, but most importantly, a symbolic, brand new, shiny sixth-form block for grades 12 and 13 had been built on the site, to the ire of all the other head teachers in the city.

Now don't get me wrong: all of these things are important, and one should be aspirational. But if the sixth form block—built with government money taken from the budgets of other schools—didn't have sufficient students with the requisite number of GCSE (spell out) passes to take the range of 'A' levels notionally on offer, then one didn't have an accessible, relevant, high-quality curriculum balanced between academic and vocational. Most importantly, one didn't have a sufficient number of high quality teachers who believed in their own efficacy, never mind in the capacity of their students to learn. This is a costly recipe for disaster, both seeming and in reality.

The demographic of the community that the school served was white, working-class, low socioeconomic background. Many of the students' parents were alumni of the school, attending back when the largest local employer was Dunlop (Dunlop Tyres? Provide context) and the expectation was to leave school and work there. Dunlop had been closed for years, but the educational offer had not recalibrated to align with the new context that children of those parents would inherit. To refuse to continue to ration education to the students of working class background, who formed the majority in my school, therefore, was a political act of moral purpose.

Working class had become workless. One of the senior teachers was still greeted as 'Sir' at parent evenings by parents who had been students of his. The community trusted the school, but too many educators and support staff treated the community with what I can only describe as 'quiet contempt'. Most of the teachers and support staff were white and mostly local, but most refused to acknowledge their own working-class roots, preferring to keep the middle-class distance that their professional status and salary afforded.

As an outsider—a Black woman with a 'middle-class' upbringing, but deep-rooted working-class affinity, and the only Black person in the school save for one cleaner—it was both a fascinating and disturbing dynamic. I was probably the only staff member who lived on the same streets as the children, but I was the headteacher, the principal.

My focus on equity and social justice in this particular context was on disrupting the deficit narrative that prevailed in the middle-class education system that was failing them. All discourse around the interface between teacher and those taught was predicated on blaming them for the system's failure to educate them. To maintain my sanity as the leader brought in to clear up the mess but set up to fail, I drew on every fibre and sinew as a Black woman to advocate for a community that had no voice. I remain eternally proud of what I was able to achieve, under the circumstances.

Fast forward to the dinner in London whose purpose was to discuss the underrepresentation of Black leadership in London schools. London is one of the most diverse cities on the planet, with a young global demographic across all stages of the education system. Far from being the 'ethnic minorities', we are the global majority in this city. Someone asked if we needed a bespoke leadership development programme to run alongside NPQH (National Professional Qualification for Headship) to catapult more Black educators into positions of leadership. Just like the system failing my White working-class children back in my school, the system here was also blaming the victims, in this case Black educators, rather than taking a hard, honest look at itself. Predictably, the majority of Black educators at the dinner were against the idea of a bespoke programme; I on the other hand was not. One thing I know for sure—you bring who you are as a school leader to what you do. You need disruptors in the public school system to *see* differently to act in the interests of the greater good.

I was one of only two people at that dinner to state unequivocally that not only did we need people from more diverse backgrounds in positions of leadership, but more importantly, we needed to create the space for them to lead differently once there. Because of this, I was invited to develop a leadership development programme for Black and (my parlance) other Global Majority aspirant school leaders. In 2003, the leadership development programme Investing in Diversity, developed for the Institute of Education, University College London, was born. Initially intended as a pilot for thirty people, it went on over several years to train 1000 educators from under-represented groups in London alone, inspiring similar programmes around the UK. In 2009, the Ontario Institute for Studies Education (OISE) in Toronto adopted this programme, but that is another story, one of sheer joy.

Fellow leaders, find your authentic voice and use your difference to make a difference!

Rosemary Campbell-Stephens MBE, having started out as a teacher of English, Rosemary is a Visiting Fellow at the Institute of Education, University College London; formally an OFSTED Inspector; Local Authority Officer; Headteacher; Consultant Adviser to the Department of Education (DFE) and Lead Associate to the National College for Teaching and Leadership (NCTL) in England. More recently, as the Director Principal of the National College for Educational Leadership in Jamaica, she developed her thinking further about leadership in post-colonial spaces. In 2015, Campbell-Stephens was awarded an MBE for outstanding service to education for over thirty-five years. She is now a freelance International Consultant on educational leadership and can be contacted by email at rosemary@2ndprinciple.com or rosemarycampbellstephens@gmail.com.

I'm *That Kid*

Lesli C. Myers

I remember sitting in my home, on the last two steps of the staircase that led to the foyer. My uncovered feet nervously traced the pentagon ceramic tiles on the floor. I quietly waited there, sometimes hours on end, until my dad came home from "work." He was a successful engineer who often stopped off at a bar to unwind from a stressful workday. My anxiety eased every time I saw the headlights approaching our home, and then immediately heighten when his bright yellow Firebird passed our driveway. Sometimes as late as two or three in the morning, he would finally pull into the driveway and I would quietly sneak into my room, relieved that Dad was finally home. A few minutes later, he would come into my room to kiss goodnight his oldest daughter, who he thought was sleeping, and then go to bed.

I would sometimes hear my mom cry or yell at my dad for his late arrival and alcohol consumption. Every morning, at the dawn of a new day, our family would break bread over breakfast and all was well, as if nothing had happened. The drinking eventually became too much to handle, and my parents separated and eventually divorced. Then my world turned completely upside down. At 13, I took on major responsibilities. I cooked, cleaned, took care of my younger sister, and was the second mom in the house. When my father stopped living in our home, the money left with him.

I want you to imagine what it was like to watch our house, custom built from the ground up, slowly crumble around me. We had limited food and clothing. One winter, we kept warm by using a kerosene lamp. For the first time in our lives, we were forced to rely on public assistance. It was extremely difficult for my mom to get food stamps and other resources because of our affluent zip code. Peer pressure was significant, and so clothing was an important part of my teenage years. My mom reluctantly told my sister and me that our clothes would now have to come from second-hand shops. Gone were the family trips to Florida, the Bahamas, and so on. I was absolutely devastated, embarrassed, ashamed, and extremely angry at the world. Those were some of the most difficult days of my life.

Why did I share this information about me? Why did I make you feel slightly to moderately uncomfortable by talking about the personal details of my life? Because I am *that* kid.

I'm that kid who was smart but sometimes showed it in disruptive ways. I'm that kid who had a stay-at-home mom who brought treats to school and regularly volunteered with the PTSA (spell out). I'm that kid who was an athlete and who responded well to her coach. I'm that kid with an alcoholic parent who was told that I would become an alcoholic as well. I'm that kid who was affluent and that kid who was economically disadvantaged. I'm that kid who was told by the school counselor to apply to our local community college, instead of university, even though my grades were above average, and my SAT scores were high. I'm that kid who had a mom with mental health issues and, as a result, sometimes I had to run the household. I'm that kid who was popular. I'm that kid who had low self-worth. I'm that kid who was bullied because of skin color by both Black and White (decide whether the author's use of race-based adjectives stands, or if there will be consistent use of related capitalization through the book) students. I'm that kid who started the minor fire in the science class because I wanted to learn about electrical conductivity first hand. I'm that kid who got on your last nerve.

Yes, I am *that* kid.

As educators, we each have *that kid* in our classrooms, in our offices, in our scope of responsibility. How do we move from intolerance to acceptance? Where do we begin? How do we start?

First, it is essential to look inside yourself. What are your beliefs, values, morals, customs, and experiences? What are your non-negotiable or absolute notions that you stand by and what are those things that completely disgust you? It is important to understand what makes you, YOU. When you understand that, it helps to clarify your approach to and interaction with the students and families you serve.

Second, it is also critically important to participate in honest conversations and capitalize on teachable moments with others. I remember eating in the teacher lounge, sitting with my colleagues, when a student's name came up and eyes rolled in disgust (including mine). A flurry of unkind words was used to describe the student. But what if that were your child or your family member we were talking about? Sometimes we must call the question and not be afraid to advocate for a student or to have an honest conversation with a colleague.

Third, we must never forget that our students live either up or down to our expectations. What we adults believe about our student's ability has a significant impact on what that student can achieve. I am grateful to have had two teachers in high school who held me to extremely high standards. They helped me to overcome all the negative talk, both internal and external.

Edward Everett Hale once said, "Now I'm a realist and I know that I can't do everything, but I can do something, and I refuse to let what I cannot do interfere with what I can do." So, I am asking you to imagine what it would take for each of us to actively engage in taking and making the steps towards understanding, information-seeking, and truly holding our "own mirror up to nature." How are you going to use your passion, your purpose, and your kindness to support *that* kid?

Lesli C. Myers, Ed.D., is the Superintendent for the Brockport Central School District in New York State. She has dedicated her life to the pursuit of high quality education. Dr. Myers was the first African-American president of the New York State School Counselor Association. Her testimony before the United States Congress helped to secure, in 2008, the largest increase (77.5%) ever to the Elementary and Secondary School Counseling Program. Her awards include being named a 2016 United States Senate Woman of Distinction, the Rochester Business Journal Forty Under 40 Award, the St. John Fisher Distinguished Alumni Award, the Urban League of Rochester Educator Award, and the Breakthru Magazine Empowering Award. She presented a TEDxRochester Talk entitled, *Racism: A Mere Pigment of the Imagination?* Her style is humorous, straightforward, and sincere, and she encourages people of all ages and backgrounds to creatively use their abilities and talents to serve others.

The Beginning...

Swaraj Chatterjee

Education is the foundation of prosperity and wisdom for any society. Education brings changes to our community and leads our life and thinking towards brightness. "Education is for all"—this is a message that my entire team and I believe in. To understand the proper meaning of life, one must enlighten one's way of living through the path of education. But our present socioeconomic conditions mean that it is often difficult to follow this path. We become distracted by the many injustices of the world and find ourselves nowhere, like a ship without its rudder. To avoid such imbalance, all teachers must take our responsibilities very seriously. To educate the entire country at the same time is quite impossible, but if we try to educate our own neighbourhood, here and now, then we may succeed.

Leading a school in a rural, rigid Indian society is a hard job. Most of the students belong to the tribal community, so leading an English middle school in such a place is particularly difficult. In our globalized world, however, English is the most important language to learn. New plans for the school have many implications: the interests of the parties involved (students, teachers, and the authorities), the environment of the school, and the conditions of the surrounding society. If any of these stakeholders disagrees, then the new plan might fail. By evaluating all the factors, we must decide whether our plan needs revision and further evaluation.

I was selected as principal of the school at a very young age. As a new school, it didn't have much in the way of resources. With just a few years of teaching experience behind me, learning to handle such a vital role was like swimming in a tsunami. Challenges included leading a school with no administrative system in place, dealing with local people, being responsible for the students, managing the staff (who were older than me) and the teachers (my age). On the other hand, my zeal to overcome these problems and my discussions with other educators enabled me to understand the role and function of a principal. Using every scrap of information I could gather, I knew my limitations. I then had to take that knowledge acquired from others and transform it using my own on-the-ground experience.

First, I began to understand the behaviour, working style, capacity to handle work load, and—most importantly—trustworthiness of my staff and teachers. After days of keen observation, I began to mix with them to assure them that I was not just their boss, but also their colleague, with the extra role of leading everyone towards our goal. Such mutual bonding allows the bridge to be set up at both ends, which allows the students to cross over towards their bright futures.

Now comes the most important part: the students. Without students there is no need for a principal, for teachers, staff, or a school building. These young minds and bodies bursting with energy are hard to control. They always seem to be hungry, either physically or mentally. Both types of hunger are equally important in the growth and development of a child and a deficiency in either area may be devastating. We must be well prepared and have a good working strategy. If we can make sure that they have healthy food to eat and interesting topics to learn, then they will surrender themselves to the teacher.

A student is like a handful of clay; however you mould them, they will turn out to be unique and worthy. Mainly our focus is to teach them, show them, and make them understand such things as the value of time, discipline, manners and behaviour, and respect for each other. One can acquire knowledge at any age, but those who are not educated when young will be at a severe disadvantage. Gradually we all learn and enrich our knowledge and wisdom with our daily experiences. It is essential to provide good guidance at the beginning of this human journey.

Swaraj Chatterjee is the principal of Living Water School, a non-profit school serving rural children since 2010 in West Bengal, India. The school keeps growing by maintaining its standard of education, thus satisfying the inner peace of anyone devoted to teaching. Before becoming principal, Chatterjee was a dance teacher at several schools and in the Department of Physical Education at Visva Bharati University. He holds a Ph.D. in Performing Art and a Bachelor of Music in Manipuri Dance. He can be reached by email at Chatterjee.swaraj14@gmail.com.

ICARE Meets "Challenging" Students

Jasmine Jackman

I have always been fascinated by students who are considered "challenging." I volunteered in youth prisons and halfway houses for several years, mentoring and supporting underserviced youth. But my strongest memory and my grounding principles for working with "challenging" youth came from an after-school program when I was 16.

I can still see her—a tall, blond, lanky, naively good-looking ten-year-old girl. She terrorized and bullied all the other students and swore like a drunken sailor. She would slap and bite at the slightest provocation and had been suspended many times. She was often by herself, twisting the heads off Barbie dolls or tearing up paper and cursing under her breath. One day, I sat down beside her. She seemed shocked that I would want to talk to her and responded begrudgingly to my questions. I praised her drawing skills. She cracked a small smile. Over a couple of weeks, she became my shadow and I gave her the special role of helping with the preparation and handing out the snacks. Her behaviour improved.

She opened up and started talking about her lack of friends. Tears ran down her cheeks as she explained how her mother had taken off, leaving her with her dad. The father was so caught up in his own grief that he was unable to show his daughter any affection other than the negative attention resulting from her many suspensions. She blamed herself. She wanted to know why her parents did not love her. I couldn't do anything other than listen and show empathy. This encounter made me reflect on my own implicit biases and how my cultural upbringing coloured the lens through which I see others. I learned to stop being judgemental when students are acting out and to separate the bad behaviour from the person.

When negative behaviour leads students down the school-to-prison pipeline, how do we stem the tide? Providing students with the necessary supports can prevent their behaviour from developing into something much more serious. In our high school, disruptions from students experiencing emotional, behavioural, or social issues were frequent, and students were sent to the Contact room—an alternate space focussed on behaviour support. No student wanted to be seen there. It was the stop-gap before being sent to the office.

Fortunately, the Contact Program was well staffed with two other teachers besides myself and four to six educational assistants. We rebranded ourselves as the ICARE Program—Improving Communication, Attitude, Respect and Empathy. Our goals were to take a proactive approach to discipline and emotional, behavioural, or social issues; reduce bias; help students rebuild relationships; encourage student leadership; and find solutions to their problems while giving positive feedback. We were like Matlock uncovering the reasons behind their behaviours and providing students with the training and skills they needed to improve.

We collected data because "what gets measured gets done." We recorded information such as dates, times, lengths of stay, and reasons for being sent to the room. This really helped to illuminate trends that we would have otherwise missed. For example, most students sent out of class were hungry; as a result, we began offering hot porridge and other healthy meals in the ICARE program. At one point I felt like a short-order cook, dishes piled up in our sink, and students coming at every turn. We addressed this problem by contacting parents when the need was frequent to see if special community support could be implemented.

We had a launch and made regular presentations in classes and at staff meetings about the program. Teachers were given referral forms to complete when sending students, and we would provide feedback. Students could also self-refer. We brought in guest speakers—elders from the Indigenous communities, motivational speakers, bereavement counsellors, and a Holocaust survivor, to name a few. By the end of year three, we had also implemented restorative practices, mindfulness support, art therapy, the Dove self-esteem program for girls, healing circles, targeted counselling, as well as monthly email tips for teachers on dealing with behavioural issues. I judge the success of the program by the improved interaction between students and teachers, the increased desire of students who came voluntarily before problems escalated, and the reduction in referrals tied to negative behaviour.

Having a preventative, supportive, consistent discipline strategy requires a whole-school approach to allow for uninterrupted learning. The program must be adapted according to the needs of the students seeking support, as well as to the strengths of the teachers running the program. Very little could have been achieved, however, without the support of a group of committed people—teacher leaders, non-educational staff, students, administrators, parents, trustees, and other stakeholders. And we need to remind ourselves that students, as Maya Angelou says, are not interested in what we know but in how much we care.

Jasmine Jackman is an acting vice principal and equity and social justice advocate. She is passionate about teaching culturally responsive and relevant pedagogy, volunteering, and working with underserviced youth. She has been a teacher mentor, a facilitator of equity and special education workshops (at the school and university levels), a summer school assistant administrator, and an active member on many community boards and associations. She is currently pursuing her Ph.D. in Educational Leadership and Policy at the Ontario Institution for Studies in Education (OISE) at the University of Toronto. Her research interests include addressing social and educational inequalities in underserved communities, culturally responsive pedagogy, social and critical theory, race and ethnicity, teacher practice, and mentoring for diversity and social justice. You can reach her at Jasminejackman13@gmail.com.

The Photograph

Darian C. Jones

" Close your eyes! Imagine I have my Polaroid camera (I've dated myself I know, right?)". I assemble a group of you and your colleagues to take a photo. "Imagine me taking the picture, on 3 . . . 1, 2, 3". (Make the noise of the self-developing film printing out.) "You know what you do: wave it in the air to help it develop. Imagine me blowing up the picture to an 8 x 10. I am now going to pass it out to each one of you, face down. Don't flip it over until I say go". (Distribute the picture). "Now flip. What is the first thing each of you just looked for?"

(Chorus) "Me. . .myself. . .what I look like?"

"Exactly! So why are your textbooks, the people in your classrooms, the print on your walls, your pedagogy any different for your kids?"

The first thing that kids do—that people do—is look for themselves in a room, a building, a line, a textbook, your language. The majority of kids are predisposed to not seeing themselves because the overwhelming majority of our representations are not about them. And what about your kids of color, your girls?

As a school leader, you have a moral imperative—especially if you want to improve student outcomes drastically—to create a culturally responsive and reflective environment. I have about 27 years of primary, secondary, post-secondary, and graduate schooling, including five major universities, and in all those courses and classes over all that time, the only African-American male teacher I ever had was my middle school band director. There needs to be a change in how we do business.

My very first leadership role in high school handed me kids from 49 different countries. The name of the school had *international* in it, but the different hues of the kids' faces were the real evidence. But nothing else on that five-building campus represented the 400 students from those different countries or the 1200 African-Americans. The name of the school had *international* in it, but we did not model what we claimed we valued.

On the day of our first open house, fifty 10 x 5 atrium flags hung down, welcoming everyone, including students from Somalia, Bosnia, Kosovo, and so on. As I jogged to the auditorium to start the assembly, I saw four girls with their arms around each other, crying. I stopped when one of them said, "Someone finally knows we are here!"

But we did not stop there. We created a student council so that the kids would have direct access to the leadership team to share what they were feeling, thinking, and experiencing in the school. We brought in a diversity and social justice organization to help train the teachers about engagement and culture. We reworked our discipline policy and used engagement strategies like mix-it-up day at lunch four to six times a month. We did comprehensive unit planning as a school and looked for outside and ancillary resources representative of who was in the classroom to supplement the curriculum. Three times a week during assembly, at least one representative of a different ethnicity received airtime to tell their story of how they got to and why they came to America. We brought in guest speakers not only for representation, but also to cross the divide of "otherness."

We became a school that modeled the value of the cultures comprising the student body, united for one purpose. All of the ethnic and gang fights disappeared within a month. Teachers engaged students in different ways, always with respect. Attendance soared, end-of-year test scores doubled from the teens to the mid-40s within one school year. Same kids, same teachers, almost the same teaching style, but what changed was a culturally responsive, representative pedagogy.

When you looked for yourself in that imaginary Polaroid photo did you perhaps become critical or disengaged if you either didn't find yourself or were out of focus? If so, how as leaders can we allow kids in

21st century classrooms to remain completely surrounded by a world that does not represent them or acknowledge that what they bring into our schools and classrooms matters?

Simply put, affirmation is cultural competence. As leaders, we are obliged to scaffold culture and diminish, to the greatest extent possible, the hidden curriculum in which most of our schools exist every day. In my experience, kids do not drop out of school; they are pushed out.

So, does your school culture say *you are wanted here, you belong*? If not, what are you going to do about it?

Dr. Darian C. Jones has spent the past 20 years searching out those "unteachable kids" and "bad schools" without success. With 18 of those years leading and learning at the school level, district level, CMO, and state level, Dr. Jones' heart work is transforming urban education. Dr. Jones has led urban high school transformations in multiple districts, yet his passion is the people and culture of schools. He works to create and design the experiences, classrooms, schools, and systems all our kids deserve, especially those traditionally denied such experiences because of their ethnicity, socioeconomic status, or zip code. Having taken part in two educational entrepreneur fellowships in Tennessee and Georgia, having successfully earned authorization for a charter petition, and having visited 234 schools across the country in the past five years, Dr. Jones has observed first-hand that leadership not only matters, but it matters most. Dr. Jones may be reached via email at drdcjones@sankorecollegiate. org.

Chinese Public Education and Global Social Justice

Spencer Fowler

D alton Academy is the international public high school program connected to the Affiliated High School of Peking University. In 2016, I made a life-changing decision by accepting an employment opportunity at Dalton Academy. Its educational landscape stood in contrast to everything I had become accustomed to after more than a decade in traditional school systems. Dalton Academy's extraordinary learning environment is fostered by a multidisciplinary team of international talents and a philosophy of education that promotes autonomy for both students and faculty. This has enabled the academic community to enact programs that are global in scale, having a positive impact on the lives of students, faculty, and partners around the world.

Students and faculty are afforded a level of autonomy and freedom I have never known before. The teaching and non-teaching faculty represent a diverse group of talented, passionate people with about half the teachers being local Chinese nationals, and the other half from various countries around the world. Many of our teachers come from academia and hold doctorates, while others have professional backgrounds.

Many of the courses at Dalton Academy explore issues of social justice on a global scale. One course developed last year by a faculty member focused on the refugee crisis in the Middle East. Students were exposed to the key issues and context of the refugee crisis in the classroom environment, while the most meaningful part of the course took place in Jordan. Students were able to meet with the Chinese Ambassador to Jordan, UN officials, NGO representatives, journalists, and writers. Traveling to the center of the crisis, students experienced first-hand the living conditions of tens of thousands of refugees who have sought refuge in one of the UN-administered camps in Jordan, such as the Baqaa Camp for Palestinian refugees or the Zaatari Camp for Syrian refugees, or in poor neighborhoods in Amman, Irbid, Mafraq, or Zarqa.

Students and faculty alike wanted to do more for marginalized youth in Jordan at the end of the course in Spring 2017. All of those who traveled to Jordan remained in contact with those they met and our students helping to set up a refugee scholarship program for our school.

The Access Dalton Scholarship will support two refugees annually, beginning in September 2018, to complete their final year of high school on our campus in Beijing. Our counseling staff will help the Access Dalton recipients find fully-funded scholarships to overseas institutions after they graduate. Seventy percent of school-age refugee children do not have access to education in Jordan. Very few have documentation or records proving their academic history, making it impossible to get into colleges or universities overseas. Our scholarship aims to support those without documentation or those unable to complete their secondary education. This is a win for our school and community. Our student body is predominantly Chinese nationals. The scholarship program enables us to add diversity. We believe the impact and contributions of these students from the Middle East will impact our entire community.

To date, many Syrian refugees have applied for the Access Dalton Scholarship. Some of them recount coming from neighborhoods in Damascus or Aleppo that have been destroyed by war. Their lives have been broken and their families split apart. For many of them, being surrounded by gunfire is still a haunting memory. Their lives in exile have been no less haunting, being bounced from what was once home to Zaatari refugee camp to poor neighborhoods in the major urban centers in Jordan.

Refugee applicants aren't only from Syria. They are also from Sudan, Somalia, Iraq, and Yemen. Some of them describe their biggest accomplishment as being alive today and making it to Jordan. Education has become their only route to bettering their condition and their social mobility. Many of them have taught themselves English after arriving to Jordan.

This scholarship initiative is extremely important to our school. A delegation of students and faculty will travel to Jordan over April and May to select the first two recipients of our access scholarship. Dalton Academy will be the first high school in China to open its doors and provide full scholarships for two disadvantaged youth in Jordan. It is my hope that this initiative will expand to include others from around the world. There is no better feeling than to know you are a part of a learning community that seeks to extend their knowledge, skills, and passion to improve the lives of others.

Spencer Fowler is Head of Dalton Academy, an elite public school distinguished for leading educational reform. He has been an administrator for over a decade in public and private schools in Chile, China, Egypt, Germany, South Africa, Spain, Thailand, and Vietnam. He is also an international education consultant on K–12 institutional reform focused on organizational change, presenting at Harvard Graduate School of Education's Learning Environments for Tomorrow Conference. He is also on the board of advisors for Partnership for 21st Century Learning (P21) and his role is expanding to CEO and Superintendent, opening multiple satellite campuses across China.

Empowering Pakistani Girls through Education

Kashif Memon

I have always been thankful that I was able to get an excellent education in a developing country where education is a privilege, not a right. Growing up in Pakistan in a patriarchal culture, I was torn by contradictions between my home and society. My parents always encouraged their children to aspire to optimal accomplishment in life. Success and service, they told us, are not measured in quantifiable terms, but in believing in equal rights for people. My father also told my brother and me that our sister shared equal status in terms of life opportunities.

My father practiced what he preached. He came from a conservative village family but married my mother, who in Pakistani terms was a liberated rebel in a male-dominated culture. She became a writer on religion, breaking the status quo against female literacy in the mid-1970s. I always believed that his decision to marry my mother was influenced by his education from the University of Pennsylvania, as he was one of the first in his clan to get a scholarship to study in the United States. However, I am left with the childhood memory that my uncles ridiculed my mother for having her own thoughts on life. There was more than subliminal bias against her educational achievements. However, my father is a progressive soul, and he always supported her.

Girls' education is still a sensitive matter in Pakistan and can lead to pitched battles in the streets, starkly contradicting my father's ideals. Some of his friends used to joke that with his values, he should immigrate to a more tolerant land. They were not wrong, and years later as a young man, I saw a society fractured by ethnic and gender hierarchies.

I saw gender inequality in education at its worst in rural Pakistan, where a son is more valuable than a daughter, where being female is a major impediment, where girls are marginalized in school, precluded from accessing equal pedagogical opportunities as boys. Why, I wondered, does my mother constantly need to prove her educational competence in a patriarchal society?

My biggest action-oriented change occurred by following my mother's life trajectory. This is not the story of my mother, but many like her who silently struggle to acquire education against a male-dominated narrative. They face religious persecution, childhood marriages, parental opposition, feudalism, and institutional bias. Many of them have been victims of acid attacks or killings, just because they aspired to attend school.

And while the world takes notice of these happenings, change will not come from outside, but must start from within the villages of Pakistan. There is a point in the development of every society when the irrelevance of groups that oppose girls' education must become obvious. My belief is that change is not impossible. I have seen it happen. Our greatest lesson comes from the thousands of girls like Malala Yousafzai, who face death every day, just for going to school.

Over the years, I have lived with and seen women who face extreme desolation in their lives. One cannot even begin to define the misery of that morning in 2005 when my wife and I were surrounded by street gangs threatening to burn us alive, as they felt betrayed by the rest of society. It was only after my wife told them that she was a doctor going to save their wives and deliver their babies at their run-down government hospital that they spared our lives. Such experiences have raised my awareness about making a tangible contribution in people's lives by taking action. But this took a certain level of personal maturity.

Women's emancipation in rural Pakistan is resisted under the guise of conservative ideologies, safeguarded by male defenders of an artificial patriarchal empire that maintains social control of females. If a change is to happen in getting girls educated in rural Pakistan, then three action steps need to be taken. First, combine indigenous solutions with international best practices. Second, iterate cycles of change and learn from people—keys to girls' educational sustainability. Lastly, society must take ownership and neutralize resistance, spreading the message that being educated is not a crime against any religion or community, and that it is time to stop treating spiritualism as a form of indoctrination.

Eventually change in rural Pakistan will come. Many generations of women have been lost to oblivion at the hands of patriarchy. It may take time, but one Malala can make a difference. We must have hope. The brave women of urban Pakistan have also shown the way. Relegated as symbols of oppression many years ago, these women achieved through immense resilience and struggle against gender bias not only the equal right to be educated, but also great success in professional lives.

Kashif Memon is a two-time Distinguished Lecturer at the University of Waterloo, delivering courses in Canada and China. He is the recipient of the Chevening Commonwealth Award by the British Government. Before joining Waterloo, Kashif served as a Country Consultant for the United Nations on Reefer Supply Chain Management. He has worked with the Pakistani Civil Service in the Commerce and Planning ministries, implementing projects of the World Bank, the World Trade Organization, and the Asian Development Bank. Kashif is passionate about travelling, spending time with his wife and son, and playing cricket.

Fighting Negative Bias
with Positive P.R.

Erica Jordan-Thomas

As a principal, I have heard lots of external messages about my school. The common theme was *"failure."* The first time I heard it, I brushed it off. But then it happened again, and again, and again. Year after year, that ugly word rolled off the lips of journalists and elected officials. What I found most perplexing was that they had never even visited my school. How could someone be so irresponsible as to assign such a harsh label to a school community they never set foot in? I suspected subconscious racial bias at play.

My school predominantly serves black and brown children. We are a Title 1 school so many of my scholars live in poverty. Our society perpetuates the disgusting racial bias that poor black and brown children can't achieve at high levels. This bias isn't overt, because then it would be too easy to recognize as racism; instead it's subconscious. I made the mistake of assuming that my school would somehow be exempt from this racial bias embedded in our social fabric.

Every day in my school building, we tear down the wall of doubt within our scholars, but this external toxic narrative was the wet cement needed to rebuild that wall. My staff works extremely hard, and every day I could point to a victory, but this racial bias made the most confident human wonder if they were doing enough. When I talked to prospective parents they might say, "We heard this is a bad school." I knew that we were doing great work and I had hard data to prove our progress, but a false narrative about my school was being built while my head was down doing the work. I knew I had to own our narrative and not allow critical bystanders to define us.

So I made a mental shift. I was now not only the principal, but I had to become the chief public relations officer as well. I had to fully commit to sharing every bit of good news about our school and not think of it as bragging, I mentally reframed it as battling racial bias. For every negative message spewed about my school, I wanted to give back three victories. My cellphone became my greatest weapon in the battle. Any time I saw a moment of magic, no matter how big or small, I snapped a picture: teachers collaborating on planning, a scholar walking down the hallway with his science project, the campaign signs for student council, or our quarterly awards ceremonies. I would share these moments with the world via our school Facebook page, as well as my personal Facebook and Twitter accounts.

I knew racial bias would assume our kids were out of control and didn't want to learn, so I created a Snapchat to show in real time what was happening in our building. I snapped moments during morning arrival of our scholars hugging their teachers, excited to be back at school. I would snap moments during breakfast and lunch to show that our cafeteria is calm. I'd snap during my classroom walkthroughs to show our scholars engaged in academic discourse. My mission was to show we were a school just like any other and our kids are no different from their white, affluent peers.

I also intentionally shared our story with my staff to affirm their work. The more affirmed they felt, the less they questioned their impact. Every month during our staff meetings, I presented the "Good News Report" of things that had positively affected our scholars. Every week I sent a newsletter with a picture that represented the magic in our building. If a parent shared a compliment about a teacher, I shared it with the teacher, the school, and the world.

During my battle, a local magazine released an article again calling us a failure. So I decided to step up my game and write an article too. My first blog post was entitled, *"You said we failed but you never visited my school."* I posted it to my social media accounts and within a day, I had over 1,000 views. My school district also shared it on their social media.

As I read through the hundreds of public comments, every single one was supportive. One even said, "Thank you so much for sharing the story about a school so many of us thought was failing."

There is an unspoken rule that principals aren't supposed to promote their own school, but only communities of privilege can afford to be silent. I challenge every school leader to not allow others to nullify your narrative. Model for our scholars the power in owning and sharing your own school story.

Erica Jordan-Thomas is a principal in Charlotte, North Carolina, where she runs EJT Consulting, LLC. Her school has grown academically and was named in "65 Elementary and Middle Schools to Visit" by GettingSmart.com. Jordan-Thomas has been recognized as an influential educational leader by many prominent organizations including TedxCharlotte, Teach For America (TFA), Relay Graduate School of Education, and the Congressional Black Caucus, and she has presented at many leadership conferences. She can be reached via email at ericajordanthomas@gmail.com and through her website: www.ericajordanthomas.com.

The Code of Conduct:
Creating Safe, Caring, and Inclusive Schools

Bob Esliger

M any attempts have been made over the past decade to address
student misconduct through the implementation of school-
wide systems of behaviour support as well as updates to various policies
and procedures, including hiring specific staff, such as hall monitors.
Despite these attempts at positive change, student feelings of safety at
school have not improved. What has provided positive results though
is a focus on using the school code of conduct for promoting new standards of behaviour, including anti-racism, anti-bullying, and general
courtesy and care for one another.

While a provincial mandate stipulates that each school have a
code of conduct, the incorporation of a district framework to guide
code development was a huge boost. An *educative, preventative, restorative practice and response* is the framework needed for this journey as
schools awaken to the issues, mobilize for action, accelerate forward,
and institutionalize the plan.

School staff understand, of course, that students need a safe,
caring, inclusive school environment in which to learn. Currently staff,
students, and parents spend considerable time reviewing and interpreting the available data from the *Student Learning Survey.* These survey
results provided a grim wake-up call to schools, revealing that students
are unclear about behavioural expectations, don't feel welcome, don't
feel safe, and don't feel a sense of belonging. In developing their codes
of conduct, schools now bring the message home by focusing on the
educative component of the desired behaviours.

Changing the way students feel about their safety at school means that staff must also change the way they respond to student misconduct. This systemic change involves interrupting the present through sustained efforts during staff meeting time coupled with focused professional development to build teacher efficacy. Research suggests that safe schools align leadership, curriculum, school-wide practices, and professional development with high expectations for all students.

Stakeholders are mobilizing to better understand the issues requiring attention and to create a clear, sustainable plan of action. Everyone must work together to address issues of bullying, intimidation and harassment, racism, sexism, homophobia, and other forms of discrimination and directly teach new skills to students so they can respond appropriately. School staff and the community must also respond appropriately and consistently to all incidents of misconduct in a fair and reasoned manner. School staff must continuously assess their school environment for evidence of improvement to recognize and celebrate achievements. Safe, caring, inclusive schools do not "just happen"; they must be developed by committed people using appropriate educative, preventative, and restorative methods in moving toward their vision for safe schools.

The map for this journey must be specific to the school and must explicitly address the issues needing attention. All stakeholders discuss the issues and take on leadership roles as they work collaboratively to implement the plan. This approach aims to change the way staff think about their various roles to engage in the change process.

A key focus currently is to further integrate initiatives and maintain a sense of renewal. A new initiative may enhance an existing program instead of adding something new. Teaching the code of conduct is embedded directly into the curriculum and the school culture rather than standing alone. Staff, students, parents, and other stakeholders all take responsibility for implementing the code.

Schools that have integrated their code of conduct into all aspects of school life provide everyone with the capacity to respond effectively to any new issues that arise. These schools make their code of conduct available to the public and review it with staff, parents, and students regularly. The code is displayed prominently where everyone, including visitors, can read it and be reminded of its purpose. School assemblies reinforce and refresh school-wide understandings of expected conduct. Institutionalization means consistent teaching and active promotion of the behavioural expectations set out in the code, thereby developing a sense of safety, caring, and belonging.

Creating a safe, caring, inclusive school is an ongoing journey with many opportunities to be involved in raising expectations for appropriate conduct. Our district's frame of reference for the code of conduct provides a consistent approach and a common language, not just in the development of individual school codes, but also in collaboration between schools.

Dr. Bob Esliger is an assistant superintendent of schools with Nanaimo Ladysmith Public Schools in Nanaimo, British Columbia. His portfolio encompasses student services, diversity, and equity. Dr. Esliger has led his district's journey in the development and implementation of a broad policy on inclusion as part of the foundational work on which to build safe, caring, inclusive schools. Dr. Esliger uses data to work collaboratively with schools as they strive to remain student-centred while addressing issues of school culture and proper student conduct.

Child's Play:
The Key to Successful Education is on the Playground

Michael Hynes

Standardized testing deprives children of many life skills considered foundational to the education of previous generations. It's time we our provided children with a learning environment that will help them compete and thrive in the 21st century.

A braham Lincoln once said, "The philosophy of the school room in one generation will be the philosophy of government in the next."

If public schools are the birthplace of future citizens and leaders, the focus on what it means to be a productive citizen must escape the contracted mindset of today's education reform. Instead, public education needs to be reassessed, with the goal of cultivating optimal conditions for all children to grow to their full potentials.

Beginning with the passage of the *No Child Left Behind Act* of 2001, and continuing through the present day with increased annual testing requirements as well as tremendous business opportunities in education, the philosophy and purpose of public education has drastically changed. Far too much emphasis is placed on test scores in literacy and math. The aftermath is that the concept of teaching children, rather than achieving scores, has been lost. While data, accountability, and assessment are important, they are not the primary means to educating our children. But at this time, at both the federal and state levels, we are experiencing a hyper-focus on ranking, sorting, and test scores, and not on fully educating students.

Moving forward, a 21st century education must consist not just of academics focused heavily on math and English language arts (ELA), but of four components of growth: physical, emotional, academic, and social (PEAS). PEAS allows children to tap into their own potential and maximize their talents. Each component is equally important and reinforces the others. And with PEAS, research shows that even with less time spent on traditional academics, academic achievement improves, along with so much more. PEAS gives direction and guidance to the "whole child" approach so often spoken about, but so rarely successfully achieved.

Recess as a Requirement

Most adults understand that a sedentary workday is far from ideal and leads to reduced output. Innovative corporations like Google design their work campuses to include gymnasiums, swimming pools, volleyball courts, and walking paths. Businesses provide gym memberships to their employees for use during the workday. With more movement comes more focus, less boredom, fewer absences, better attitudes, and more positive outlooks.

The trend in public school, though, has been the opposite. As the emphasis on attaining high scores in math and ELA grows, the reaction has been to increase classroom time, on the assumption that the more time spent on these subjects will correlate with better performance. All too often, that extra classroom time is pulled from recess time, or from physical education time. At the same time, the childhood obesity problem in the United States has continued to grow, being cited as parents' number one health concern last year by the American Heart Association. Recess can no longer be thought of as a throwaway. In fact, recess is critical to children's healthy growth, and to their successful performance in school. Children run, play, climb, swing—and smile. They connect with their peers. They are out of breath. When they finish their play, they are ready to be in a class again, ready to focus. And they are happy.

Research repeatedly supports that increasing physical fitness opportunities for children leads to not just improved physical health but also to increased academic growth. The Center for Disease Control reports, "There is substantial evidence that physical activity can help improve academic achievement, including grades and standardized test scores." The CDC further notes that physical activities "enhance concentration and attention as well as improve classroom behavior." Even simply incorporating physical activity breaks during class increases student performance.

In addition, recess lets children actively develop the 21st century skills so often discussed in the education world: communication, critical thinking, collaboration, and creativity. These skills are best learned and honed not in a classroom exercise, but rather on the playground, by creating an imaginary kingdom out of a shade tree with kids wearing crowns made of autumn leaves. They learn problem solving and collaborating when they figure out how to share a space or decide how to choose who participates in a game. The playground is its own microcosm, where children are the governors and citizens, who learn to play in their world together, with goals of kindness and support.

We understand that physical growth—via recess, physical education, and participation in afterschool sports—is just as important as academic teaching, and in fact is integral to maximizing academic success and improving student health. When physical activity is relegated to being just a disposable, non-essential filler, our children suffer. It's time to right the wrong of reducing children's physical activity that high-pressure testing has caused. It's unhealthy on too many levels. The United Nations Standards of Human Rights endorses that prisoners have at least an hour of outdoor exercise every day. Why don't we allow the same right to our children in schools?

Laying the Foundation

As schools, we are remiss if we don't ensure that children, especially our youngest, are learning in ways that create emotional health, because, in fact, a strong emotional basis is the groundwork for the academics that will follow. This emotional strength will allow a child to continue to strive even when he or she is frustrated. Emotional well-being gives a child permission to fail along the route to success. Children will understand that feelings both positive and negative are part of the human experience and aren't something to be feared or repressed.

To combat excess stress and foster emotional well-being, schools also need to offer outlets and life-long methods of coping, such as yoga and mindfulness training. These activities help children develop healthy relationships with peers and teachers, and be able to self-regulate emotionally, mentally, and behaviorally. I believe that integrating mindfulness and yoga into curriculum creates a number of other benefits, including improved academic performance.

By prioritizing the importance of emotional growth, and reducing the emphasis on testing, we help our children grow into more secure, well-balanced adults who can thrive in a diverse global society, able to navigate the multitude of opportunities and challenges that they encounter. And we also help improve their academic careers. For students' overall health, both emotionally and cognitively, it is imperative that we focus on emotional growth.

Rethinking Common Core

The mandates of the Common Core Learning Standards enforced by high-stakes tests have led to dramatic changes in our classrooms, to the detriment of our children. With a school's very existence riding on the outcome of grades 3–8 standardized tests, and with teachers' jobs dependent on these scores, schools have been forced to narrow their curriculums to focus far too heavily on just these two subjects, neglecting science, social studies, art, music, and so much more. Fix spacing below

It is time now to recalibrate and move forward with research-based methods of teaching that we know will improve our children's academic lives. We must abandon one-size-fits-all lesson plans and stop drilling to create high scores on year-end standardized tests. Instead, children should be involved in play (especially younger learners), project-based learning, cooperation, collaboration, and open-ended inquiry.

As pressure has mounted to achieve high test scores, focusing on a child's social growth has been shunted aside. But study after study shows that social learning is critical, in more ways than intuition suggests. It isn't surprising that integrating social and emotional learning within a curriculum leads to improvements in positive self-image, positive connections with school, reductions in discipline issues, and reductions in substance abuse. It makes sense that children's overall behavior and wellness improves when they can navigate social issues, from sharing to teamwork, from collaboration to work division, from conflict resolution to managing within a group.

An added bonus to this healthy sense of being, though, is that academic achievement also improves—significantly. A recent study involving almost 100,000 students concluded that children who had the benefit of curricula with social and emotional learning opportunities placed well over ten percentage points academically above their non-trained peers.

Today's heavy pressure on ELA and math test scores has made fostering emotional growth an afterthought, if that. Twenty-first century skills of collaboration, creativity, critical thinking, and communication aren't learned by testing and drilling. They are truly learned when done in the context of social and emotional learning—and it is long overdue that this learning be prioritized. As one educator noted, if our children had sufficient social and emotional learning opportunities, "we'd live in a better world with far less hate and far better social and emotional health."

Teach More, Test Less

Our current system has led to a situation that is no longer healthy or productive for our children. We must create a new philosophy of what it means to be truly educated and how we plan to achieve that. There is a loud call from education leaders, families, students, and community members to end the current system and strive for a way to educate children so that they become engaged, life-long learners.

By truly focusing on the whole child, we are finally acting in the best interest of all children, supporting their physical and emotional health, and at the same time, setting the stage, as research strongly supports, to maximize academic achievement.

Unfortunately, the new normal is to teach less and test more. And because of the high stakes attached to these tests, schools are forced to focus on academic outcomes at the expense of a child's social and emotional growth. Under the current model, teachers rank and sort children based on a proficiency model instead of how much growth each individual child may show. Our emphasis on well-being is a much-needed new narrative that will inevitably swing the educational pendulum back toward a balanced state of the true purpose of education.

Michael Hynes, Ed.D., is an educator, scholar, and thought leader. A superintendent of public schools on Long Island, New York, it's his mission to spread the importance of a holistic approach to educating children. Dr. Hynes, an innovative public school advocate and university lecturer, has made contributions regarding the importance of play and recess in schools as well as yoga and mindfulness in the classroom. He has also published numerous articles and featured in numerous podcasts on school leadership.

A Fish Out of Water

Debbie Donsky

One of the roles of a school leader is to ensure that school is a place of inclusion that honours not only the diversity of those within the school, but also the community and the world beyond. As classroom teachers, if we are truly committed to equity, you will see the evidence in our resources and assessment practices, in how we communicate with children and families, in how we approach discipline, and in how we work within the school and in the community. As leaders, we must do all this and more. We must use the positional power inherent in our role as school leader to create a culture that strives for excellence for all learners, honours community, and pushes the limits of what is possible. We create our own microcosm of the world of which we wish to be a part—or, as Gandhi said, "Be the change you want to see in the world."

When we think about meeting the needs of our students, staff, and community, we must also think about how those needs are met. Do we wait for a crisis or complaint? Do we go expecting what Human Rights calls "undue hardship"? Do we ask ourselves what is the easiest way to respond causing the least amount of disruption? Or, do we think about what we can do to support others based on an open, critical, ever-evolving discourse catalyzed by our own willingness to be vulnerable, question our own practices and assumptions, and inclined to change?

To call oneself an equity leader is to be willing to make those changes. It is about a commitment to go beyond compliance and minimum disruption to a place of flexibility and responsiveness. It means taking the leap and trusting what others tell you when you can't see it.

As a white woman with privilege, I trust my racialized students, families, staff, and colleagues to tell me about their lived experiences. I listen to what they need and make changes to improve their children's school experiences. When leading a workshop about white privilege with a group of school principals, I use the Marshall McLuhan quote, "I don't know who discovered water, but it certainly wasn't a fish." Just because we don't see the environment of another person, doesn't mean it isn't there.

A few years ago, a new staff member joined our school. She was an educational assistant who had worked at the local high school, but after having been injured by one of the older students, she required a placement with smaller children where the physical demands would not be as extreme. I was glad to meet her and we talked about the school. She was Muslim and wore a hijab, so as I welcomed her to the school I let her know that we had a prayer room upstairs. The school had grown from 400 to 800 students in the four years that I worked there, so we had a new addition that I had helped to plan. When I told her about the prayer room, she started crying. I asked her why she was crying and she explained, "When I found out I was coming here, I told a few colleagues and one of the teachers at my last school told me to be careful. She was concerned about my wellbeing because she told me you were Jewish. Then, without even asking, you tell me that you have a prayer space for me."

It moved her. It changed how she saw me as a Jewish woman and as a leader. It changed how she perceived the other educator and the advice she had received. So, while I used my positional power to create invitational inclusiveness, my own experiences of marginalization in belonging to a minority faith group fuelled my empathy for the need for an appropriate space not only for this woman, but also for our students, staff, and community.

When we make decisions as leaders, we must never dwell on ideas of how things have "always been done" or on not fixing what "isn't broken." We must always seek answers about *who does it work for* and *who is silenced and marginalized* by this action, structure, or practice?

And then, with those who have been disenfranchised, create a new reality where we can reconcile all manner of inequities.

Dr. Debbie Donsky is an elementary principal and a Student Achievement Officer at the Ontario Ministry of Education. Throughout her 25 years in education, she has worked throughout the greater Toronto area. Donsky is the mother of two amazing teenagers and loves to read, blog, and draw in her free time. She has made a career focused on creating spaces of possibility— whether as an advocate, leader, writer, or artist. She believes that stories are what connect us. Check out her website at www.debbiedonsky.com or follow her on Twitter @DebbieDonsky.

Peer Learning in Practice

Nils Wedel

After 25 years as a teacher myself, it is always inspiring to see just how young the important teachers in our lives can be. Often the teachers we can relate to most are our peers rather than our elders, and we can gain much from them, opening up and letting them help us much more easily than we would allow from someone we look "up" to. Researching and writing about peer learning and peer assessment is one of my specialties, and it involves lots of classroom observation. Recently I observed two fifth grade students, Peter and Sofie, help teach a physical education class to the second grade students. Later, I also watched the interaction between Peter and Sofie in their own class.

In teaching students three years their junior, Peter and Sofie wanted to provide some warm up and training courses. Peter wanted to develop an obstacle race with the start and finish at the same place; Sofie wanted to develop a jumping course with different jumps. The conversation and feedback with the second graders afterwards was one of the most important aspects of learning for their fifth grade teachers: What was good? Was something too difficult? Was something too easy?

For my first observation, I came into the gym 30 minutes before the start of class. The jumping course and the parkour course (military-inspired obstacle course) are both set up. Sofie and Peter have designed and placed the courses. Now, with focused concentration, Peter and Sofie are practicing their courses themselves. The mood is high and the motivation is exceptional. Now we can hear children outside the gym. Jesper, the gym teacher, says, "Peter, you welcome the students!" With the same intense focus, Peter gets ready to welcome the second-grade students.

Soon, the warmup begins. The second-graders must be organized into neat, military rows. Peter's clear voice is heard and the students now stand in rows, arms outstretched to ensure the distance between them. At the end of row, a little boy sits out on the trampoline. Sofie approaches the student, gently taking him by the arm, leading him into line. The boy follows cooperatively and begins to do the exercise together with the others.

On the second Thursday that Sofie and Peter teach the second-grade students, Jesper helps them set up the parkour course in a U-shape with Sofie's jumping exercises in the middle. It is Sofie's turn to lead the warm-up. The second graders are very active even before the warm-up begins, but this time the "surprising" thing is to see how fast they comply with Sofie's instructions. Once warmed up, the students decide for themselves which of the two courses they will use and Sofie and Peter support them actively. Sofie and Peter work well together, stepping in to help whenever needed.

Back in their own class early one morning, Peter sits at his desk playing on his computer. Sofie sits at her desk working on a Rubik's cube. After about 15 minutes, Peter says, "Now I think I will do a little Danish." Peter goes to his drawer, looks at his book, and quickly closes the book again. He then shuts the book back in the drawer saying, "Done!" But Sofie has risen from her seat. She opens Peter's drawer, takes out Peter's book, and opens it. Sofie says, "Peter, what about me helping you with your book?" Peter looks up. Without hesitation, Peter says, "That would be nice." Peter seems happy. Sofie sits down next to him and together they read his book.

The next day, I invite Peter to talk about what I observed. I ask him if wants help from Sofie in Danish on a regular basis. Peter replies without hesitation, "Yes!" Later in the day, I ask Sophie whether she wants to tutor Peter in Danish, she also accepts positively. The effect of peer learning is significant. Peter, it turns out, would much rather accept help from Sophie than from me. Sophie, for her part, will learn more herself as she teaches Peter. For both of them, the opportunity to teach has also given them more interest in taking an active part in their own learning, and more self-confidence as well.

I hope you will be inspired by Peter and Sophie to work with peer learning yourself. For my part, I would love to give you feedback on your own proposal for a peer learning course.

Nils Wedel is a Danish special education teacher, learning advisor, educational researcher, and author, who has been working as a teacher for more than 25 years. He has a Master's in Pedagogical Sociology, has worked with the Melbourne Educational Research Institute, and is a member of the Challenging Learning Professional Development group. Nils has written two books: Peer Learning (Hans Reitzels Forlag, 2017; in Swedish, 2018) and Peer Assessment and Self-Regulated Learning (2018). Wedel has also written a number of pedagogical articles published on www.Linkedin.com and similar platforms. How can readers connect with Nils? he has offered to give readers feedback on their own peer learning proposals.

Empowering Leadership

Carol Hunter

As a young teacher with all of ten years' experience under my belt, I was appointed principal of a small school in the Edmonton Public School Board (EPSB). Little did I know then the impact that first leadership experience would have on me.

The school was in a mobile home park with the majority of families living from paycheque to paycheque. The range of student needs could have been overwhelming. Instead, we were able to work as a team with our community to create a school culture and programs that maximized the potential of everyone. The key was empowerment—of self and others.

Perhaps the most important factor in our success was the fact that EPBS was a world leader in site-based leadership. In this model, principals are empowered to organize and operate their schools in whatever way best addresses the needs of their community, while achieving the goals of the school board. One of the key differences in the model is that principals have control of the complete operating budget and they are empowered in areas of staffing and programming. We were not told how many teachers or educational assistants we were allocated based on a central staffing model. We could staff our schools in whatever way best met the needs of our students.

The school board had a robust strategic plan and all principals were required to develop an aligned site-based plan. Staff, parents, and community worked together to develop our plan. At first, many parents didn't feel they could add value or help to make a difference for their children. They soon found out that their input was important. Together, we developed our mission statement: "To maximize student learning through students, staff, parents, and community working together in an atmosphere of mutual respect and shared responsibility."

Within this empowering framework, we were able to make lasting, important change. First, we created a general learning profile of the students we were serving. We knew that the challenges they faced required a different learning profile for each. To fully understand the importance of developing personalized learning profiles, we studied Rita Dunne's 21 elements of learning style, Marion Diamond's research into brain plasticity, Howard Gardner's multiple intelligences, and Joseph Renzulli's revolving door model of gifted education.

With this knowledge and our shared understandings as the base, we created individual learning profiles for each student and removed the grade levels from our primary division to allow students to progress through the curriculum at their own best pace. We also created a gifted program that welcomed each and every student at some point in the year, based on their motivation and commitment to a particular issue or project. We also ran parent education programs to help them better understand what we were doing and to help them find their place in the process.

The results were astounding. Our students actually improved their scores on the Stanford-Binet Intelligence test over a 3-year period. They performed at average and above on other standardized tests. We focused on developing their capability to solve problems, think creatively, and think critically. Most importantly, all students saw themselves as being smart and good students. The kids and teachers loved to come to school. Parents felt comfortable asking for and giving advice.

After five years, I moved to a school district in Ottawa, Ontario. They were organized very traditionally, with limited opportunity for site-based leadership. Not knowing any other way of leading, I continued to empower those with whom I worked as well as myself. I always felt and communicated that we were working toward common goals and that we were simply taking a different path to get there. Our path has always been very successful. After working within Excellence Canada's leadership framework for the education sector, we ultimately achieved the Order of Excellence award for our very significant accomplishments.

Interestingly, senior administration and the school board did not always recognize or value our success. Education is both bureaucratized and politicized, which makes real change very difficult. We were seen as outliers and were confident enough in our path to be proud of that label.

The point is not that all school districts should operate on a site-based leadership model but that all should understand the importance of empowering people to make a difference. Personalization is central to effective empowerment.

Nurturing a culture of empowerment is the key and requires a deep sense of trust in people's motivation, capabilities, and commitment. No matter the organizational structure, people must feel empowered to be their best and do their best. When empowered, people will solve problems, be creative, take risks, and love learning. We need this if public education is to remain relevant and meet the needs of all of our students.

Carol Hunter is a retired elementary school principal, author of "Real Leadership, Real Change: Moving beyond Research and Rhetoric to Create a New Future for Public Education", and recipient of the Order of Excellence in Education from Excellence Canada. Carol has been interested in change and empowerment since the early days in her career and has shared her knowledge at many major conferences. More information is available from www. impactleadership.ca.

Leadership in Rural Education

Matthew McCarty

Education is about meeting the social and emotional needs of our students as well as their academic and intellectual needs. My career has been spent in rural schools, and in both general and alternative settings, which has allowed me the opportunity to grow my leadership skillset and effect change through non-academic leadership opportunities. My current leadership assignment involves supervision of our secondary Special Education department. My school division has one comprehensive high school; therefore, I attend every meeting, monitor every caseload, and consult on every Individual Education Plan (IEP). As a result, I have been able to guide the leadership process from the classroom to the community.

I am a firm believer in open and honest communication. The Special Education department at the high school had functioned on a proverbial "island" for many years. Academic and Special Education teachers did not communicate, did not share information on student growth, and did not consider their job roles to be on equal footing. I began supervising Special Education this fall and instituted a departmental policy of open communication through a viable and official chain of command. I actively encourage all department members to communicate their concerns, suggestions, and ideas to their department chair as an initial point of contact. The department chair is responsible for answers to any questions within their purview, referring staff to building administration, or the district office for resolution.

As I am the building-level administrator in charge of the Special Education department, I am the next point of contact. My role is to manage personnel, oversee instructional practices, provide professional development, and be a parental liaison. I also interact with every member of the department daily and require department members to update me regularly on the progress of students on their caseload. The concept of open communication has been a foreign one for many in the department. They have been used to functioning as individual educators with a minimal amount of collaboration.

The division has instituted a co-teaching initiative with the goal of providing the best education possible for every student. This includes instruction for students with disabilities in the general classroom throughout the school day with services provided by both a general and Special Education instructor. My department members have been able to collaborate through planning with their co-teachers, discussing their caseloads, reaching out to each other, and communicating with parents frequently. They feel comfortable and are becoming a cohesive department and an essential element of our success. My leadership has been that of a servant leader, with a clear intent of allowing department members the opportunity to grow and develop as leaders in their classrooms and in our school.

Matthew McCarty, Ed.D., is the interim principal of Pulaski Middle School in Pulaski, Virginia. Dr. McCarty has almost twenty years of experience in education, including Social Studies instruction, Special Education, at-risk education, and administration. Dr. McCarty holds a B.A. and M.A. in History and Specialist and Doctorate degrees in Educational Administration. Dr. McCarty is an aspiring school superintendent with research interests in rural education, Social Studies education, and at-risk education. Readers can reach Dr. McCarty at mmccarty@pcva.us.

Culturally Responsive Pedagogy and Math

Gianna Helling

For principals, some pivotal learning experiences are not only professionally satisfying, but help to shape your identity as a leader as well as the identity of the community you serve. This is the story of a co-terminus collaborative inquiry that I helped organize with my Student Achievement Officer, Nancy Steinhauer, in collaboration with superintendents, ministry staff, central staff, principals, teachers, and parents. This inquiry began by investigating culturally responsive and relevant teaching practices in mathematics and then extending the inquiry to include social justice initiatives that use mathematics as a tool for both sociopolitical critique and to reconfigure society to be more ethical and just (#TM4SJ—Teaching Math for Social Justice).

As a result of several collaborative inquiries over a two-year period, students, educators, and parents explored the big ideas in math and pedagogy including student voice, a growth mindset, rich math conversations, and culturally responsive pedagogy and math. These experiences extended the learning by reaching out to local communities. By responding to student voice and wonderings, educators, parents, and students co-created rich, cross-curricular math tasks that empowered student learning and improved student engagement and achievement in mathematics. The learning was extended to superintendents, principals, teachers, and parents through a co-terminus collaborative inquiry involving over 49 educators, coaches, ministry staff, and parents from both Toronto Catholic District School Board (TCDSB) and Toronto District School Board (TDSB) communities. The project is documented through two video series on the Learning Exchange entitled *Culturally Responsive: Educator Mindset and Action* (2016), and *Math Lives Here: Helping Social Justice Take Flight* (2016) as well as through board publications, a number of professional publications, and research conferences.

This project began with the analysis of data, including attitudinal and achievement data. Student learning and conversations about math problem solving were captured and shared through various digital means (video, audio, blogs, and the use of apps like "Explain Everything" and "Aurasma"). Online pedagogical documentation was used—including video, audio, and product documentation—to triangulate our results and inform our teaching and learning. Students were encouraged to document their responses using technology in order to monitor and refine their answers. Parents and community members were invited to participate in the learning through blogs, social media, experiential learning, and involvement in school and after-school projects.

Michael Fullan writes that "our main goal in education is to provide immediate opportunities for students to help humanity…students have a role as change agents" (see www.michaelfullen.ca) Students need to believe in the impact of their learning, that their learning can change their classrooms, their school, and their local communities. Through culturally responsive pedagogy, students and teachers co-created rich cross-curricular learning opportunities based on students' wonderings and lived experience. We set high expectations for students and co-created rich math tasks that were relevant to students' lived experiences. For example, through an inquiry into the proposed Metrolinx project in the Davenport area of downtown Toronto, students learned through measurement and mapping the location of the proposed commuter train and then commented on the distance between the track and their homes/school.

Students asked questions such as "Whose house is closer to the school? Further away? How does that affect your day?" Being made aware of an issue, students then needed the tools to affect real change. Through social media, students used their learning in math to affect change in their community. When the students learned through their graphing and data analysis that the community lacked information on the Metrolinx project, they advocated for more information and helped organize with their parents and the school trustee a series of community meetings to discuss the project. This is one example of the many cross-curricular math projects that transformed teaching and learning across two school boards and raised achievement, engagement for learning, and well-being for students.

By posing interesting questions based on students' lived experience, celebrating the search for answers, and giving permission to explore mathematics in meaningful and innovative ways, we transform learning, not only for students, but for staff and parents as well. The use of technology allowed us to document, monitor, and reflect upon our learning, leading to greater student achievement. It also facilitated the exploration and extended the learning by reaching out to parents, and the local community.

Gianna Helling has been a teacher and a principal with the Toronto Catholic District School Board for over 26 years. She is currently acting as Student Achievement Officer with the Ontario Ministry of Education. She has authored a number of articles on student voice, mathematics, leadership, collaboration, blended learning, and student transition initiatives including "Establishing Successful Transitions for Intermediate Students" in Perspectives on Schooling and Instructional Practice (University of Toronto Press, 2013). Helling has presented to administrators across Ontario and internationally on a variety of topics including math and social justice, a growth mindset, strategies for students at risk, ELL learners, personalized student learning, inquiry, collaboration, and 21st century learning.

What I Learned from Grandma

Darian Jones

Let us call him Jobias. He was off the chain and with only one year of assistant principal experience, I became the newly appointed principal of one of the lowest performing high schools in North Carolina. This school had had five principals in the past eight years who had all tried to establish order and culture while trying not to suspend kids for trivial matters. Jobias reminded me of myself in many ways, save for my middle school years when I received daily paddling, until one teacher finally figured out that I was bored—not bad—and extended lessons for my brain instead of paddling for my behind. It changed my life, but that's another story.

Jobias cut-up in every class, was labeled Special Ed due to his behavioral and emotional challenges and practically *lived* in the main office when he was not in chill-out or in-school suspension. He was hilarious when he was not cursing at adults or trying to start fights with kids twice his size, but he was the example cited by teachers arguing that the school was out of control. I created new schedules, had one-on-ones with teachers about how to work with him, did two whole-school sessions on classroom management and building relationships with students. There was a great deal of *them vs. us* in the school and the kids felt it—but Jobias just happened to be the one sparking and would react at any perceived slight. The teachers called home and both the head counselor and program assistant for Special Ed had had several meetings with his grandma to no avail.

One day, having run out of options, I decided that we were going to resolve the problem and deal with this young man. Up until then, the staff had been raising hell about my youth and inexperience and how I was the new superintendent's "golden boy" sent to "get rid" of them all. So in late September, I sat behind my desk and practiced my principal voice, intending to make the call just after 7:00 a.m. I was taught that you call before work and school, when folks want to get you off the phone, so that they understand your seriousness. This has not failed in 20 years.

"Hello?"

"Yes, ma'am. This is Darian Jones, the principal at Smith High School, may I speak to Ms. Brown?"

"This is her!"

"Are you the grandmother of Jobias Brown?"

"Uh-huh!"

"Well, Ms. Brown, I am calling because. . ." (and I proceeded to list all the things he had done in the five weeks since the school year started and all the things we had done to help Jobias) . . . "and I was calling to get your help, to see if we could meet and come up with a plan for Jobias because this is his junior year and it's so important that he do school. I am new, and I do not know the context of last year, so I am not carrying over any issues. I just want to get him onto the right foot." (Talk about that long pause and having enough wait time in a classroom—that twenty seconds of listening to her breathe but not say anything was about to kill me.)

"Ms. Brown, you there?"

"I'm here, but you say, you that new principal they got up there at the high school where Jobias go, that young man?"

"Yes, ma'am."

"And you say, Jobias been cutting up and acting a fool all year?"

"Ma'am, he has been acting out, but I didn't say acting a *fool*."

"Yeah, yeah, same thing, but here is what I can't figure out. You the principal, right? The young man I hear so much about?"

"Yes ma'am."

"Well, you know I pretty much raised Jobias since he was about eight by myself and during the summer he is all mine. I heard tell you been up at that school since May and it is now September and Mr. Jones

I need you to realize, you been at the school all summer and I have been dealing with Jobias all summer and not one time did I pick up the phone and call you for help." Dial tone. She hung up on me.

As I sat looking at the receiver. I was suspended somewhere between annoyance and fighting back a laugh at the way in which she spoke, because she was graveyard serious!

"I had that boy all summer and I didn't call you, not one time."

I repeated that story three times that day (and still years later) as the audience of assistant principals and several teachers hurt themselves laughing, in part because of what she said, but mostly I suspect because of the look on my face at the realization that my title and a phone call didn't mean what I thought it would. My feelings were hurt. This was a reality check.

Yet, still not having a resolution to keep Jobias from heading to the alternative school or not graduating, I found the gateway to the solution: my beliefs and values about my role as a high school principal and leader.

What do you believe your role to be as the leader? Are you simply there for the title and the pay, the power, or the promise? Are you a servant leader? Are you a gatekeeper or a dream keeper? I developed my actionable educational philosophy that day because of what Jobias's grandma shared. I recalled that somewhere in North Carolina State school law was a phrase about the principal being "in loco parentis"— in absence of the parent—that we have a singular obligation to ensure that each of *our* children not only have access and opportunity to learn and to achieve but that *we* must bring that access and opportunity to fruition.

I learned from Jobias's grandma that as leaders we have to stop looking out the window for our solutions and instead look in the mirror and ask ourselves, "What can I do? What am I doing, messaging, modeling, or communicating about what I believe in my children, my school, my teachers, and this work?"

Fast forward four years: Grandma gave me a huge hug at Jobias's graduation and as the three of us embraced she said, "We did it."

Darian Jones, Ed.D. has more than 14 years of experience as an educator and administrator in Virginia, Georgia, and North Carolina. From 2003 to 2005, Dr. Jones served as director of minority student achievement for Williamsburg James City County Schools, working towards community solutions to improve a significant achievement gap. As principal, Jones helped Ben L. Smith High School earn the distinction of Most Improved High School, in addition to creating an International Baccalaureate Program. After earning a B.S. in psychology and a B.A. in philosophy from Tulane University, Dr. Jones received his doctorate from the University of North Carolina at Greensboro where he studied curriculum, teaching and cultural foundations, and urban studies.

Not Here:
Principal Power Meets Relationship Power

Alison Gaymes San Vicente

"Are you serious; are you going to let that student come to our school?" pleaded one of the staff. "This kid is trouble; everyone knows this. Just tell them no and to find another school in *their* area."

While I could have unleashed a tirade about how we did not *own* schools in public education, I knew this response would not address the needs of this staff member. Nor would such an approach shift the thinking or bode well for our relationship. I needed to balance staff needs with my belief that principals should leverage their positional power with staff relationships to advocate for underperforming and/or disengaged children. This is particularly important given that the education system is complicit in all educational outcomes.

A second staff member entered the conversation with another passionate argument about why this student should not attend *our* school. I remember glancing around my office at quotes that embodied my belief as a leader. One caught my eye: *Education is the most powerful weapon which you can use to change the world*—Nelson Mandela. I thought to myself, how can we use education to be transformative in this case? If education was complicit in causing underperformance/disengagement, then all educators surely needed to be part of the solution.

While hearing the growing number of concerned voices in my small office, I have to admit I smiled, wondering why I had created an open-door policy. Truth be told, I really just wanted to pause, drink my latte, and engage in some deep reflection. I think I briefly zoned out, deep in my own thoughts. Then I posed a question, "Where does this child belong?" No response at first. Then, after a pregnant pause, one voice emerged with a less challenging, somewhat inquiring, "Not here…?"

"I'm not sure I agree," I said with a smile. "What a gift it is for any child to attend school here, with educators who possess the power to foster belonging. Can we talk more about this later?"

"Sure" they replied. And off I went to do my classroom rounds.

Principal power is complicated. We have to be cognizant of how we use it and question the impact of that use. Are we using it to alienate or to embrace … to build or to tear down … to provoke cognitive dissonance with staff and therefore foster new thinking or to maintain the status quo … to challenge barriers that impede children or to maintain those barriers? In this context, I couldn't help but think that this student needed more than a school to attend; the student needed a school to which he belonged. I believed that schooling, the system, and/or society had failed this child. How could I do the same?

But now what? Having this principal power doesn't feel so powerful if the staff does not agree with how you use it (not that you shouldn't go against the grain when needed). This was a real dilemma. If I accepted this child into our school, he would be placed in the classroom of one of the teachers opposed, perhaps the one who said, "*Not here.*" And if the teachers didn't feel he belonged, what was the likelihood of his success? All of their biases attached to this belief would be at play. They would expect him to misbehave, they would expect him to be "bad," and they would probably judge him more quickly. The sick feeling in my stomach told me he didn't stand a chance unless we challenged the thinking we had constructed about a child we hadn't even met. I wonder how often we do this to children. Allow our biases to define them and then invoke structures and situations for them to embody these biases?

Even though I knew the staff trusted me and would ultimately respect my decision, this was not enough. It was my job to create the conditions for the teachers to think differently about this student— to embrace him. Therefore, I needed more than positional principal power. I needed relational power; this would allow staff to hear me and me to hear them.

So, together we explored. We reasoned about the purpose of education and considered our purpose as educators. We engaged in those uncomfortable conversations about the points in our own lives where we felt included or excluded in response to bias. It was the staff who finally pushed the conversation to how we might include or exclude the children in *our* own building through attitudes, beliefs, structures, and actions.

In the end, the student did attend our school. The intentional use of principal power and relationships challenged bias and fostered a foundation for him to have a school in which he belonged.

Alison Gaymes San Vicente works to disrupt educational practices that continue to disadvantage historically marginalized/underserved students. Her passion for equity and justice has led to a secondment at York University's Faculty of Education and her current position as a Principal Coach for School Improvement with the Toronto District School Board. She is the recipient of the Queen's Diamond Jubilee Award (2014) and Canada's Outstanding Principals Award (2016). In addition to being a member of the provincial writing team for the Principal's Qualification Program (2017), her writing also appears in the following books: Our Schools, Ourselves—Community Watch: Marginal at Best, A Narrative on Streaming in Public Education (2016); Restacking the Deck: Streaming by Class, Race and Gender in Ontario Schools (2014); and Rhymes to Re-Education: A Hip Hop Curriculum Resource Guide for Educators with Social Justice Activities (2014).

Leading in a War Zone

Wendy A. Dunlop

My experience as a principal in Kuwait was replete with a succession of unexpected events and challenges split into two by the terrible events of 9/11. Before the Twin Towers in New York City came down on September 11, 2001, my focus as principal was on learning about the expectations for the quotidian running of an "American" private school in a Muslim country. Post-9/11, after the United States invaded Iraq in 2002, my focus shifted to be guided by safety alerts from the Canadian and American embassies, as well as directives from the Kuwaiti Ministry of Education.

Pre-9/11

As an educator in Ontario's secular public schools, I initially had a great deal to learn about leading a private school where Islamic values and tenets informed curriculum content, as well as expectations for staff and student comportment. My teachers and students were all female, predominantly Kuwaiti, and Muslim, with a handful of Palestinians and children of the North American teachers in the school. English-speaking teachers were a mix of Canadians and Americans. Arabic staff came from Egypt and neighbouring countries in the Middle East. The "American" curriculum was taught in English. Arabic language and Islamic religion classes were mandatory.

As a neophyte to the tenets of Islam, I had to learn quickly about such events as the holy month of Ramadan and its effects on the rhythm of the school day; the importance of scheduling time for the highly esteemed Qur'an recitation competitions; the alignment of

American-based textbooks with Islamic values; and understanding the religious significance of the hijab. There was no clear vision of which Islamic values must be followed, however, as the various religious leaders assigned to the school never arrived at a consensus.

During Ramadan, I had to ensure that all school members—including non-Muslims—did not consume food in public during the school day. For the duration of Ramadan, my office was offered as the place of refuge for non-fasting staff to eat lunch in private.

School days were altered in other ways during this holy month. We came to expect that all activities and classrooms operated at a much slower pace. The Muslim students and staff were tired from fasting from sunup to sundown, feasting in the evening, and then celebrating with family and friends late into the night. Although it was supposed to be school business as usual, in reality, the rhythm of each day slowed for us all during Ramadan. We grew to appreciate this and enjoy the respite.

Scheduling time for Qur'an recitations and competitions also became part of my principal duties, with the Islamic teachers guiding the process. I was impressed by the skill and dedication of the students, as well as our teachers. I was also impressed by how the student body would sit quietly and respectfully on the floor of the gymnasium while their peers took turns reciting the Qur'an on stage. The pride reflected in the faces of the students who received prizes for their memorization of the Qur'an rivalled any awards conferred for academics or athleticism.

The alignment of American-based textbooks with Islamic values presented a unique mandate. As principal, I oversaw the alteration of books by teachers. This sometimes meant tearing out pages, whole chapters, or blackening out images and terminology deemed offensive to Islam and/or to Kuwait itself. For instance, if Israel was named, we had to cross it out and write "O.P." for Occupied Palestine. References to the "Persian Gulf" were blackened and "Arabian Gulf" was inscribed above. Any depictions of prophets, including Jesus Christ, had to be removed by tearing out the pages, or covered with marker.

The majority of our students wore hijabs that matched the colour of our school uniform. To encourage modesty and to de-emphasize body shape, blouses could not be tucked in. When a girl chose to begin wearing a hijab, she was feted by her peers. The mothers and maids brought in copious amounts of food and special sweets to the school as part of the celebration. It was a joyous and proud occasion for the student. Even as a non-Muslim, I was caught up in this religion-based coming-of-age celebration.

I also was witness to the converse. The decision of the school's student president to no longer wear a hijab created both drama and upset in in the school. It was an incredibly brave action on her part, given the environment. The student was supported by her mother, an American married to a Kuwaiti. Despite the mother's support, however, the matter had an effect on the entire school. Removal of the hijab was considered "haram" (forbidden by Allah). I had to navigate the outcome carefully and nothing in my principal training courses in Ontario had specifically prepared me for this type of event. After consultation with the student, her mother, and her teachers, I issued a judiciously worded memo asking students to speak to their teachers, or to me, about their concerns, to respect the student's difficult personal decision, and not to address her directly. After a week, the matter seemed to have dissipated. It both surprised and relieved me that a decision to permanently remove a hijab did not become a divisive issue.

Hijabs and other matters pertaining to Islamic protocol in the school, however, were completely eclipsed by 9/11. On September 12, 2001, the Arabic teachers mounted a huge banner in the mailroom. It read, "We are very sorry." Students expressed fear that the North American teachers and I would pack up and go home. At the end of the day, we all gathered in a large circle, holding hands in support of one another.

Post-9/11

Even though it was Iraq that President Bush invaded in 2002, its proximity to Kuwait resulted in our school being on high alert. In consultation with the Canadian and American embassies and the Kuwaiti Ministry of Education, we quickly devised external and internal safe-haven protocols. We practised numerous drills with our students in preparation for potential threats, or actual missile attacks. Two different times, our school was shut down and we were evacuated from Kuwait because of perceived danger. Aside from the evacuations, two scenarios involving students remain vivid in my mind.

First, as principal, I tried to recruit students of different nationalities to our school of predominantly Kuwaiti girls. I was overwhelmingly unsuccessful. I did, however, meet several times with the parents of one girl from India who were all keenly interested in our school. The first day this student joined her Kuwaiti peers, the entire school had to be evacuated to a nearby safe haven because of a threatened attack. The new student was profoundly traumatized by the experience. She sobbed and shook inconsolably. As we were unable to quell her fears, the girl's parents were called to take her home. Sadly, she never returned to our school.

The second memorable experience occurred after the American soldiers had been in Iraq for several months. Our handful of Palestinian students did not hide their dislike for the United States. Some of them began to wear a keffiyah, the checkered black and white scarf of the Palestinian leader Yasser Arafat, and the symbol of Palestinian nationalism, as a belt on their school uniforms. Although the student action was interpreted as political protest, I chose not to engage in a discussion with them about their intent. It was too potentially volatile. Instead, I used the school handbook. I gathered the Palestinian students and calmly asked them to show me on which page it stated that the keffiyah was part of the school uniform. I also offered to invite their parents to the school to discuss uniform protocol. The students offered no counter-arguments, and ceased wearing their non-sanctioned "belts."

Postscript

Our two evacuations from Kuwait presented some unsettling social justice issues. As North American hires, the teachers and I had our flights home (and return flights to Kuwait when it was deemed safe) funded by the school board. Support staff, mainly from India, Pakistan, and Egypt, had to pay their own way home, if they could afford to leave. Many of the Palestinians did not have passports (or a homeland), so they had to remain in Kuwait.

Once the school was closed and the students gone, there was no reason to remain in Kuwait. My students were safely in the hands of their Kuwaiti parents. They could exit the country, if they chose. Leaving behind our staff members who were less privileged, however, weighed heavily on me.

After five eventful years, I finally returned home to Ontario in 2004. My experiences as a principal in Kuwait greatly influenced my ensuing life choices. My interest in social justice was so greatly piqued by living in a war zone and witnessing differential (unfair) treatment of some groups that I decided to become a lawyer. Equally, my introduction to Islam while in Kuwait influenced the subject of my doctoral thesis—the legal duty to accommodate faith and religion in Ontario's public schools. It is said that teachers learn from their students, and I certainly learned lessons from mine that changed my life.

Dr. Wendy A. Dunlop was an educator with the York Region District School Board for twenty years. During that time, she was Lead Teacher in French on the elementary panel, taught French as a second language in two high schools, and served as Ontario Secondary School Teachers' Federation branch president. Dr. Dunlop was also appointed by the Canadian Teachers Federation as part of the Project Overseas initiative to collaborate with educators in India and Nepal on professional development methodologies. Following these assignments, she participated in a one-year exchange to Queensland, Australia, where she worked with at-risk students as a behaviour management co-ordinator. Dr. Dunlop then relocated to Kuwait for five years where she was a principal in a private school. Post-Kuwait, Dr. Dunlop obtained her J.D. from the University of Western Ontario and was called to the bar in 2009. She currently practises law in Toronto. In November 2017, Dr. Dunlop earned her Doctor of Philosophy from the Ontario Institute for Studies in Education, University of Toronto. Her doctoral thesis is a qualitative case study on the legal duty to accommodate faith and religion in Ontario's public schools.

PART IV

Practices of Community:
It Takes a Village

Schools and school systems exists to serve school communities. Educators are not co-parents, they are educators. Leaders must cultivate and establish relational trust with the communities that they serve. Trust cannot be assumed; it must be earned and never be taken for granted. Trust is sometimes tested when systems mandate leaders to manage communities in a way that is incongruent with community aspirations. When trust is compromised, feelings of betrayal emerge. Communities have voice, agency, legacy, and stories which need to be respected and honored. It takes a whole village to raise a whole child. Multidisciplinary teams are mobilized to meet the needs of children and communities in crisis. Truly accomplished individuals make themselves available in support of student learning. We have heard narratives of annual celebrations and we have heard narratives of how leaders mobilize community in support of children, community, or colleagues in pain. Our school communities become our families.

Only Flowers Bloom Silently

Tony Lamair Burks II

At the ripe old age of 27, I accepted my first principalship; since then my life hasn't been quite the same. One evening after a fairly long day at work, I reread an email message I'd sent to family and friends a few weeks after I began my first principalship:

> dear all: last sunday sometime after church, i made my way to work. i'd initially planned to file away mounds of papers, but found myself being drawn to our grassy playground. i yielded to temptation and decided to take along my kite. now, you must understand i've not flown a kite since "dog was a pup". i placed my multicolored piece of therapeutic equipment on the ground; commenced to unravel a bit of string; and wondered seriously if i could write-off my kite on this year's taxes.
>
> the southern winds were terrific and the sun was beaming. in an instant my kite was airborne. things went well. the truth is, my mind began to "drift" once i got the kite up. it wasn't long before i began to compare leading a school (or any organization, for that matter) to flying a kite. you need more than favorable winds to keep a kite afloat. like the playground field where i flew my kite, my job comes with specific parameters. i—as a principal—and we—as a school family—can only go so far. once the kite's in the air, it [can] take on a life of

its own. and what's more, when you think you're controlling it, you really aren't.

so, what keeps our high-flying friend in the air? of course, a good gust of air and string tension are essential. give the kite too much slack and it dips and drops. pull it too tight, the string snaps and you lose your whole enterprise. ahhh, but when it's really up there and the wind is to your back, no one sees you. folk only see what's really important. they see your kite flying and soaring—a thing to behold.

Two days after sending out this email message, Sterling H. Hudson III, the man who is largely responsible for my entrée into education responded to my "update." Dean Hudson wrote,

Very interesting analogy. When I think of kite flying, I think of Charlie Brown whose kite always seems to end up in a dreaded tree. But you know what, Tony? Charlie Brown never hesitates to loft another kite even with the prospect that yet another tree might eat it. This is the epitome of perseverance. Stay encouraged. Remember, God's supply of kites (and trees to eat them) is unlimited.

And did I ever have an unlimited supply of kites and trees during my time as a new principal! I wasn't looking for a principalship and I could've easily stayed at the University School of Nashville teaching history and philosophy until retirement. Because of this, I had yet to take the state's required administrator licensing examination.

Before I started my first day on the job, an article about me appeared in the local newspaper, emblazoned above the fold:

"Hiring of young principal prompts call for new policy"

Tony Burks, 27, principal designate for Crockett Elementary School, is a history teacher at University School of Nashville and has served as headmaster for the summer session. But his youth and years of experience have one school board member saying the principal standards should be tougher.[1]

A photographer had even managed to snap a shot of me in the school cafeteria having a lunchtime conversation with kindergarteners as they queried me about becoming their new principal. Parents questioned my credentials and educational pedigree. A few even contacted the superintendent to ask why he'd hired a "n**ger principal" to lead a school that was 98% white.

The scrutiny didn't end there. Some parents were concerned about class assignments, others were concerned about new teachers, and still others were concerned about grading practices. Two veteran teachers challenged almost every classroom observation and evaluation I completed. Several teachers packed their bags and transferred to work with their former principal.

We had three educators die in the span of 14 months. One student died tragically in a car crash with her mother. Many of my elementary school babies witnessed the play-by-play reporting of the tragedy on September 11, 2001.

Someone vandalized my reserved parking sign, scrawling vulgar language about me. A band of parents secretly met with the new superintendent to question my fitness for duty because two third-grade students plotted an escape from campus. I spent a full year with two central office administrators monitoring my every decision. And a special educator falsely accused me of sexual harassment. She said I'd invited her to spend the night with me in a hotel. A lot of learning and leading was compressed into 3½ years.

For every negative experience, I encountered students who were appreciative of my ability to connect with them and observe them as learners and leaders. Because of my students, I honed my craft of telling and reading stories (what I now call "storyWeaving") through weekly All School assemblies. I vividly remember Alexandria Peyton Kennedy, a precious little kindergartener, wondering aloud within earshot of me if it was permissible for her to like the former "girl principal" and me,

---

1   Nancy Mueller, "Hiring of Young Principal Prompts for New Policy," *Tennessean*, December 10, 1998, first edition.

the new "boy principal" at the same time. I assured her she wouldn't betray Dr. G. by liking me as her new principal.

For every negative experience, I built strong relationships with staff—from the custodian and the main office team to the classroom teachers and the school counselor. I remember welcoming a veteran educator who had been mistreated by her principal. She was crestfallen and apprehensive in the aftermath of her experiences. She joined our team and I invited her to give our students her very best. She took the yearbook home that night and mastered the names of every student in the school! I remember two teachers—they dubbed themselves "The Bookends" because they taught the same grade level and came as a set—who took me under their wings and exposed me to teaching at its best. They reminded me that classrooms should gush with healthy noise because "only flowers bloom silently."

And now, many years later, I reflect on those times and the lessons learned. Even now, I often travel with a kite. Whether in a city park after a day of work or on an island for vacation, I still find kite flying to be a meditative experience. The twists, surges, and turns my kite makes as it encounters the ever-changing wind invites a deeper reflection on lessons learned. It is so important to seek out and embrace the challenges of life. It is through them that we develop as individuals.

From Bought Wisdom: Tales of Living and Learning [Interactive Leadership Memoir] by Tony Lamair Burks II published April 2017 in Atlanta, Georgia by LEADright.

Our Community Needs Esperanza

Eulogio Alejandre

"Esperanza" means "hope" in Spanish. Hope keeps people walking in the darkness. Hope keeps people working in jobs they do not enjoy. Hope keeps people in failing relationships. When the long-distance runner's rigor fades, hope keeps her moving forward. We want students to work hard even when their energy evaporates. When the rigor increases, we expect our students to persevere with confidence. Our students will become biliterate in Spanish and English. They will contribute to their local and global communities. That is not only our vision, but also a reality that we pursue daily. Thus, the name of our school, Esperanza Elementary School, is fitting.

In January 2014, however, there was no hope. There was no building, and there were no students, no teachers, and no administrators, but the school opened anyway in August 2014. The board of education hired me in February. Since they had no money, I worked without salary for a month. Accordingly, I asked for free advertising at all local media outlets and the Spanish media responded. Several stories ran on the local stations of Univision, Azteca America, and Telemundo.

Since I had plans to go to the Soccer World Cup in Brazil in June, I was abundantly motivated to find teachers and students. The building was well on its way by mid-May, and by the time I left, there were over three hundred students enrolled and 75% of the faculty and staff already hired. If I could not find a qualified teacher for a specific subject, I looked for a college graduate with a passion for helping students learn. A license would come later.

By the time the first nonexistent bell rang on the first day of school, we had a teacher in each class. The beginning was not easy. We forgot to establish routines, like where to line up after lunch and recess, what to do for recess on rainy or cold days, and many more. However, we didn't forget breakfast and lunch. We had the school fully functional.

Esperanza is a dual immersion school that follows the 90/10 model. In kindergarten and first grade students, learn content in Spanish 90% of the time. Learning time in English increased by 10% each year until grades 5 and 6, when students spend 50% leaning in Spanish and 50% in English.

Only 5% of the students in grades 3 through 6 were at grade level in mathematics at the beginning of the first year, but by the end, it was up to 9%. In May 2017, students scored 22% proficiency in mathematics. Similar results were evident in English language arts and science. Most importantly, social and cultural literacies have improved more dramatically. The choir, chess, dance, and mariachi clubs no longer have to beg students to join.

Esperanza uses four philosophies that underpin everything we do. Most importantly, we believe that belonging is a prerequisite to achievement and success. Just as basic human needs like air and water precede safety needs on Maslow's hierarchy, students cannot learn if they frequently face microaggressions that make them feel as if they don't belong. To create a positive environment, we adopted the elements of Invitational Education to support our efforts. We adopted the Sheltered Instruction Observation Protocol (SIOP) as our primary pedagogical philosophy. All teachers received extensive training in SIOP (although to save money, we had to use early editions of the SIOP materials).

Managing a growing staff is like pushing a bus up a hill. Everyone has a job to do in getting it to the top. Some had to push, and I begged them to push unconditionally. Even if some people appeared to push less than others did, I asked for their trust. I also promised them that nobody was going to lose their job, unless the law required it. I told them that some people may appear to be doing little, but their job was to look out for dangers on the mountain, like boulders, rocks, trees, hikers, or cliffs. I could not do my job without the faith, support, and trust of all the staff. Once we started pushing up the hill, we could not stop. We had to push harder when it rained or snowed. If we stopped doing our individual responsibilities, our progress would stop or slide and our community would suffer greatly.

The trajectory of Esperanza Elementary School is clear. We now need to purchase our building from the developers. Purchasing the building will save the school thousands of dollars a year, which can be invested in better salaries and benefits for faculty and staff. Additionally, owning the building will help us create the equity that will secure the future of the school and our community. Passion and hard work made it happen. Our community needs Esperanza!

Eulogio Alejandre is the executive director and principal of Esperanza Elementary School in West Valley City, Utah. Alejandre emigrated from Mexico in 1977 and spent 25 years in public schools as a teacher and administrator. He earned Bachelor's and Master's degrees from Weber State University and is currently a doctoral student at the University of Utah. Alejandre's research interests include education equity, undocumented students' access to education, language acquisition, dual immersion language education, and teacher preparation. He plans to open other schools around Utah.

Developing Deeper Learning through Global Education

Rob Ford

"The World is a book and those who do not travel read only one page"
                                        — St. Augustine

$\mathbb{A}$s Principal of Wyedean School, I take a couple of critical think-ing groups each week here in this corner of the Welsh–English borders. We meet in my study and, over a cup of tea, we put the world to rights—discussing topics from philosophy to current affairs. We've attracted a good number of students and are never short of viewpoints, but I am always having to apologise to colleagues when we run over our time and students are late for lessons! Developing critical thinking groups has been something I've implemented in any school in which I've taught. It develops students' leadership skills, offers a forum to stretch and challenge learning, is great curriculum enrichment, and allows the development of global learning. As a school principal, I have taken on this initiative for a number of reasons, not least because it allows me to have regular formal educational contact with the students in an otherwise organisational-heavy time-consuming day.

When I talk to my teachers, I also need to know that I can look them in the eye with the integrity of a fellow educator. I see it as an opportunity to develop a crucial but increasingly sidelined element of education, which is the Socratic dialogue with students that fosters the development of discussion and debating skills without the pressures of the "will this be on the exam?" question. The development away from the abstract is where global learning plays a crucial role in relating these skills to the world the students live in.

At Wyedean School, my students regularly hold discussions with their counterparts in France, Moldova, Russia, India, and Indonesia to name but a few. Wyedean is now developing some of the International Baccalaureate (IB) programmes for its curriculum and we are working to become an IB World School here in the borders of England and Wales, where the border under a fragmented, post-Brexit "Global Britain" may become more of a reality.

At the beginning of my school career, I was fortunate enough to start work in education at a UK Quaker independent school, Bootham School in York, which counted historian A.J.P. Taylor and diplomat Philip Noel-Baker amongst its alumni. Noel-Baker helped found the UN in 1945 and won the Nobel Peace Prize for his work. Only later in my career did I realise that part of Bootham's culture and ethos that I so admired was the safe space it provided for students to explore ideas, to be challenged, and to hold constructive healthy dialogue, often with a range of opposing viewpoints. This safe space needs to be resurrected in an age of fake news, post truth, false dichotomies, and binary positions.

I am also lucky enough to be involved with two global educational organisations that have aided deeper learning: the British Council and the International Baccalaureate (IB). The British Council has influenced the global learning dimension in schools across the globe to an incredible extent over the last few decades. Through the British Council, I've had the privilege of being able to work with schools from around the globe as a British Council ambassador, using educational programmes that connect classrooms on a range of projects using innovative technology. The power of this international education is phenomenal in terms of the impact it has had on developing global citizens and a shared understanding of global issues. It's also brought an incredible amount of fun and wider opportunity into the lives of all those involved, not least the students.

If we are to design an education system for the 21st century then it must be anchored in global learning. Whatever the current nationalist populist zeitgeist in Europe and America, the world will continue to become more globalised and interdependent through trade, culture, ecology, travel, resources, and technology. The challenge in our education system is to celebrate local culture and identity, but also not to be afraid of the other influences and benefits of globalisation that have been evolving for over 500 years, ever since European sailors went off to discover new worlds. When I had my own history classroom, I had this quote from H.G. Wells on the wall:

Civilization is in a race between education and catastrophe. Let us learn the truth and spread it as far and wide as our circumstances allow. For the truth is the greatest weapon we have.

In a post-truth world, the educator's prayer must be that education win that race for all of our sakes. Global learning is one of the key elements of holistic education for our students and future generations.

Rob Ford is the principal of Wyedean School in the UK. Rob has been a senior leader in various state and independent schools and has a background in international education, leadership, curriculum, and the International Baccalaureate. Rob believes passionately in the transformative power of international learning on young people, educators, and communities. He has been working with schools, teacher training universities, and school boards on these areas all around the world for over 20 years. More information is available here: http://www.wyedean.gloucs.sch.uk/.

The Why, the Need, and the How of School Vision

Em Del Sordo

When looking to co-create a school vision that acts as a daily filter to our actions and our work, we need to explore "the why," "the need," and "the how." The result? A school vision reflective of all stakeholders that inspires the hearts and minds of the entire school community.

As a first generation Canadian, I had a different sounding name from my neighbours. I remember watching Romper Room and never being "seen" through the magic mirror, so I felt invisible. But I developed resiliency and a passion for social justice and for the underdog. This personal history fuels my sense of self and my work.

As the principal of the brand-new Dundas Valley Secondary School in a small southern Ontario town, we were in a rich spot to create something new and meaningful for the 21st century. We needed to think of what we wanted to be known for in order to centre our work and thinking. My job as principal was to coach the committee of teachers working through *how* they wished to create "the school of our dreams." As our vision, the committee concluded that human rights were actually the focus of our work. *Why* focus on human rights? They discovered a program called Global Connect and related strongly to its goals: acceptance and well-being for all; creating citizens who are aware, engaged, and seek to have a positive impact; and alignment with the *Canadian Charter of Rights and Freedoms*. Having the school focus on human rights also brought the *Ontario Human Rights Code*, the Truth and Reconciliation recommendations, Aboriginal education strategy, antiracism and ethnocultural equity, anti-bullying, and the UN Sustainable Developments Goals into the discussion.

The *need* for a human rights focus as a school vision meant that we could address the essential character traits of building a culture of empathy for kids and staff alike. We wanted to look at what was needed in our society to best support our students and staff. Our chair of the school vision committee solicited the voices of all our feeder schools as he collected data from the various elementary schools within our catchment area. We wanted to create a momentum so that our future students saw themselves as part of the journey to create a new high school in the town. The most important thing was to collect their voices to inform our vision.

The committee also explored all the curricular connections feasible with a human rights focus. When exploring the *how* of creating a school vision, we discovered that human rights and the 17 UN Sustainable Development Goals crossed *all* subject areas. Each Ontario curriculum document allowed many entry points for students and teachers to access the UN Sustainable Development Goals. As principal, I coached staff to filter their interests and passions so that they had autonomy in accessing the curriculum and the school vision. For example, I would ask, "How might you use the school vision to teach the curriculum? How might you use student interests and passions to access the curriculum and school vision? How might you allow student voice to drive student inquiry within the curriculum and the school vision?"

Many teachers who harnessed the school vision found that student engagement and achievement increased. Teachers created exam questions that spoke to their students' interests and passions and, as a result, discovered that students would make connections with our school vision on their final exams.

Our school vision committee chair also solicited the voices of our parents and caregivers. During school council evenings, we would ask for community voices of what they wished to see in their town school. The committee then created a "think tank"—displaying pictures, lyrics, poetry, artwork, posters, and the *Canadian Charter of Rights and Freedoms* on its walls—to share their data and ask for community feedback. Questions that that the committee asked included, "How would you describe DVSS? What are the multiple voices in our school community? What would the best school in the world look like? What do you want the vision of DVSS to be? What would a school with a human rights focus look like?" The committee's draft statement echoed the voices from feeder schools, school council, staff meetings, and community outreach. The result was a collaborative effort that speaks with the voices of all.

The school vision at Dundas Valley Secondary School focuses on creating "An empathetic culture of respect and learning through the lens of human rights." The teaching staff works every day to create a school that teaches "empathy" and gives "respect" while "learning" as we explore our thinking and work through the lens of "human rights." As a Canadian principal, I am honoured to support staff and student thinking driven by their passions and interests in the support of human rights for all.

Em Del Sordo, M.Ed., has been a secondary school principal and a Student Achievement Officer for the Ontario Ministry of Education. His awards include a YMCA Peace Medal, a Premier's Award for Accepting Schools, and The Learning Partnership Canada's Outstanding Principal Award for 2018. He is a human rights advocate who co-created a school vision that filters curriculum and student curiosity through the UN Sustainable Development Goals and the Canadian Charter of Rights and Freedoms. His passion for student learning and student voice fuels his purpose and passion for education.

The Joys and Challenges of Opening a New Campus

Glenn Odland

A ny challenging goal that we work long and hard to achieve is of monumental significance for the whole community. What isn't so obvious is that the victory of achieving the large goal can sometimes cloud the judgement of a leadership group, causing unnecessary pain.

I was the head of a medium size international school (1500 students) on its way to doubling in the span of six years. The challenging goal was that we needed a new home for our expanding community. The short-term strategy had been to splinter off into increasingly stratified communities on separate, interim campuses. At our zenith, we were on four campuses, three of which were targeted to be consolidated onto one large, purpose-built campus housing a full K–12 program. The fourth community would continue on its own, as it was on the other side of the island.

The journey of planning this new school, raising funds to build it, and actually seeing it to completion was a veritable marathon of over five years. To be fair, we were just nicely completing the piling works (sub-surface foundations) when the financial crisis of 2008 struck. Our financing fell apart, and we had to pause construction. You can imagine the angst that grew among our faculty and parents, to say nothing of the leadership team, over the 18 months of that pause.

As a privately-owned school, our only recourse was to find investors willing to join us. Ultimately, that is what allowed us to resume the project and move into a stunningly beautiful new campus.

As is often the case, construction delays prevented us from taking possession on an optimal timeline. In fact, we had to use our October break to pack up, move everything, and resume classes in the new building. I don't recommend that plan.

Many people worked around the clock to be able to conduct meaningful instruction to the last day on our old campuses and continue with meaningful instruction on the first day in our new campus. I remain extremely proud of and grateful to all my colleagues, both academic and support staff, for their dedication and commitment. It was only through their Herculean efforts that we were able to pull this off.

Ironically, while the seamless and uninterrupted continuation of learning deserved to be celebrated, in a way it contributed to some of the mistakes I committed. Focusing on victory in the classroom without balancing several other crucially important perspectives meant that I did not prioritize and plan for addressing other key areas of our transition.

Of course, I was not the only one involved, but I accept responsibility for the mistakes I made. Two specific examples are:

- Given the astronomical cost, our new partners were understandably keen to protect their investment. They decreed (and I supported) that there would be nothing affixed in any way to any wall in the building. Only bulletin boards could be decorated. This mania to preserve walls kept us from creating a home for our community. It felt institutional, cold and in very subtle ways undermined our core values.
- We decided to throw an elaborate opening ceremony, including government officials, dignitaries and many VIPs. The scope of the guest list, and the limited capacity of our flashy new auditorium, meant we could only accommodate some parents, but none of our faculty. Gulp. You got it … by the end of that first exhausting year they felt (understandably) marginalized and unappreciated.

While it may seem simplistic, I now realize that I allowed the preservation of undoubtedly the most important goal (preserving effective student learning) to blur my capacity to see that other goals were being compromised. As always, these decisions were deeply value laden. When my leadership colleagues and I acknowledged that our core value of caring for and supporting all members of our community had been compromised, we made changes. I apologized for the oversight of not hosting a staff opening ceremony, we solicited their requests for how to support them more effectively, and we honoured many of those requests the second year.

It took a little longer to pry loose the grip our new partners had on the "nothing goes on our walls" policy. By the end of the second year, we had overcome that barrier as well, and pursued a variety of strategies to ensure that our new home looked and felt like a school that is proud of its students and their work.

The take-away? Don't let victory, however significant and worthy, blind you to other areas needing your attention as a leader. I know I will never forget that lesson.

Dr. Glenn Odland has been an educational leader for more than 25 years in Canada, Singapore, and India. After 11 years as head of the Canadian International School in Singapore, he is now the Managing Director for the Global Schools branch of Velammal Educational Trust in Chennai, India. He has been a keynote speaker at educational conferences around the world and his work is published in the Journal of Research in International Education.

Championing Our Students

Lynn Leslie

K nowing the importance of a child being connected to a positive
adult role model in their lives, as part of our Student Wellness
plans, our school district challenged each school to ensure that every
child is connected with an adult champion (advocate, mentor, difference maker, coach etc.). In our diverse K–9 school with over 750 students and 60 staff, creating a safe and caring culture in our school was
already a high priority. Using the idea of championing students, our
school community set out to focus on ways to bring a climate of caring
to life.

We started with staff members choosing one student per week to
connect with, have conversations with, and write a personalized card
with positive comments about the student. Students usually responded
in two ways—surprised that an adult was showing interest in them and/
or humble about the strengths we identified. This year, we grew into
a more student-centred, integrated Champion vision, "Let your Light
Shine." To further tap into our students' talents and gifts, we provided
many opportunities for student involvement and connection—through
leadership, service, positive relationships, mental health awareness, and
community.

Connection with Staff: Last year, adults chose the student they wanted
to champion; this year, students chose their adult champion. This was
no easy task in a school our size, so each staff member created a personal Google slide about themselves, sharing favourite quotes, families,
pets, hobbies, and so on. In homerooms, students viewed these slides

and picked six possible adults to be their champion. Every child was connected with one of their chosen adult champions. Groups of about fifteen students and one adult champion meet monthly for "getting to know you" activities. Informally, students know they have someone at the school who cares about them, someone they can connect with at any time.

Engagement in Leadership and Service: Almost three-quarters of our students are diverse learners, for language, learning, and/or social emotional needs. Sometimes, shining at purely academic tasks can be difficult for students, so we wanted to ensure equitable opportunities for all. In Junior High, we designed our Career and Technology Foundations (CTF) course as a student-centred career simulation with the purpose of students designing and hosting a family event called Ignite the Night. Teachers held a career fair, students created resumes, completed applications, and were hired for a job (CTF course). Classes were composed of students from grades seven to nine. Teachers were worried about handing over control and responsibility to students; however, students really stepped up! Our evening event was a huge success with over 75% of our families attending. Student event planners were the organizers and others created and ran makerspace challenges, hair salons, video game arcade, boot camp, dance, medical studies, technical theatre-design, art design, and MasterChef. Parents, teachers, and staff were so proud, as students who had not previously thought of themselves as leaders began to shine with confidence and excitement!

Mental Health Awareness: Knowing that students often go to other students before an adult, we championed students to support one another in positive, healthy ways. Two students from each of our 17 Junior High homerooms were chosen by peers to be community helpers. Thirty-four students were trained by the Canadian Mental Health Association's YouthSMART (Supporting Mental Health And Resiliency Together) program, learning peer-helping skills in order to develop confidence in their abilities to help others and to build mental health equity into the school. Our counsellor established a Student Wellness Advocacy Team (S.W.A.T.) where 11 students attended a citywide wellness summit and planned a wellness event. Elementary students learned about positive relationships during clubs like Friendology, Fair Play, Positive Vibes, Fun Friends, Virtues, and Secret Kindness. Seeing students engage in helping others is so heartwarming, especially when they seek adult support, share compliments, or perform random act of kindness!

Community Connections: We have been lucky to have a community partnership with Calgary Bridge for Youth who provide an after-school program one day per week for English language learner students. This year, we expanded our after-school programs to offer two additional opportunities: Junior High students can participate in the City of Calgary, LEAD program—Leadership, Empowerment, Achieving a Difference. Elementary students can participate in Families Matter, Front Runners program focused on respect, self-awareness, responsiveness, interdependence, and playfulness. Now, almost 100 students are connected with community role models and mentors.

We believe that part of creating and sustaining a culture of caring is implementing practices like the Champion vision where students have positive relationships, feel included, and develop into healthy and productive citizens. Still in its early stages, one thing is for sure: we are starting to see our students truly shine when they are championed. They get involved and step up as leaders, becoming confident in recognizing and sharing their gifts and talents with others.

Lynn Leslie is a K–9 principal with the Calgary Catholic School District. As a former school trustee and current Ed.D. student at Western University, Lynn is a passionate lifelong learner, who believes in leading collaborative, caring schools where all students have opportunities to succeed. She has received Alberta's 2014 Distinguished Leader award (Council of School Leadership) and Canada's 2016 Outstanding Principals award (The Learning Partnership). When not working on her studies, Lynn enjoys reliving her younger days through the adventures of her two adult children and traveling to warm destinations with her husband.

It Takes a Community
to Raise a Gosling

Andrea Taylor

Developing a positive school community was one of my primary visions when I started my first principalship at a high school. I had visions of collaborative learning commons both inside and outside of the school, especially when I had to work with architects and facility planners to renovate space in preparation for welcoming a special program, the Community Pathway Program (CPP) for students with exceptional learning needs. Little did I know that my school community would involve wildlife.

In preparation for the CPP class, a new larger elevator was required and the only place the architects could find to build a 3-storey shaft was in the old rundown weed-covered courtyard. I worked with the architect and facility people to renovate the entire outside space to become student-friendly and fully accessible to all. It turned out to be a beautiful outdoor classroom and learning space, so much so that our annual pair of nesting Canadian Geese started to use the space for their own life lessons.

Each spring the same pair of geese returned to the school grounds to find a nesting spot for their new gaggle of offspring. The school grounds would become their "territory" and the students and staff would learn to monitor, observe, and study their every movement for both authentic learning opportunities and self-preservation. An angry mother goose is not a creature we wanted to cross!

The return of the geese also attracted a beautiful red-tailed hawk—another potential authentic science lesson in discussing the concept of ecosystems and food chains.

As the spring season warmed, the gaggle of goslings got bigger each day and ventured further away from their nest to learn new life lessons. As the weather warmed, more students also ventured into the new Outdoor Learning Commons courtyard to read, write, take photographs, and practice oral presentations. One lovely day a few years back, a Grade 9 French Immersion class was outside practicing their presentations when one observant student noticed the mother and father geese on the roof of the school. One after another, the students, and even the teacher, gathered to watch the geese and wonder what they might do next. As the whole class looked up towards the sky, they noticed the goslings waddling towards the edge of the roof. Before the humans realized it, the goslings were dropping from the sky! It was their first "Fly and be Free" lesson! The class did not know what to do except cover their heads and find the nearest door into the school.

From behind the glass, the French class watched as the little birds either flew well ... or not. Oh Mon Dieu! As mom and dad watched from the roof, each little bird plunged down, caught some air, flapped madly, and for some of them, landed with little damage. All except one gosling that hit the ground with a thud, watched stoically by its parents and hungrily by the red-tailed hawk. The students watched in horror, some frantic to help while others warned them to stay back. The teacher tried to stay calm and re-direct the students back to class. One student, however, ran to the office and wanted to know our policy for protecting the goslings. I don't remember reading that one in my administrator's handbook so we improvised—quickly!

By the time I got to the Outdoor Learning Commons, the mother and father goose were on the grassy slope with their gaggle of goslings. I counted how many were present (cue our zoo fieldtrip flashback here), and one was missing. The red-tailed hawk was still perched in the pine with nothing in its talons or mouth, so I ventured outside. I was not sure what I would do if I found a dead gosling. All eyes, wildlife and human, were on me and then I saw it ... the last little gosling madly trying to make it up the slope back to his family. Phew! But how did it even survive the fall? I'm thinking, *Way to go little guy!*

The students, so relieved, made out-of-bounds signs for the outdoor space reading "Stay Away—Geese Flying Lessons!" The signs stayed up for the next two weeks while the Outdoor Learning Commons became a viewing exhibit for the whole school community on a key life lesson: "Step carefully; that first step is a doozie!"

Andrea Taylor *is a secondary school principal in Burlington, Ontario, Canada. Andrea started her career as an elementary school teacher in 1990. She spent nine years teaching grades 5–8 in math, science, and physical education before moving to high school. She began her administrative career in 2003. As vice-principal, she worked in four different regions of the school board before being promoted to principal in 2012. Over the last 28 years, Andrea has worked with students of all ages and abilities. She continues to enjoy working with staff to hone their skills in meeting the needs of all students.*

Closing a School

Simon Goodacre

As a vice-principal, I was moved to a high school that had just undergone a very contentious closure process. The school was designated to close and the student body would be merged with that of a nearby school. I was the lead administrator, but also an alumnus of the school. I had just been assigned to close my former school.

I had also worked through a school closing as a teacher and one salient memory was that the students had shown more resilience and adaptability than the adults (both staff and parents). I reflected on this experience and worked to incorporate it into my current role. A guiding principle for the leadership team at our school was to involve students as much as possible in all aspects of the closure process, both formal and informal. While having formal student involvement was important, maintaining a constant openness towards student conversation was even more valued. We spent considerable time walking the halls at lunch, wandering into classes and the library, and talking to students as they waited for the school bus home. The value of this time cannot be understated; it created a lot of trust and openness with students. It also helped me to understand what issues were important to students. When you can speak knowledgably from a student perspective, it goes a long way in comforting many parents.

The community of a school slated for closure will experience intense emotional swings. Each person will have unique emotional reactions; usually a roller coaster of them as the process plays out. During this time, a school leader must be willing to spend considerable time just listening and being supportive. Your job is not to support the decision to close the school. Your job is to help move the community through a difficult process with as much dignity and support as possible. Providing time to allow students, staff, and parents to express emotions and feel valued goes a long way. Despite the huge demands on your time during the closure process, it is important to prioritize the time to listen.

One must respect the feelings of communal grief while also subtly shifting the narrative to a focus on a positive future. A tricky balancing act indeed! The choice of language around the closure proved to be incredibly significant. Many people in the community wanted the history of the school to be extensively celebrated. It is a tricky balance to recognize the significant history of the school without dwelling on it. Helping the community through the closure process requires leaders to keep the focus on the future. The school leader must recognize the importance of the school history while steering the conversation towards the opportunities of the new school; a separate but related process was operating concurrently to develop the structures and vision of the new school. You need to present the benefits of the future opportunities respectfully and carefully, noting that many people will disagree with this direction.

The job uncertainty of a school closure process can have a profound impact on staff. While all staff members were guaranteed jobs within the school district, the different employee group contracts each had a separate staffing process so many were unsure of their placement the following year. This created a lot of angst. One had to be acutely sensitive to these feelings. The balancing act of being the onsite manager for the school district and maintaining quality working relationships with staff took considerable effort. As with students, the key was to be always available to listen and discuss issues. It was important to have relationships with individual staff, teacher union representatives, and school board Human Resource staff. Being open, transparent, and accessible was important in building as much trust as possible in a situation where people are inclined to be distrustful.

Throughout the process, the other leaders and I tried to communicate more than we thought necessary. No one complains of too much information in this type of situation. The community came to trust that information was being made available. We were honest when information was not available and strived to provide answers to questions when posed. We tried our best to develop trust with the community as individuals, even if the school board was not trusted as an organization. It is never easy being the one to deliver unpopular information, but trust can still be maintained if one is open, transparent, and honest.

Simon Goodacre was a secondary vice-principal for nine years and is currently a principal at a K–8 elementary school in Ontario, Canada. His areas of interest are Special Education and blended/e-learning instruction. He has been an instructor for the Guidance Additional Qualification program through Queen's University and is currently enrolled in the Ed.D. program at Western University.

PART V

Leading in a Culture of Status Quo

Organizational improvement planning is the work of leadership. Leaders understand that organizations exist within organizations. Leaders are frequently called upon to lead change in an organization that appears to embrace status quo. "Well, this is always how we've done things around here." Evidence-informed leadership requires an assessment of cannot versus will not when faced with the opportunity to leading in the status quo. Cannot is a capacity issue. When faced with *cannot*, leaders tactically, strategically, and collaboratively develop and implement improvement planning processes for both individuals and organizations based on clearly delineated goals. Improvement plans require monitoring, evaluating, and communicating over several iterative cycles. When faced with several options, maintaining the status quo is typically not in the leader's repertoire, mindset, or moral purpose. By definition, maintaining the status quo does not represent change. When faced with *will not*, leadership response balances empathy and tenacity with high expectations. Exemplary leaders shift the paradigm from leading in a culture of status quo to leading in a culture of change courageously taking a road less travelled.

The Snowball Effect

Isabel Oliveira

Twenty years into my leadership in the classroom, in the community and at the Ministry of Education in Portugal, I decided to apply for the position of principal to lead a high school that had lost its once-renowned national reputation of excellence. Encouraged by school colleagues, I applied for the position with the optimistic idealism that I could quickly turn the school around to its former glory and ranking as one of the top high schools in the country. For decades, students from all over the region had once competed for admission and the alumni included nationally renowned individuals, from politics, literature, science, and the arts.

I was the successor of past leadership attempts—including a state-of-the-art school rebuilt, with unsuccessful results—at regaining that successful academic history and tradition. I began to lead the school with the four-year school plan of action that had been a requirement of my application. All aspects of school life engulfed me; I immersed myself in every small detail that I believed could improve the learning environment, the school climate, and the teaching conditions and practices. I worked day and night and night and day, and yet, the school remained stuck in time; entrenched in a culture of out-dated practices and methodologies. I was frustrated that I had a skilled staff that lacked the enthusiasm, and in spite of all my efforts to create change, they kept themselves isolated.

In time, the shear resistance to the changes became almost overwhelming. Anything and everything that hinted at novelty was shut down swiftly and quietly. I tried to assimilate into the existing staff culture, to show them that my intentions were not personal, but rather professional. I kept praising their skill set, and yet, the resistance kept increasing. Staff clung even more to past practices and to their low expectations of themselves and of the students. Even moments of exceptional teaching and learning remained isolated, locked behind classroom doors.

In spite of improving the school's climate for students, staff, and families—through radical changes in school routines, a student code of conduct, and emphasis on staff and student social gatherings and celebrations—self-doubt in my ability to turn the school around settled in, shrinking my once-high enthusiasm. I felt unable to influence the staff's mindset, to lead them to new ways of thinking about the teaching–learning process in a progressive 21st century way.

Then, in one opportune moment, something began to stir. I summoned the courage to have an earnest conversation with one of the most vehement resisters. Her main objective, as far as I could see, was to constantly march into my office to protest my plan to provide our students with opportunities to extend their learning by participating in national and international academic competitions. Despite her past critical observations of my leadership, I invited her to discuss her consistent, unwavering objections. Then, I asked her *why* she objected. Her fears were my fears: she was afraid of failure, of being blamed for her students' lack of success. I assured her that I would walk with her, support her, and take equal responsibility if the risk did not have positive outcomes. She agreed to take on the initiative for one year. This one step forward was the beginning of many changes to come.

Our collaborative work and the national and international success of her students created a snowball effect of change in the teaching culture of the school. Not only did this one teacher continue, year after year, to innovative, but other teachers from her department began to follow suit. The snowball effect gained momentum as it began to spread to other staff, in other departments, increasing collaboration and innovation.

In one conversation with one resistor, I understood the power that one individual can have, negative or positive, as a collaborative change agent. Schools are organizations of individuals and sometimes not even the most well intentioned, detailed plans, hopes, and skills are going to inspire people to change, even if they understand that the change is needed. By listening, by being present and walking with resistors, sometimes they can become your greatest allies in the change process.

Our students have since won local, national, and international competitions in Literature, Biology, Chemistry, Arts, Sports, Entrepreneurship, and Innovation. Our European exchange program morphed from one activity to six per academic year, providing our students and staff with increased learning opportunities with students and staff from Belgium, Finland, Italy, Holland, and Germany. Equally important, the snowball effect that one conversation triggered continues to lead my staff and myself to continued innovation in our practices, and regaining the history and tradition of our school, as a school of excellence.

Isabel Oliveira was a French and English high school teacher for eleven years. She also worked as a pedagogical specialist and coordinator at the Ministry of Education of Portugal for nine years. She is currently in her fifth year of leadership, and second mandate, at Escola Secundária Rodrigues Lobo, Portugal. She is currently completing her doctorate in Education at the University of Coimbra.

A Lesson in Deficit Mentality

John P. Portelli

I had almost given up completely. The nasty and meaningless bureau-cracy of doing administration at an educational institution had exhausted me. I had just finished yet another inconclusive meeting where the majority of my colleagues were objecting to policy changes that would bring about more equity in the institution. Their argument was that diversity would lower standards. They could not or would not understand that having a variety of equally valuable standards does not amount to lowering standards. Old habits are very hard to change. How can they be so closed-minded and blind to the dangers of deficit men-tality?

I was so passionate and enthusiastic when I started my administra-tive role. I knew it would not be a smooth ride. I hoped that gradually I could shift the organization towards being a more just institution. I believed that critical work without hope and action is not possible. I believed that, as an administrator, my main role is to open up possibil-ities for students and colleagues to achieve equity and social justice in practice. I had acted on these beliefs, but I was on the verge of losing all hope!

In such moments, I usually either go to a coffee shop and try to engage in a meaningful conversation, or find a good book to read. In desperation, I walked towards the bookstore to search for something that would intrigue me and, at least, free my mind from such miseries. Being a poet myself, I headed to the poetry section. A book entitled *The Rose that Grew from the Concrete* intrigued me, and the title immedi-ately gave me a sense of hope. I grabbed the book, sat in a corner, and began to read. Halfway through, I found the poem with the same title as the book. The poem ended with these lines:

Long live the rose that grew from concrete

When no one else even cared!

Suddenly I was revived and hopeful again. And I realized that I was so engaged with the poetry that I had not even checked who the author was. To my great surprise, I discovered that it was rapper Tupac Shakur. In amazement and disbelief, I whispered, "Tupac Shakur?!" I exclaimed it as if I never expected that Tupac Shakur would have been able to write such poetry, even though rap is an immensely complex poetic form with echoes of the Irish bardic oral tradition.

But, why, I asked myself? What do I really know about him? Why did I carry such negative expectations?

Suddenly I realized that the experienced administrator who had written about the problems of deficit mentality had himself fallen prey to it. We are all vulnerable to this deficit mentality—thinking that others cannot possibly achieve, prejudging them, having low expectations—and, with humility and courage, we need to be continuously on the lookout within ourselves for such prejudice! Or, to end with another two lines of poetry from a Scandinavian proverb:

In every man there is a King.

Speak to the King and the King will come forth.

John P. Portelli, Ph.D., was born in Malta where he completed a B.A. (Philosophy & Maltese). His Commonwealth Scholarship took him to McGill University in Montreal where he earned his M.A. and Ph.D. He has published 10 books including Key Questions for Educational Leaders (Word and Deed Publishing, 2015). Two of his books won the American Educational Studies Association Critic Award, and another won the Canadian Association for the Foundations of Education Book Award. He is now a professor at the Ontario Institute for Studies in Education (OISE) and Co-director of the Centre for Leadership and Diversity. Since 1982 he has worked closely with teachers and school administrators in Canada and internationally.

We're All in This Together:
Collaborative School Leadership

Sarah Mullin

I firmly believe that there is no greater resource than our collective skills and experiences. We would not be where we are today if not for the guidance, wisdom, and support of those who mentor us, challenge us, and give us the opportunities we needed to flourish as leaders in education. It is our responsibility to grow future leaders by providing a range of opportunities to enable colleagues to develop skills in resilience, resourcefulness, and reflection. We need to encourage colleagues to step out of their comfort zones and challenge themselves, leading to positive mental and physical growth.

When I was appointed as the assistant headteacher of an independent Catholic secondary school, one of my responsibilities was to lead the curriculum for Personal, Social, Health, and Economic Education (PSHEE), a planned programme of learning that allows pupils to acquire the skills, knowledge, and understanding that they need to manage their lives. An early audit of the curriculum included meeting with a pupil consultation group and gathering staff feedback. It soon became clear that the existing programme would benefit from a revamp. Some pupils admitted that they did not find the lessons engaging and some teachers did not appreciate the value of such a curriculum, thinking the time would be better spent preparing for examinations. I knew that things had to change.

After some careful research, sharing ideas with other colleagues, and exploring a range of widely available resources online, I delivered a training session for staff where teachers considered the merits of a

PSHEE curriculum, thinking about the core values of the school and their personal philosophies as educators. Teachers were encouraged to think about the tremendous power that they have to enable learners to blossom into critical thinkers, independent enquirers, and confident, articulate citizens. It was important for me to instill in teachers a sense of responsibility so that all staff could adopt a positive attitude towards the PSHEE curriculum.

My next challenge was to ensure that we revised the programme, producing carefully planned lessons to meet the needs of all our learners. I wanted the lessons to be fast-paced and engaging, with an appropriate level of challenge. Most importantly, I knew that teachers needed to feel empowered by the lessons. They needed to be enthused and passionate about delivering the key messages and moral values. I could have put metaphorical pen to paper and written every lesson plan for each of the five years' worth of the PSHEE curriculum myself (as a former Head of English, I had enough lesson planning experience to do so). This was not what I wanted for my team, however. I made the strategic decision to adopt a devolved leadership approach, carefully distributing key areas to each member of staff so that our community could take ownership of the curriculum.

There were many different reactions to my strategy. There were the self-motivated teachers who could not wait to share their ideas. There were those who could see the benefits but needed further support and coaching to help them along the way. Then there were those who were reluctant and did not welcome the responsibility. Confident in the belief that a collaborative planning approach would ensure that everybody could share in its success, I gave clear guidelines as to what was needed, set timelines, and offered an open-door policy of support.

A year later, the transformation is evident. Some staff members who initially showed reluctance are now openly positive about the contributions they have made. Colleagues are publicly praising one another for their commitment and hard work and the culture of sharing good practice has rippled across the staff room. There is a noticeable improvement in pupil engagement and pupil behaviour. Feedback from staff, parents, and pupils has been increasingly positive. In this /

For this (otherwise subject "I" refers to being a self-improving school) self-improving school, I will continue to review and revise the curriculum to meet the needs of our current cohort, but I will also continue to empower and motivate staff to play a proactive role in its development at all times.

At a recent interview for a middle leader position, an internal candidate was asked to share an example of where they had made a significant contribution to the school community. They enthusiastically discussed their experience in planning the PSHEE curriculum, showing their teamwork skills, creativity, and the positive impact that they had on others. The candidate got the job and attributed this success to being trusted with the responsibility of trying something new.

We never really know what we are capable of until we try. Let's provide opportunities for our colleagues to show us what they can do!

Sarah B. Mullin is Assistant Headteacher at Priory School, Birmingham, UK. Mullin is passionate about raising standards in education, having trained several teachers across the UK. After gaining her M.A. in Education and becoming a Chartered Teacher of English and a member of the Teaching and Learning Academy, she is currently working towards her Doctorate in Education.

Plant a Seed

Shaunna Finley

As instructional leaders, we want to make a positive impact on the education of our students, but also on our teachers. I am an instructional leader for a predominantly low-income high school in an urban district. Our teachers come to work ready to change the lives of students. Due to the nature of our community, students miss a lot of school. This impacts both students and teachers. Our students are unable to stay after school to make up tests and participate in extracurricular activities like clubs. This has a negative impact in so many areas of the school.

Last school year, I attended a conference and participated in a session focused on an initiative called Power Hour, originated in a rural high school in Florida. The idea is that students have an hour in the day to eat lunch, make up missed assignments, participate in clubs, register for the ACT/SAT, meet with guidance counselors, or any other school related business. The pioneer of the concept presented at the conference. I spoke with her immediately after the session. I was so moved by the concept and the reasons behind this intervention to support students and staff that I decided to present it to my administrative team.

As soon as I shared it with the team, they all gave excuses as to why it could not work. I knew I had to figure out a way to get them to see how this would benefit students and teachers. There was plenty of evidence to show that our current plan was not working. It was time to plant a seed or two! I found some teachers who thought outside the box and who would share this idea with others. I told the administrative team that I would share it with teachers to get their feedback.

At our next professional development session, I showed a video about Power Hour and asked the teachers what they thought. Wow! The positive feedback was overwhelming. The seeds planted received a little water and light and started to grow before my eyes. The teachers had ideas as to what they could do with their time during our new "Cardinal Hour" intervention. The deans of students even chimed in; they saw an opportunity to institute a lunch detention. The teachers looked to each other to figure out office and lunch hours. Some teachers wanted to keep their classrooms open the entire hour to provide academic support to students. It started to sound like they were focused on something else our students needed ... *college* and *career readiness*! Students would be learning how to manage their time as if they were in college or in a career, all business taken care of during Cardinal Hour.

Instructional leaders, do not be afraid to try something new. Most importantly, be organic and expect great things to happen! We are in week four of Cardinal Hour. It has been positive for everyone in the building, from cafeteria workers to maintenance to guidance. We all receive some benefits, but the most important beneficiaries are our students.

Shaunna D. Finley, Ph.D., is the principal of East Chicago Central High School in Indiana. Dr. Finley also has an extensive background in career and technical education, non-profit and business management. You can follow Dr. Finley on LinkedIn and Twitter.

George Webster:
Achieving Together to Build a Better School

Nancy Steinhauer

I arrived at George Webster as Principal in 2008. At the time, our motto was "Working together to build a better world." The staff was lovely, energetic, and committed. They were working hard. But we soon realized that "working" was not enough. We needed to succeed. Fewer than half of our students were meeting the provincial literacy expectations. For many of them, school success would be a ticket out of poverty. So, after an elaborate, collaborative process, we agreed to change our motto to "*Achieving* together to build a better world." Student achievement needed to be our number one priority.

When I arrived at George Webster, it was a JK–5 school of about 450 students, most of whom were living in poverty. At George Webster, there were approximately 30 languages represented and 35 different countries. There were many communities within the community, including newcomers, refugees, and white Canadians who had lived in poverty for generations. We had interactions with the child welfare system on a weekly, sometimes daily, basis. This was a community where children were faced with very challenging circumstances. For some of them, a good education was a life or death proposition.

During my first year at George Webster, we allowed ourselves to experiment freely with different methods, programs, and approaches, and we made a few important discoveries:

1. **We Needed to Aim Higher**: We compared how our students were doing on the provincial standardized tests compared to report cards. Based on report card results, it appeared as if our students were doing just fine, but when compared to other students across the province, our students were failing. We had to ask ourselves hard questions about this discrepancy and began to realize that we had been setting the bar too low for our students. By scrutinizing provincial results, examples of student work, and the curriculum expectations together in small teams, we were able to redefine our expectations for our students. We became aware that we were over-valuing knowledge and comprehension, and under-teaching students how to work with ideas and concepts.

2. **Social Justice is about Action**: We started to think about the difference between charity and social justice. We were committed to teaching about social justice, teaching through the lens of social justice, but we realized that we had to make a shift from "doing for" our community to supporting its members to take action. The staff had always been extremely generous in its devotion to the community, collecting food and clothes for families in need. We still believed that the students' basic needs needed to be met, and supported the establishment of nutrition programs, a clothing closet, and even an on-site pediatric clinic. At the same time, we shifted our focus from giving *things* to developing *skills*, and over the next four years, we would provide many opportunities for students and parents to make change in their school, community, and the world.

3. **Focus on Learning**: Finally, we made a very conscious effort to shift our focus from teaching to learning. As the "lead learner," I understood that we needed to build in time to learn together about our students and their learning. We needed to look at student work together and, like scientists working in a lab, cooperate to find solutions to problems students were having. Working as a team, where every student was our student, and

every teacher was everyone's teacher, we could investigate ways to ensure that students were meeting success more reliably.

We spent considerable time during my first year at George Webster reflecting on our own assumptions about our students, their families, and each other. We engaged every staff member in equity training: teachers, educational assistants, office assistants, caretakers, and so on. This was puzzling to some, as there were some divisions among the staff based on role (and possibly class), and it was not typical in our board to train across unions like this. Nonetheless, if we were truly going to tackle issues of equity in the community, it seemed critical that we first break down any barriers that existed within our own team.

Learning together, regardless of role, was a powerful action. What I learned was that we cannot expect equity for our students when inequities exist among the adults in a school community.

Before we could raise our expectations for our students, we needed to have higher expectations of ourselves and each other, applying both pressure and support and believing in our collective ability to enact change. As our staff felt more empowered to take action, so did our students and so did their families. Over time, we were indeed able to achieve, together, towards making a better world. In the end, every member of the community was required to make our new motto a reality.

Nancy Steinhauer *is currently the principal of The Mabin School, one of Canada's first Ashoka Changemaker Schools. An educator with over 20 years of experience, Nancy has worked in both independent schools and public, inner-city schools. Nancy has also served as a Student Achievement Officer at the Ontario Ministry of Education. In 2012, she was recognized as one of Canada's Outstanding Principals by The Learning Partnership. She was also awarded the Stand Up for Kids Award by the 4 Children's Aid Societies of Toronto. Nancy is one of the authors of the critically-acclaimed book Pushing the Limits: How Schools Can Prepare Our Children Today for the Challenges of Tomorrow (2017).*

Intercultural Dialogue

Marta Milani

"I was a stranger and you [only] welcomed me."
—Matthew 25:35

My desire to explore issues around interculturalism was sparked by something that happened about ten years ago when I was teaching secondary school in Verona. At the time, the presence of foreign students—particularly in the upper grades—did not yet have the structural character it has today, but was seen as exceptional. Consequently, it was quite uncommon to have proper training in that respect. I was teaching Italian, history, and geography, and I was also running the theatre workshop. It was in theatre where I came to understand the need for a radical shift in our pedagogical paradigm, but first in my own mindset.

We were working on a scene with seven students, six of whom were acting as tipsy customers in a bar; one was a female student playing the role of a waitress. At one point, I asked the girl—a young Muslim woman with a Tunisian background—to serve some alcoholic drinks to the customers so that she could really get into the character. Unexpectedly, the student refused to touch the bottles with alcohol in them because it would have been an indefensible violation of her religious beliefs. I remember feeling bewildered, embarrassed, and inadequate. I tried to remedy the situation by casting her in a different role, which seemed the proper way to overcome the impasse.

Later, I often thought about that episode and the way I handled it. Perhaps I had sidestepped the issue rather than resolving it. Did the new part I assigned to the student fulfil her expectations or put her in a position that she could not refuse due to my being her teacher? What kind of message—though sparked by good intentions—had I conveyed to my students? These and other related questions preyed on my mind in the years that followed since I had failed to capitalise on a 'critical incident' from which we could have drawn invaluable joint reflections.

I had made two notable mistakes in handling the situation. The first was to invoke a universal moral precept assuming that the *other*— being like *us* and sharing *our* societal values—would necessarily accept the solution as required by the supposed common (European/Western) ground of efficiency. The second mistake was that my decision was a symptom of a resigned relativism of differences being both inevitable and inescapable. My student was in an awkward position and my choice of solution contributed to relegating her culture to a fixed, *other* state. Not only that, I had somehow avoided the crucial issue of coexistence, and failed to trigger a fruitful discussion on this point with my students.

Several years after this episode, and after completing a Ph.D. in intercultural pedagogy, I understood the urgency of adopting a positive anthropological perspective that does not look down upon, conceal, or remove differences, and at the same time does not glorify them. As Clifford Geertz puts it in *Available Light: Anthropological Reflections on Philosophical Topics* (2001), the 'supremacy of the familiar' ultimately makes everyone poorer. We must rethink differences by engaging in dialogue based on a two-way negotiation process that allows for the repositioning of different interests while striving to reach points of equilibrium. Regarding the episode I described at the beginning, this would require me to allow the student a say in the solution to our mutual problem. Obviously, in the high school setting, there was no alcohol involved and so the dramatic exercise would detract nothing from the orthodoxy of her beliefs. In other words, there is a need to re-calibrate and rewire convictions and ideas sometimes etched in stone, reassigning to them their "specific weight."

Truly intercultural dialogue provides us with tools for interpreting events and nurtures enlightened ideas, investigating—as Foucault would say in *Discipline and Punish* (1977)—truth by means of its effects on power and power by means of a discourse on truth. This does not mean being perplexed out of prejudice; it means, rather, embracing Kant's dictum *Sapere aude* ("dare to know"), to unshackle ourselves from surreptitious ideas that are frequently nothing more than the by-products of political and social short-circuits. *Tertium non datur—* the third option must unite the other two.

*Dr. **Marta Milani** is a post-doc fellow at the University of Verona (Italy), where she is involved in research and educational consulting at the Center for Intercultural Studies. She is also a member of the Cooperative Learning Study-Training-Research Group, where she works as a vocational training expert. Her research focuses on intercultural education, especially the development of intercultural competence at school. Dr. Milani may be reached via email at marta.milani@univr.it.*

"We Are Safe Now. We Have a Voice and No One is Afraid to Use It."

Diane Charles

Kelly Clarkston's 2011 hit "Stronger"—celebrating German philosopher Friedrich Nietzsche's 1889 saying "That which does not kill us, makes us stronger"—speaks to my experience in leading a culture of change when assigned as a principal to a new school. Change is hard, even for those tasked with creating the conditions for change to occur.

As a seasoned principal, with experience working in multiple schools with various teams, I was ready for the challenges presented to me by the district to help to move my new school forward. As with all principals assigned to a new school, I knew I had many things to learn and very little time in which to learn them!

My first impressions of the school were positive. Academically, the students were doing quite well. There was a strong sports tradition with high participation in extracurricular activities. The hallways looked wonderful, full of beautiful displays of student work. Yet there was something missing. There was no joy, no freedom, and no spark in the building. Staff were reticent to share on any level. What looked like a wonderful place to learn was actually a place where fear and mistrust ruled, and where collaboration and positivity were vacant.

It was not my goal to change long-held practices immediately. Yet, there were fundamental issues that could not be ignored or go unchallenged. The more I brought these issues to light, the more pushback I received. "That's not the way we do things around here" became the rallying call of many staff during the first few months of the school year. Staff meetings became contentious. There was loud opposition to changes needed to bring school practices into alignment with the widely held expectations for all schools in the district. However, the pushback was not staff-wide. A silent minority would nod in meetings, and would speak openly with me when others were not present. I listened carefully and began to take my lead from them.

The work was hard; by the winter break, I was exhausted. I was seriously questioning myself as a leader. However, instead of wallowing in self-doubt, I took the opportunity of the break to reflect on what I was doing. I connected with the premise of *Start with Why* from Simon Senik, and wrote about what I most valued about being an educator. I now had a renewed sense of purpose and was ready to return to work with confidence.

The next six months of the year moved forward with equal challenge, yet less personal strife. I was more confident in the path we were taking to open what had been a closed school site, and I was seeing evidence of a subtle shift towards a more collaborative relationship among staff. They were open to exploring ways to support all students instead of focusing on the needs of their individual classrooms.

There were a few milestones that year that provided solid evidence that a shift in culture was occurring. Through work in our Professional Learning Community (PLC) sessions, I was able to introduce a full plan-do-study-act cycle to the school team. Through this work, we were able to implement a school-wide numeracy intervention process with participation from all staff! Another celebration occurred when my primary staff agreed to become part of a pilot program on early literacy, allowing me the opportunity to attend a conference with them. Magic happened! We were actually talking about student learning, and ways to support each other in moving forward.

I would be lying if I said all staff supported the changes that were occurring. However, the majority began to see the value of student-centred dialogue, the strength in "we" versus "I," and the value of building community. At the year-end staff meeting, I shared my personal vision for the school—every adult would know every child, and every child would know every adult. The years of being a closed system were over.

Three years in, the school is now a vibrant, open learning community, centred on trust and collaboration. The staff truly values working as part of a team. They listen to each other and honour each other's voices. Students are part of a community, not a class. Learning happens in all areas—sometimes it is even a little loud and messy!

As for the staff, some left after the first year, but the majority stayed. Some questioned how I kept coming to work each day that year. My response is always, "I believed in the school." One staff member, in reflecting on the changes in the building shared that "We are all safe now. We all have a voice and no one is afraid to use it."

Dr. Diane Charles is an elementary principal in British Columbia, Canada, and a strong advocate for supporting the needs of marginalized students. She has spent the majority of her thirty years in education working in inner-city school settings. Charles holds a Doctorate in Education Leadership through Western University. Her passion is for creating teams and developing programs to move student learning forward. She fully embraces the adage that learning is a lifelong process—she is excited about where the journey will take her next!

Building Trust Spawns Results

Kenneth M. Jandes

For me, leadership is all about building trust, knowledge, and confidence.

I had just been appointed to my second superintendent position in the suburbs of Chicago in 2001. The students, parents, teachers, and administrators were great, as was the Board of Education. As the school year began, I spent much time listening to my colleagues and community stakeholders to glean perceptions from them about the school district, student achievement, and the school improvement process.

Although each of the five schools had two teacher leaders, voted in by the faculty members at each school, and these ten teacher leaders met at least once a month with the curriculum director, there appeared to be no overarching district practice driving the school improvement process to increase student achievement year over year. My leadership style has always been collaborative, and so we began the conversations that would ultimately lead to an amazing district-wide transformation.

The district's collective bargaining agreement allowed teachers to take part in professional development (PD) activities during off-site "day trips." While PD is always encouraged, to receive the most benefit from these activities, teachers and administrators should develop a system for "sharing the knowledge" when the teachers return to the district. One of the first processes we collectively undertook was to create a strategic vision and mission for the district and to involve all stakeholders (students, teachers, board members, parents, community members, and administrators). Our goal was to decide what we wanted to do as a district. We then prioritized those goals into three categories:

instructional, building and grounds, and personnel. It took us three months to agree on our plan of action. We also agreed that all future endeavors and decisions would be viewed through the lens of the plan we had just created, including best practices and long-term research.

The first instructional goal was to find a long-term research study that we could use as the foundation for our instructional improvement process. We formed a team of stakeholders and off we went. After months of critically assessing several best-practice research models, the team selected the Professional Learning Communities (PLC) model by Dr. Richard DuFour. Several "how-to" books were given to our staff and other stakeholders including *Professional Learning Communities at Work: Best Practices for Enhancing Student Achievement* and *Getting Started: Reculturing Schools to Become Professional Learning Communities*. From that point forward, our PD activities concentrated on PLC activities. We collaborated the rest of that first year to read, digest, discuss, and "live" PLC. That summer we used the money from our Title II professional development grant to send 35 teachers, administrators, and board members to the weeklong PLC National Conference at Adlai E. Stevenson High School in Lincolnshire, Illinois. At dinner meetings each evening, we discussed what we had learned during the many sessions we attended during the day and planned implementation strategies for September when the students would return. For the next four summers, teams of 30 new stakeholders attended the PLC conference and returned with knowledge and confidence to enhance the district's PLC culture.

Teachers selected math as the first core subject area to tackle district-wide. From the PLC conferences, we learned that we had to provide teachers and administrators with time to meet. Negotiating with the teachers' union to have staff members arrive 10 minutes before the start of classes in the morning, as opposed to 30 minutes, allowed the district to "bank" an extra 20 minutes of time each day, which was used to create "common" time for teachers to meet. During many grade-level team meetings, teachers finally agreed on the 16–20 major, in-depth math aims they would teach at their grade level each year, down from the 120 they were currently trying to teach. In addition, grade-level teams needed to meet all together to discuss the grade level where each math goal would be placed. As well, these discussions were taking place with district-level teams during the four in-service days held each year.

These discussions were not easy. Teachers wanted to hold onto "pet projects" they had taught for years. During these multi-grade level discussions, however, several teachers at adjacent grade levels realized they had been teaching the same units—a mind-opening revelation. Overhauling the math curriculum into a PLC best-practice product took about 14 months of "kicking and scratching," but we eventually succeeded. In the process, we learned much that we could transfer to each of the other core learning areas. Each of the next revisions only took about three months to reorganize into best-practice PLC models.

The rewards of this overhaul were many. All students, including special education and ESL students, were receiving on-grade level instruction in the district for the first time, because we kept mastery as a constant instead of time. Curriculum maps and pacing charts allowed almost 100% of each core curriculum to be taught, and student achievement skyrocketed. In school districts where trust, confidence, respect, and collaboration can flourish, amazing results will occur!

Kenneth M. Jandes, Ed.D., is Senior Director for the Office of Academic Excellence, American College of Education, Indianapolis, Indiana (www. ace.edu). His educational experience at the Pre-K–12 level includes teaching science for eight years, serving as a school principal for 21 years, and as a superintendent of schools for 12 years in two suburban Chicago school districts. His research interests include school leadership and effective schools. He serves on several non-profit foundation boards and is a professional jazz saxophonist (www.churchjazz.com). You can reach him via email at kenneth.jandes@ace.edu.

Don't Expect Board Trust, Earn It!

Teena McDonald

Superintendents need to be reminded that moving to a new district means starting over. Trusting relationships need to be built with the board, staff, and students, no matter how wonderful you were in your previous district. The first week of school in my new district went smoothly. It was the second week when all hell broke loose. When I arrived at the high school, three sheriff's officers stood in the Student Commons where close to 200 students were engaged in a sit-in. The tension was palpable, and I knew this situation could quickly escalate out of control.

Because the principal was out of the building, the first thing I did was ask what was going on. The assistant principal and officers had asked students to go back to class and students refused. They were in a virtual standoff. I asked them to let students sit there, while I took a small group of student leaders into a conference room. The students told me they felt branded as "bad kids" by the school, the community, and the administration. Because of a few incidents the year before, the school got a police officer, security cameras, and became a closed campus—changes that were made without dialogue with students.

I told the students that they needed to be heard, so part of the solution was to let staff know when issues arose. I explained that I was their advocate, and that our Constitution allows for peaceable assembly; however, they were breaking school rules by skipping class and there would be consequences. I assured them that I valued their passion for standing up about an issue and appreciated their respectful way of discussing it.

I helped them formulate a petition asking the administration and eventually the school board to hear their concerns and seek ways to address those concerns. I walked to the commons and spoke to the entire group, sharing the right way to effect change. Students signed the petitions and returned to class.

Work did not stop there. I went back to my office, called the principal, and discussed ways to proceed. I composed a letter to teachers at the high school, explaining that this was a perfect opportunity to use the momentum to have deep, rich discussions with students regarding social justice and equity. I was pleased when a Black (black?) English teacher described how she told students about the time she was arrested because she questioned an officer about the way he treated a fellow graduate student. She shared with students the deep feelings she had of not being heard and of being discriminated against. She told students that she stood up for what was right and faced the consequences for her actions. She described the rich dialogue with students that followed her sharing. I got goosebumps as I listened to story after story of how teachers used this potentially volatile situation as an opportunity to discuss equity issues.

I was pleased, and I shared a lengthy email with the school board after my initial phone call about what happened. I was sure that they understood I was working to make the most of the situation. What I didn't know was the history that preceded this event. Hannah, a longtime school board member, said, "Teena, it almost seems like you and your new principal want to come in on a white horse and be the heroes. It's tough when the board looks like the bad guy in this situation. I know you didn't mean for us to feel this way, but that's how it feels to me."

My intentions were not to put the board in a bad light; on the contrary, I worked to talk to students and tell them that the board had to make previous decisions based on evidence and recommendations from the previous principal and superintendent. What this event reminded me, however, was that even though I was providing a long-term solution to the situation, I needed to build up trust with the board *first* because I was brand new to the district.

It took the students almost three months to prepare their data. They developed a PowerPoint and a tri-fold display board, presented first to the principal, then to me, and then to the school board. At the board meeting, students thanked the board for listening and gave an insightful, compelling argument for having a modified open campus. The board was impressed and voted unanimously to open the campus, following the guidelines that the student privileges committee recommended. When I talked to Hannah later, I think she understood I was not trying to malign the board. However, this experience taught me a valuable lesson: build trust first, act second. This situation ended well, but it could have gone the other way had a board member not been honest about how she felt about my decisions.

Teena McDonald is an Associate Clinical Professor at Washington State University (WSU) in Spokane, Washington and enjoys working with her great colleagues and amazing students in the WSU principal program, of which she is Director. She is also President of Washington Education Research Association. Before moving to academia, McDonald was a school superintendent. Her own Ed.D. is also from Washington State University in Educational Leadership and Administration.

Supporting Teachers is Top Priority

Felicia Durden

Being an educational leader is not for the faint of heart. I began my journey in educational administration as a district level administrator in the curriculum department. This job was wonderful, as it allowed me to work on my love of teaching and learning to the benefit of our district on a large scale. I adored this job and was blessed to be part of some important initiatives, like the roll out of the Common Core Standards. After being in this position for five years, I knew I wanted to go back as a school level leader. I was fortunate to be placed as the principal of an urban K–5 school in my district.

My first order of business as principal was to explore the culture and climate and figure out what my best moves would be, based on the students, staff, and community. For my first year, I merely watched and took note of who I was leading and the best way to lead them. This was no easy task, as I saw many things that needed to be addressed, but I knew that time was on my side and I had to know them, and they had to know me, in order for my leadership to have impact.

After the first year, things were in place to start making big decisions. This is where instructional leadership became my key focus and goal. I had worked in educational curriculum development and support for over ten years. This love of curriculum, teaching, and learning are what set me apart as a leader. I am comfortable working with teams of teachers on lesson planning and truly enjoy classroom walk-throughs and observations as a time to learn about best practices and impart what I know to help support my teachers in their craft.

As a leader, your teachers are incredibly important stakeholders and supporting them should be your number one priority. Remember that teachers stand in front of the students every day and thus have an everlasting effect on students. Do you remember an awesome teacher who touched your life versus a teacher who left you feeling unworthy or depressed? As a principal, never forget how hard it is to be that awesome teacher. I make it my business to get into classrooms daily so I can assess the culture and climate of learning. This helps me support teachers and give them the feedback necessary to grow in their practice.

Since teachers hold such impact on student achievement, putting your efforts into molding your teachers into the best practitioners they can be will prove most worthwhile. This can be achieved by providing in-the-moment feedback to your teachers, which can only happen after you have established rapport and trust. This is why I spent the first year just getting to know my staff. I can confidently say now that I can tell my staff anything and they know it comes from a place of positivity and wanting only the best for our students.

Another way to impact teachers is to celebrate their commitment and hard work. Everyone likes to be recognized; when people feel appreciated, they will achieve more. We celebrate our teachers on every occasion possible. During staff meetings, we give out carnival treats like cotton candy, snow cones, and popcorn. We go all out with our decorations and make a big deal of celebrating our teachers' hard work. Of course, a big part of the reason we celebrate hard work is to reinforce our expectation for hard work. Let's face it—teachers have to work hard these days in order to make an impact. Our students come in with so many different deficits and challenges that only hard work can begin to turn them around. Creating a culture of working hard and playing hard will be prudent in your work as a principal.

Finally, just as teachers motivate their students, do not underestimate the power you hold to motivate your staff. Being an instructional leader, cheerleader, and taskmaster is a hard job, but if you are realistic in your expectations and clear in your message, carrying out these tasks will be easier. Start by getting to know your staff and letting them get to know you. Do not be afraid to be vulnerable. Create that culture of celebrating hard work for yourself, students, and teachers and keep up to date on new instructional practices with which to lead your school. Being a principal is truly the best job in the world, but it requires a brave soul with vision and might.

Dr. Felicia Durden is an accomplished educator with over 16 years of experience in education. She holds a Doctorate of Education in Educational Leadership, a Master's in Curriculum and Instruction, and a Bachelor of Arts in English Literature. Dr. Durden has taught grades K–12, served as an assistant director of reading and writing, and currently serves as principal in a large urban school district in Arizona. She also taught English composition at the college level as an adjunct instructor. Dr. Durden has a passion for assisting student growth in reading and writing. She can be reached via email at fdurden77@gmail.com

The Art of Change:
A Lesson Learned

Donato Di Paolo

I was in my first year at an inner-city school in an up-and-coming neighbourhood that achieved some very good results in the provincial assessment of Mathematics and Language. The staff included teachers who had worked together for several years and the school had not experienced significant staff turnover during that time. The staff were comfortable in their routines and generally reluctant to change. Many felt that they were meeting their students' academic needs and wanted to continue with the status quo.

Fundamentally, the status quo conflicts with what I believe in as an administrator—that schools must be places that embrace "a constant cycle of improvement" model. I believe that all schools need to undergo some degree of change regularly to address any deficiencies. It was difficult for me to resist the urge to make immediate changes. I did not want any unnecessary time to pass before bringing my ideas forward. At the first staff meeting of the year, I remember going through the agenda that I had prepared—*very enthusiastically*. By the end of the meeting, the teachers' reactions surprised me. They were very concerned with what they had just heard. After the meeting, a few teachers approached me and wanted to discuss things further. From my perspective, I could not understand their concerns, especially since the information I shared at the staff meeting would help to bring about much need change and improvement, or so I thought.

The changes that I had spent time planning for included the implementation of a new mathematics resource for all grades. I redesigned the Special Education Support Model and created block scheduling to facilitate what was, in my opinion, a much better delivery of Special Education support. I also made some changes to the entry and exit procedures as well as the recess and yard duty schedules.

I did this all at once, very earnestly, and based upon the information shared with me by the outgoing principal during a transition meeting, but without my having spoken to any of the staff. At the time, it had not occurred to me to seek staff opinions; I was completely focused on the need to make changes to the school now that I was the principal. I wanted to address what I believed to be inefficiencies prior to the start of the school year. I thought that the staff would be just as excited as I was and very impressed with my ideas. I did not consider that perhaps they would have appreciated an opportunity to add their input.

To be an effective leader, you must learn from your mistakes, as I did. It took some time for me to repair the relationships that became strained that day. Eventually the changes that I implemented were embraced. It took time and effort on my part to establish a new and more positive dynamic. In retrospect, I know now that change is something that should not carried out too quickly. I still believe that change is necessary, but it can only work when there is open communication and an opportunity for collaboration and discussion. Like with any good relationship, communication is the key.

I have learned these lessons on leadership through experience, through trial and error. School administrators will inevitably make mistakes during their careers. The key is not to repeat them. Although change may be necessary, it does not have to be immediate. A period of observation means that an administrator can learn the school culture and norms of practice; once relationships are established, staff can be invited in for consultation.

I have tried various leadership styles and experienced very different outcomes. What you say and do as a principal has a great impact upon staff, so it is essential to ensure that staff have had an opportunity to contribute to changes implemented at the school level. Clearly, of the many tasks that a school administrator is responsible for, building, fostering and sustaining meaningful relationships with staff, is of paramount importance.

Donato Di Paolo *works for the Toronto Catholic District School Board and holds a Master of Education degree with a focus on critical literacy and specialist qualifications in Religion and Special Education. Di Paolo is passionate about school improvement and is a strategic, results-oriented instructional leader with developed EdTech skills, strong curricular knowledge, and a demonstrated ability to build trusting relationships and engage all stakeholders. Di Paolo embraces change and builds staff capacity through mentorship. He can be reached at donato.dipaolo@tcdsb.org.*

On Finding Meaning

Manuela Sequeira

So many people walk around with a meaningless life. They seem half-asleep, even when they're busy doing things they think are important. This is because they're chasing the wrong things. The way you get meaning into your life is to devote yourself to loving others, devote yourself to your community around you, and devote yourself to creating something that gives you purpose and meaning.

Mitch Albom, *Tuesdays with Morrie*

To give meaning to my leadership is a daily journey of reflection. I am a passionate Catholic leader, driven by moral purpose, and committed to creating the necessary conditions for the success and wellbeing of every student, regardless of socioeconomic circumstance, ethnicity, gender, or ability.

Through this journey into the true meaning of leadership, I am constantly seeking self-improvement through continuing education, inquiry, and careful readings of my amassed collection of leadership literature. These are non-fiction stories detailing research-based narratives of epic leadership, from respected and renowned worldwide authorities on educational reform—to the last, all impressive stories of success; narratives of the personal and professional absolutes of leadership. However, despite the knowledge I have gleaned from them, there were not contextual; they were often not in harmony with my leadership landscape. Despite this, in challenging times, instead of seeking guidance and inspiration from within, from the lessons learned through my own successes and failures, I often return to those safe, successful narratives, where I hoped to find the answers.

In 2015, fourteen years into my leadership journey, I began to wonder if another path would bring added value to my leadership. It was this introspection and a chance encounter with a very special person that brought renewed meaning to my vocation. During the preparations for the school's 100th anniversary celebration, by chance or by fate, I came to know of a past leader who in 1953 had been the first teaching principal of the school in its current location. Intrigued by the historical value of the story, I reached out and was invited to the abbey for a half-hour meeting.

I have read and reread *Tuesdays with Morrie*, but it was not until I sat across from Sister Mary, by the light of a late autumn sun, that I was certain that art does indeed imitate life. In leadership, there are multitudes of books, and many inspirational quotes and phrases, intended to provide guidance and inspiration. Yet, there, in her presence, I lived the meaning of "standing on the shoulders of giants," and experienced the power and simplicity of true Catholic leadership.

With raw emotion, she narrated her life in vivid color and detail, where the professional and personal intertwined with one sole mission, to serve, to leave her community a better place for the children. She narrated endless stories. Stories of successes, challenges, partnerships, advocacy, self-doubt, and stories of persistence; not for self-promotion, but rather for the still evident passion for her vocation, for community, and for the children whose education she was entrusted with. The children inspired Sister Mary. Children *who had the whole world ahead of them, who had so little and deserved so much.* Yet, of all her accomplishments and her years of service, she remained humble. In her eyes, she was simply fulfilling her calling to the best of her ability.

When she spoke of family, the old neighborhood, and her devotion to her calling, I sat in silence, inspired and in awe of a life lived, not weathered by loss or time, but still hopeful, with an undying faith that *"there is always more out there,"* that *"God is always present, always guiding us in our purpose."* Time passed. The half hour turned into hours. In the silence between the words, I wished that I could have spent my

Tuesdays with Sister Mary, to be inspired, empowered, and to capture her life in print: the story of a strong, resourceful, passionate, and unwavering woman in Catholic leadership in the 1950s.

As our time ended, I had to ask, *"How did you accomplish so much and overcome so many challenges, without ever losing hope?"* Quietly, firmly, with teary eyes, she stated, *"when you care about the children, you find a way."* At that moment, I knew that I was exactly where I was meant to be.

Manuela Sequeira is an educational leader with sixteen years of experience in diverse inner-city schools. In 2016, she was the recipient of Canada's Outstanding Principals Award by The Learning Partnership. In 2017, she was the recipient of The Leading Women, Leading Girls Community Award by the Ontario Government. In the same year, her work was published by Dr. Ken Leithwood in Even More Real Stories: How LSA Participation has Improved Leadership, Teaching and Student Achievement.

PART VI

Only the Beginning: Moving Along Transactional, Transformational, and Transformative Continuum

L eaders thrive along the scholar-practitioner continuum. Theory informs practice and practice informs theory representing a reciprocal process. Exemplary leaders and leadership teams demonstrate a deep understanding of the leadership theories informing their leadership practices. Over time, leaders develop an increasingly nuanced, integrated, and sophisticated understanding of leadership theory, often combined with theories from other fields of study. The choice of leadership theory aligns with leadership context and worldview. Leadership decisions are theory-driven and embedded within all dimensions and processes of organizational improvement planning. Readers of this volume are encouraged to stop and reflect upon those leadership theories and theorists who have been most influential in their leadership thinking. Leaders recognize when the decisions of individuals and organizations are incongruent with espoused theories. Riel and Martin's (2017) *Creating Great Choices: A Leader's Guide to Integrated Thinking* demonstrates how exceptional leaders combine complex theories and models in response to leadership opportunities and challenges. Intuition isn't random; it is an outcome of a lifetime of navigating dynamic and fluid leadership contexts framed by the scholar–practitioner continuum.

Rookie Season

DeOtis Williams Jr.

I am speaking to you in my rookie year as a principal. Stepping into this role, you don't know what you don't know. I am not writing this with double-digit years of experience as a leader. However, I have a few insights on what I have learned within the first 100 days of my principalship.

One of my first tasks was to hire the vice-principal. This was an extremely difficult decision due to the level of respect I had for each of the candidates and their amazing skill sets. One piece of advice that I received from a fellow administrator was to ensure that my administrative team was comprised of people who I could trust. It was put to me this way: "So many things are going to come at you from many different angles. You want to ensure that the people on your team support you and have your back."

Transparency is critical. Keep your staff in the loop on how changes within your organization may affect them. The more details the better. Err on the side of providing more information than necessary. We started a few initiatives within my organization this year. Although the staff was informed of the initiatives, they did not know how to recognize when and if the new initiatives were working. Share what successes and setbacks look like. Share where you have been, where you are currently at, and where you are going as an organization.

Be your authentic self in your role. Avoid being an imposter. Leaders are not cut from one mold. Some best practices in leadership work anywhere; others require custom fitting. Figure out how those best practices merge with your personality. If you are a leader who does not micromanage, then do not micromanage. Your efforts will not come across as genuine if you try to use someone else's tools.

Commit to taking care of yourself. Education is a selfless profession so it is easy to fall into the habit of doing for others and forgetting to do for yourself. As in an airplane, put on your own oxygen mask first before helping someone else. In order to give people the best "you" possible, ensure that you are the best "you." Start by getting adequate sleep. Can you work on less than two hours of sleep? Maybe. Will you be at your best? No. Be intentional about eating breakfast in the morning and refuel to sustain yourself throughout the day. Exercise regularly. In this world of technology, it is easy to become sedentary while working (checking and sending emails, writing articles and reports, making phone calls, and so on).

Stepping into the role of rookie principal, I knew my work as I once understood it would change, but I did not know how. As a teacher, I was concerned with my students and their families. As assistant principal, my lens shifted to focus on the students, their families, the teachers, and the community, completely widening my perspective. As principal, it widened again to include the building, human resources, operations, athletics, broader stakeholders, and more.

Keep in mind that the work you do is not about you. I structure my day a certain way to get my work done. Now remember, this is me offering insight in my rookie year ... I made a habit of getting to work early to check morning emails. When the students and teachers are in the building, they are my priority. I typically stay at my desk for at least two hours after class is out to check emails, make phone calls, and take care of other administrative duties.

What does all this have to do with leadership? Well, through trial and error as a rookie leader, I found it beneficial to be mindful of the following: the people you bring on your team, transparency within your organization, being your authentic self, taking care of yourself, and keeping your role in perspective.

Lastly, I suggest seeking mentorship from within and outside of your organization from people who have been there and done that. Within my organization, I have been fortunate enough to be surrounded by staff who share their expectations of a leader and supervisors who provide mentorship, helping me to avoid making the same mistakes they once did. Ultimately, find what works for you. Or, in the words of Bruce Lee, move like water my friend.

DeOtis Williams Jr. was raised in a military family so is no stranger to serving communities across the nation. Williams has served for three years as an AmeriCorps member, taught middle school and high school Social Studies, and worked as an adjunct instructor at the University of Missouri–Kansas City. He has a B.A. from Georgia Southern University, an M.A.T. from the University of Central Missouri, and an Educational Specialist Degree in Educational Administration from the University of Missouri–Kansas City. Williams is currently a high school principal and a doctoral student in the College of Professional Studies at Northeastern University.

Turning the Ship
Without Losing the Crew

Elliot F. Bolles

When educators talk about turning a school around, they discuss school improvement plans, effective use of data, collaboration, and teaming. We eventually got there, but our journey started with a less traditional focus. It started with the school mascot.

I had been a principal for eight years in a neighboring district, but got a new assignment in a new district, where the school population had changed significantly in the previous two years. It had been a middle-class/upper middle-class school scoring consistently in the 90s on state assessments but now struggled to get out of the 70s. Our community had shifted from white to minority, with 38% economically disadvantaged and 30% English language learners. Not quite Title I, but a school with challenges nonetheless.

One of the first things the district leadership told me was not to change too much the first year. Get to know your school, your staff, your community, and give them time to get to know you. Building trust is a necessary first step. Good guidance!

We reviewed the previous year's results during that first summer and the scores were still discouraging but, the leadership team said, not indicative of "who we are." It became apparent that there had been few adjustments to instruction despite the changing needs of our students. Many of our teacher leaders were convinced that this was just an "isolated storm" or "rough seas" and things would be okay if we just stayed the course. To me, these were not just rough seas, but an entirely new ocean of challenges threatening to swamp us.

I also met with all the staff individually that first summer. Whenever I mentioned the school mascot, people became uneasy. At my previous school, we had been the Wolves, a powerful image tied to our staff and students in many ways. The students all worked to earn PAWS and our younger students were cubs. Our mission was to turn young cubs into strong young wolves. Our staff used Kipling's famous statement, "The strength of the Pack is the Wolf and the strength of the Wolf is the Pack." When you joined our staff, you joined the Pack; you were not alone. As a Pack we tackled the challenges of student learning. I knew the power of a symbol.

At this new school, our mascot was based on a pen and inkbottle to encourage writing, and had been created nearly two decades before. Although it was obvious during my summer interviews that it was not a favorite thing, messing with a mascot is always a risk. A mascot can be a school's heart and soul, embodying the history of a school and its community. Changing the mascot would directly challenge the current culture and history of our school. Despite central office's guidance not to do too much that first year, I began questioning the appropriateness of the mascot. Most staff thought a change would be a good thing. I wondered, were they just agreeing with the new boss? What did they really think?

That first December, I formally raised the mascot issue with the staff, the Parent Teacher Organization (PTO), and our Parent Advisory Council. Again, most thought something different could be positive. But what would the new symbol be and how would we roll it out? We needed student input—if the students were excited about it, the parents would follow. I limited the choices to ones I knew would work for our purposes, and the students voted on the animal and the name. That spring we rolled out Paws the Panther. Our school was now The Home of the Panthers. A paw print became the symbol for our positive behavior interventions and support program, PAWS: "**P**awsative" Attitude, **A**ct Responsibly, **W**ork Together, **S**elf-Control". Both classes and individual students could earn PAWS. I referred to the students as Panthers every morning on announcements.

The PTO bought T-shirts for the entire student body with an image of our new Panther on the front and "I'm an Original Panther" on the back. The shirts were very popular and proudly worn. We purchased a Panther costume for Paws and the mascot was a hit at all our school functions and a matter of pride for our students. Everyone wanted to take a picture with Paws.

This was the start of the transformation our school needed—an important symbolic step in "turning the ship without losing the crew." Becoming the Panthers signified to the community that change was coming and we worked to include all stakeholders in the effort. The students and staff liked the feel of it—the excitement, and the fun that came with it. The Panther permeated our school culture. A teacher leader shared with me two years afterwards, "The mascot change was huge! It affected the entire feel of the school."

Some may think of a mascot as mere "window dressing," but we needed to improve our student, staff, and community connection and our morale. In the following years, we worked hard to change "how we always did things." The collaborative learning teams have grown in effectiveness and our school has become a true professional learning community. We are still on our voyage of change that all started with the Panther.

Elliot F. Bolles, Ed.D, is an elementary principal in northern Virginia, and an Adjunct Professor for Virginia Tech and James Madison University. He teaches graduate students in Educational Leadership and Principal Preparation programs and he researches educational leadership. He earned his Doctorate in Educational Leadership and Policy from Virginia Tech in 2014. He came to education 20 years ago through the Troops to Teachers program, following a 20-year career as a United States Marine Corps pilot. You can reach him at bollesef@jmu.edu or bollesef@pwcs.edu.

Essential Ingredients of Principal Success

Arvin D. Johnson

My formal leadership preparation started in a university educational leadership program. I learned leadership theory and specific tasks related to serving as a building principal. My most relevant and significant preparation, however, came through job-embedded learning experiences while serving as a principal. These experiences provided me with opportunities to explore and experiment with multiple combinations of what I consider "essential ingredients to principal success."

While some essential ingredients are universal and transferable, many are local to the school, district, and region, and may vary greatly depending upon the setting. One of the roles of a principal is to concoct the proper combination of ingredients to maximize the learning experience for students, faculty, and staff. Some schools may require unique ingredients not found anywhere else.

Principals must actively lead in three essential leadership areas—instructional, operational, and environmental—to be successful in their role. Each contains many micro-ingredients essential to the overall recipe for success, including school and district needs, state educational infrastructure, and the demands of local stakeholders. Accordingly, micro-ingredients will look different depending upon the dynamics of the educational setting. The three essential ingredients for principal success, however, are universal and wide reaching.

There are many aspects to leading a successful school, but the ability to demonstrate instructional leadership is a general requirement. By definition, instructional leadership is an elusive, ambiguous construct. An instructional leader must be attuned to the many aspects of pedagogy within the school, beginning with setting the expectations for the instructional culture. This culture involves both school-wide academic commitments and daily classroom expectations. Principals cannot be content-area experts in all areas; however, the principal must guide the overall academic infrastructure of the school, including analyzing and revising curriculum, planning and delivering instruction, studying and triangulating the data that informs instructional practice, monitoring instruction, conferencing with teachers to provide meaningful feedback, and building instructional capacity in assistant administrators and teacher leaders. Leading the instructional climate begins by setting the ongoing pedagogical expectations. At a minimum, these expectations should govern the typical time and stages of classroom instruction (i.e., a gradual release of responsibility model), the daily cognitive demands placed on students, student engagement practices, differentiation of instruction, data usage, and how student learning will be assessed daily (formal or informal). The principal should not curtail teacher creativity by demanding universal delivery of instruction, but should expect certain instructional elements to be implemented in all classrooms daily.

Every operation in a school should support, directly or indirectly, the learning experience of students. More than academic achievement, the learning experience is multifaceted and includes the systemic student experience. Breakdowns in operational leadership will usually lead to breakdowns in the student learning experience. Principals must ensure that school facilities are intentionally arranged to support students including safety and security (external and internal), building maintenance, and budget resources (human, infrastructure, and instructional). Principals need not attempt to oversee all of these areas personally, but can delegate some of these responsibilities to assistant administrators, faculty, and staff. It is important that any such delegation come with clear expectations and supervision.

Environmental leadership requires establishing and maintaining strong, healthy, productive relationships with students, faculty, staff, and all stakeholders. In addition, the principal must serve as both mentor and coach to many individuals in the school. The ultimate goal of environmental leadership for principals is to build capacity in students, faculty, and staff.

Three foundational ingredients—instructional leadership, operational leadership, and environmental leadership—are essential to any recipe for school success. And every school principal worth their salt needs to learn how to blend them to perfection. Remember, school can be bitter or sweet for your students, teachers, and staff depending on the flavour of your leadership.

Arvin D. Johnson, Ed.D., is an assistant professor in the Department of Educational Leadership at Kennesaw State University. He is also the founder of the Principal Academy at Kennesaw State University, an ongoing professional learning academy for partnering school districts. His research interests include principal professional learning, student achievement, school climate and culture, and teacher retention. Prior to his higher education career, he successfully served as a principal for six years in Jacksonville, Florida.

Leading with Optimism:
How a Mentoring Partnership Transformed Leadership Development Within a School District

Matthew Ohlson

In the spring of 2015, I was asked to help support the leadership development of a cadre of new principals within a district of more than 16,000 students in Florida. My focus was to share my experience as a former principal and leadership development consultant to support and guide these beginning principals. Yet, what emerged from this process became a mutually- beneficial learning experience for both the mentor and those being mentored, reaping significant benefits for students and teachers. This reflection will share a few of the lessons learned and best practices from this unique leadership-mentoring model that can be used and replicated by school leaders.

My focus was to train the school principals to know what they were doing well in hopes of creating a culture of optimism within their schools. This focus was based on my years of research and practice that examined the lack of optimism and hope as a key indicator for teacher retention, discipline, and attendance issues, and an overall lack of achievement and success for both students and educators. When a school community believes in themselves and each other (parents, teachers, students, staff, administration) there is a sense of purpose within every activity, event, and initiative. The feeling of optimism must start with the school leader. When teachers and students only hear about the lack of resources, unavoidable mandates, and challenges ahead—that optimism gap permeates the entire school community.

Best Practices: Weekly Success Stories

To begin this optimism coaching, we implemented a process where the school principals would document their successes and achievements of the week. Using an electronic calendar invite every Friday at 5 p.m., the principals would share artifacts and testimonials highlighting their impact as school leaders that week, including classroom visits, celebrations, events that they had coordinated, and new initiatives they were spearheading. This simple task allowed each principal the opportunity to reflect upon their week, document what they had accomplished, and appreciate their role in leading, not just managing their school.

In addition, these weekly success stories were shared within our principal network. Initially, many were hesitant about bragging, but when I reminded them that their goal was student success and that we learn from each other, the ideas began to flow. Principals visited each other's schools, shared resources, replicated best practices, and gathered new strategies from their collective expertise (e.g., "Have you thought about including your guidance counselor …").

In many of our schools, the principals began to ask teachers to send them their success stories of the week—a student they helped, parents they connected with, or colleagues that supported them. This simple practice helped to spread all the positive things happening in school and served as a reminder to administration and staff that they were making a difference throughout the school year, not just the standardized test scores at the end of the year. Interestingly, the schools that participated in this process also achieved the highest school culture scores and teacher attendance rates within the district.

Best Practices: School Community Recognition

We also challenged our principals to create success charts that documented the progress school leaders were making in celebrating the positive things happening at their school. Each time the school leader took time to celebrate a teacher, staff member (cafeteria worker, bus driver, office staff), community stakeholder (parent, business liaison, school board member)—they would place a green Post-it on the board documenting the positive action. When the school leader needed to participate in a negative action and/or comment (disciplining a student, correcting a teacher action), a red Post-it was placed on the board. At the end of the week, the principal and team of administrators (assistant principals, deans, etc.) would compare the ratios of positive actions versus negative and determine if they were maintaining an ideal ratio of 5:1 (Losada & Heaphy, 2004). This process also celebrated their own roles and impact as school leaders.

This clear focus on increasing joy and optimism was instrumental in enhancing the school culture and positive leadership styles of our participants. In this era of negativity, with fewer people choosing education as a career, the focus on optimism and hope for our leaders is essential. These few examples illustrate the importance of making people feel valued and significant in their roles. It also demonstrates the mutually beneficial growth of learning with and from other leaders.

Reference

Losada, M., & Heaphy, E. (2004). The role of positivity and connectivity in the performance of business teams: A nonlinear dynamics model. *American Behavioral Scientist, 47*(6), 740–765.

***Dr. Matthew Ohlson**, a former teacher and school principal, is a faculty member in the Department of Leadership, School Counseling, and Sport Management at the University of North Florida. Dr. Ohlson's scholarship and service focuses on leadership development and developing organizational culture to increase outcomes. He also works extensively with schools and universities throughout the nation to establish college and career readiness partnerships.*

Turning Around
a Leadership Deficit

Brian K. Creasman

In the summer of 2007, I was completing an interim middle school principalship that was widely seen as successful by students, teachers, parents, the board of education, and the district administration. I had been named interim middle school principal after the principal had retired. At the time, I had only two years of experience as an assistant principal in a very tough middle school. The school's culture had changed dramatically over those two years because of the school leadership's focus on teaching and learning instead of all the weeds that often derail student success.

The school was now moving in the right direction. To my surprise, that summer was also my last at the middle school. While attending a summer dissertation conference, the district superintendent called to tell me that I would be transferred to a high school that had just entered school turnaround status—which meant the state was closely monitoring the school's student achievement, graduation rate, and other critical school data.

The district had been forced to change the principal at the school, which is where I came in. After speaking to the district superintendent, I learned that he had been eyeing me for the position for over a year because of my work as an assistant principal for curriculum and instruction and then interim principal at the feeder middle school. The superintendent needed someone who knew the students' parents and was energetic enough to change the school culture. Being a former high school teacher and instructional technologist, I had no desire to go back to the high school level. I was comfortable at the middle school and with the middle school structure. Additionally, I felt the middle school was ready to transform and reach the next level.

The high school I was transferred to was in some disarray. The previous principal had been absent regularly from school, leaving assistant principals in charge. Students and parents recognized that the school was suffering from a leadership deficit, leaving it with no clear vision or purpose. More and more students were dropping out of school or just not attending. The morale of teachers and staff was at an all-time low, and many of *them* were not attending school either. All of this negatively impacted student achievement and the graduation rate, which ultimately placed the school in North Carolina's turnaround program.

To be clear, before becoming principal of a turnaround high school, I had no prior experience of leading a high school, much less a high school in turnaround status. I had only taught at the high school level for three years so had no experience with graduation requirements, high school master schedules, or leading school transformation from the ground up. Sure, I had experience leading small-scale transformation at the middle school, but high school was different.

When I walked into the high school on the first day with my assistant principals, it looked like someone had dropped a bomb on the school and the faculty, staff and students had all abandoned it. It was mid-July; the last day of school had been the first week in June. Papers littered the floor, trash all over the place, the office had stacks upon stacks of files. But what stands out most in my memory is what I found in three of the classrooms—the American flag stuck into the ceiling tiles, hanging there as if to say, "We surrender."

The leadership team and I had just four weeks to transform the school and make it ready for the first day of classes. The superintendent gave me unbelievable freedom to do whatever I needed to get the school back up to operational status. I thought there would be no way we could open the school in four weeks. Summer cleaning and maintenance was three weeks behind, there were several teacher vacancies in critical subject areas. In addition, the student, staff, and school handbooks had to be completely redone, and I had yet to meet any teacher or staff member. The odds were obviously stacked against the school and many in the community—including students and parents—had written it off, but were willing to give it one last chance. The pressure was on.

We had to act quickly, strategically, and collaboratively. I suddenly realized that to tackle this mammoth task, teachers and staff members had to be empowered to be transformative leaders. The condition of the school required a team approach and four assistant principals and I were not a big enough team. We needed an army to get the school back on track and the clock was ticking.

That summer helped to shape my thinking about shared, collaborative leadership. Too often, we school leaders think we are superhuman and can lead alone. My experience as a turnaround principal taught me that leadership is collaborative and must be shared. Over my five years as principal of that high school, graduation rates and student achievement improved dramatically. We were able to transform the school, expanding many programs and hiring some excellent teachers and staff members. More importantly, our team of school leaders, teachers, and staff members worked together to graduate more students and assist them in going to some of North Carolina's top universities.

Brian K. Creasman, raised in Nantahala, North Carolina, is now Superintendent of Fleming County Schools in Kentucky. His degrees include an A.S. in Education, a B.S. in Public Administration, an M.Ed. in Instructional Technology, and an Ed.S. and Ed.D. in Educational Leadership. He is also the co-author of three books with publisher Rowman & Littlefield: The Leader Within (2016), Growing Leaders Within (2017), and Can Every School Succeed (2018). You can follow him @FCSSuper.

Becoming Batman

Aaron J. Griffen

I came into education with a belief that I could make a difference. However, making a difference, I learned within the first three years, is not sufficient. To truly transform the lives of those we touch and to truly transform the system, we have to become the difference. *Becoming* the difference and *making* a difference are two different things. Making a difference means putting ideas into place and managing outcomes. Being the difference means being part of the idea and manifesting the outcomes. This sometimes means putting our careers on the line for others and for ideals, which is the exact opposite of what "effective" means to most people.

During the 1980s, I grew up watching Superman, the Super Friends, and Batman. We all wanted to be Superman. Superman could fly, bullets bounced off him, and he had the desirable Lois Lane. Who did Batman have? Batgirl, Robin, and Alfred. Batman was human and could be killed with a bullet or knife. Superman had Kryptonite, and it took other super individuals to defeat him. As children, of course we wanted to fly and feel invincible like Superman.

Fast forward to my life as an educational administrator, first as an assistant principal and then as a principal. With both promotions, I was expected to perform certain duties and be the answer to a long-held issue or problem. It both cases, what folks wanted was Superman, but what they got was Batman. Several years ago, a documentary called *Waiting for "Superman"* (2010) chronicled the many failings of the American education system and the leaders brought in to "save" it. After reflecting on the documentary, I decided that we experience high anxiety and frustration, without being able to focus on long-term results versus short-term gains, because we don't appreciate Batman. Nor do we understand that there really is no Superman, no "super fix."

Rather that swooping in to save the day and move folks out of harm's way, we mingle with the community as one of them, providing ways for them to help themselves. Our bravado does not leave us when we leave our role; we are Batman and Bruce Wayne. Although our Batman or Batgirl suits hang in our closet, our everyday suit still exudes confidence and reckoning. Superman on the other hand saves the day and destroys the villains, but then turns into a bumbling, clumsy, regular human named Clark Kent. Education has no room for Clark Kent. We cannot pretend to be weak so that others are not intimidated.

The problem that waiting for Superman causes is that while we Batmans are constantly thinking of ways to improve the condition of all, our approaches are often viewed as non-essential or too slow. As in *The Lego Batman Movie*, Gotham City complains that Batman never actually gets rid of the villains. What society wants is for us to pulverize the problems right now, never acknowledging that the problems will not go away so long as we continue doing what we are doing to cause them in the first place—achievement gaps and funding inequities, for example. The problem manifests in new and frightening ways, such as the "school to prison pipeline."

As Batman, I see this. I work with my staff and community on the problems we face together. I train our students to be proactive, to fight for justice. I collaborate with parents to celebrate even the small successes of our students and staff. I exit before anyone can thank me for a job they can do themselves. It is not about me; it is about all of you. That is why I have accepted my role as a vigilante for education. I cannot swoop in to save them. I cannot get immediate results and fly away. Education is our Gotham City.

I came into education to make a difference. I soon discovered that making a difference was not sufficient. We *are* the difference. Our role is to show others the way and clear a path. But, we are not alone. We may not have Batman's awesome car, but we have a utility belt for every situation and must use every tool at our disposal. We also have our entourage: Robin (assistant principals) to challenge our thoughts, Batgirl (department chairs) to save us all, and Alfred (parents and the community) to support us and provide wisdom. When they need us, they will light the Bat signal. We are Batman.

Aaron J. Griffen, Ph.D., is the Principal of Sierra High School in Colorado Springs, Colorado. He received his Ph.D. in Curriculum and Instruction from Texas A&M University. Dr. Griffen Co-Chairs School and Community Partnerships for the American Educational Research Association (AERA) Special Interest Group #27 (SIG)—Critical Examination of Race, Ethnicity, Class, and Gender. He is the 2013 recipient of the Urban Education Teaching Award from Texas A&M University for Outstanding Teaching of Urban Education at the University Level.

Focused Leadership:
Putting It All Together

Samuel P. Scavella

I nstructional leadership means focusing on factors that promote and support teaching and learning. It is generally defined as the management of curriculum and instruction by a school principal. In my 19 years as a school-based administrator, I have found that certain processes precede a principal's ability to become a truly effective instructional leader. To that end, creating a shared vision has been my priority in the schools I have led, as principal, for the past 13 years.

To help this process, I create intentional protected time to get to know the professionals (i.e., teachers, paraprofessionals, instructional coaches, administrators) who will engage in this critical work. Usually this work begins during the summer months. In the last few months of the fiscal school year, I engage the building leadership team along with school partners to plan a summer institute for staff to promote team building, reviewing, and revising the school vision, engage in data analysis for school improvement, curriculum and instructional planning, and professional learning. It is vital to include the voice of all members of the school community. I invite key members from the local school council, PTSA, and student government to study the data, shape the vision, and clearly identify the purpose and direction of the organization. This data could include attendance and discipline, student learning results, program evaluations, and a variety of stakeholder feelings.

The next critical step is to engage school community members in structured activities to develop school goals and action plans. I utilize SMART goal statements: specific, measurable, attainable, relevant/

results-based, and time bound. Multiple data sources help us to collectively develop these goals, focused on student success and school improvement. My mission has been to communicate to all stakeholders that learning is the most important charge of the school. This cannot be carried out unless leadership is shared. I involve staff in every aspect of the decision-making process, empowering them to lead specific action teams for school improvement, known as Better Seeking Solution Teams. These teams are made up of staff with specific ability and passion to positively affect change. As a trained Critical Friends Group Coach, I lean highly towards using the National School Reform Faculty's protocols to keep the work focused and driven towards naming root causes, coupled with instructional and organizational grappling to arrive at expected results. It has also been a successful practice to create teacher leaders willing to take on added tasks and responsibilities beyond their required classroom duties to benefit the school and empower other teachers (i.e., team leaders, department chairs, student support team chairs, webmaster, etc.). Marrying professional growth with learning is essential to reaching school goals.

As instructional leader, I must also function as the lead learner. I have found that the two critical school functions are 1) teaching and learning, and 2) organizing for teaching and learning. Prioritizing student learning means paying attention to curriculum, instruction, and assessment. Visibility is also critical. The leader's focus largely determines staff attention. Therefore, a platform for collaboration and professional learning is required, such as common planning times in the master schedule. Meeting protocols helped teachers share best practices and explore ideas deeply through dialogue, artifacts, texts, and student work. Administrators also regularly took part in these sessions to create a culture of collaborative work. Individually, each teacher and administrator used a self-assessment tool to identify areas of professional growth needed. Teachers lead and take part in professional development sessions to promote the practices that lead to effective teaching and learning.

Monitoring the implementation of curriculum and instruction to identify instructional strengths and weaknesses is also key to instructional leadership. Adhering to a classroom visitation schedule means that I can keep abreast of instructional practices. Implementing a continuous improvement model (i.e., plan-do-check-act) coupled with instructional frameworks (i.e., gradual release of responsibility model), classroom visits ensure that the correct curriculum standards are being taught and learned. The plan-do-check-act cycle requires teachers to collect and disaggregate student learning and assessment data in order to differentiate instruction by content, product, process, or the learning environment. Utilizing a backwards-mapping approach, teachers use district and state curriculum maps as well as scope and sequence documents to prioritize curriculum standards coupled with a timeline for the standards to be taught and assessed.

Reflective teachers are effective teachers. Teachers sharing best practices and receive training on how to utilize high-yield instructional strategies in their content areas is paramount. A standards-based instructional framework incorporates specific strategies and learning activities to be incorporated during the various phases of a lesson (i.e., focused instruction—I do it; guided instruction—we do it together; collaborative learning—you do it together; independent learning—you do it alone). Once effective lessons are planned and instruction provided, the process requires teachers to check student levels of understanding and performance using formative and summative assessments. Assessment data is then collected, disaggregated, and analyzed to decide if students have mastered the standard(s) being taught. Students are then grouped into four levels and provided with remediation or acceleration activities. Teachers must act correctly based on the data. Flexible grouping is one way teachers can provide re-teaching or enrichment activities and strategies. The cycle then repeats itself as teachers enter the planning phase to re-teach concepts and skills until all students have demonstrated an appropriate level of mastery. Throughout this process, teachers provide appropriate challenges for students by building coursework and designing learning tasks around critical and creative thinking, interpretation, decision making, and problem solving. Active learning opportunities authentically engage students in an environment where it is clear that teachers care about *what* they are teaching as well as about *who* they are teaching.

Samuel P. Scavella, *Ph.D., is a principal and principal mentor/coach in the Aspiring Principal Program in the Cleveland Metropolitan School District. He is also a BRIGHT Fellow Program Mentor/Coach with Ohio State University. He serves on the Board of Directors for the Ohio Association of Secondary School Administrators, the Cleveland Transformation Alliance, and the Cleveland Council for Administrators and Supervisors. His research and practice include educational leadership and policy, school reform, continuous improvement and assessment, instructional coaching and pedagogy, equity and social justice, and "students at risk."*

PART VII

To Thine Own Self and Community Be True: Leadership Lessons and Reflections

One defining characteristic of outstanding leaders is their deep commitment to ongoing learning, and their deeper commitment to the ongoing capacity building of others. Individual and collective reflective practice is the work of leadership, whether it is formal or informal, individual or collaborative. Cultivation of legacy is a holistic process. Leaders are sometimes asked to share their most impactful leadership development experiences. Often these conversations can be heard at the end of a formal leadership program. Examples of these may include completion of graduate degrees, supervisory officer certification, executive leadership development programs, district-mandated professional development sessions, and communities of practice. Leadership development wisdom informs life-embedded practice and vice versa. You will often see a human element to leadership development experiences. People may not remember the content, but they will remember the level of engagement and enthusiasm within the sessions, and they will remember those who took the time to first learn about them as characters, and then as leaders in training. Upon reflection, powerful leadership lessons are learned from elders and our children.

Aspire to be Outstanding

Neil Hendry

I have been fortunate to work with many exceptional leaders over the years, each of whom helped me develop my own leadership style. However, in the summer of 2006, as an aspiring head teacher, I was given the opportunity to attend a Columba 1400 head teachers' leadership academy in Staffin, Skye. I have no doubt that my Columba experience had a significant impact on how I led the young people, staff, and community of Northfield Academy, Aberdeen, when I was appointed as head teacher six years later.

Columba 1400 is based on six core values: awareness, focus, creativity, integrity, perseverance, and service. Head teachers leave Columba equipped to lead transformation in the culture of their school and community. This desire to change the culture was crucial to my leadership style at Northfield Academy.

When I first arrived at Northfield, a school that serves several areas of multiple deprivation, rather than finding a school with a reputation of challenging behaviour and recruitment issues, I found a community of young people with great potential, a management team that quickly bought in to my vision, and a committed staff. However, a few challenges over the years had contributed to a significant lack of aspiration, confirmed by looking at achievement data and discipline. Northfield Academy needed to renew its sense of pride.

I began by holding daily staff briefings; two- or three-minute updates bringing all staff together at the start of the day in a collegial fashion. I was highly visible at the school gates when the children arrived, greeting them and picking up on latecomers, and I was at the gates again at 3:25 p.m., ensuring a calm finish to the day—most of the time! I drew a clear line in the sand with many hard-hitting assemblies, openly stating the expectations of staff at Northfield Academy. I re-established the dress code, which brought the Academy in line with the other twelve secondary schools in Aberdeen and I increased using the school badge to create a sense of identity, which the school had lacked for many years. However, I had to do more. I had to create a positive ripple from the school out into the wider community.

I began with the local primary schools and worked collegiately with head teachers to improve educational outcomes and raise the profile of schools in the area. We introduced an annual Northfield schools Christmas concert where all the feeder schools performed. The concerts brought the community together and celebrated the amazing talents of the children. We introduced a summer fair, based at the academy, inviting different community groups to take part. These events were attended by hundreds of pupils, alumni, and local people. We introduced open mornings to allow parents of current and prospective pupils to see the school operationally, certain that if twenty parents enjoyed a positive experience, they would go out into the community and tell their friends and family and spread the word.

To encourage a positive mind-set at the school, we had posters produced showing pupils being successful in a variety of different activities. Initially, the young people were embarrassed to see themselves on the walls; being successful was clearly not cool. However, recognising the small achievements along the way had a cumulative effect and it wasn't long before the pupils were pleading for their pictures to appear whenever a camera was produced! We also worked hard with the local press to celebrate school success and change the perception of the school within Aberdeen.

We were beginning to see the positive ripple from the school out into the community as I used social media to share everything positive. A pivotal point came when we created a new school hash tag, 'Aspire to be Outstanding'. It was used on social media and appeared around the school, on classroom walls, and even on teachers' lanyards. I used Aspire to be Outstanding whenever I worked with pupils, parents, and the community. My message was always, 'Do we aspire to be OK? Average? No, we *aspire to be outstanding!*' Over time, *Aspire to be Outstanding* became clearly associated with Northfield Academy and pupils, parents, and partners were regularly hash-tagging it.

The feel-good factor was back, and Northfield Academy was sitting proudly in the local community and beyond. Students, parents, and staff were working together to deliver positive outcomes for all.

Neil Hendry has spent the past 20 years teaching in several schools within Aberdeen. He began his teaching career at Robert Gordons College as a Physical Education teacher. He moved to St. Machar Academy before being seconded to Aberdeen City Council as a Quality Improvement Officer. He then became head teacher at Northfield Academy until he left for Lochside Academy, a new £48-million academy, bringing together both Kincorth and Torry Academies. Neil is a keen athlete with a very successful rugby career captaining Ellon Rugby Club during their most successful period. Too old for rugby, he can now be found on the golf course, still as competitive as ever.

Living in Two Languages

Lorraine Cruz

As I reflect on my life and journey, I feel grateful and blessed. I wouldn't change a thing ... well, maybe I would change the structures by which I had to learn, work, and teach, but I wouldn't change the lessons and the people that I met along the way. I was born to islanders. Although they were born American citizens, moving to the mainland, meeting, falling in love, marrying, and having children took on a very different shape in my upbringing.

My parents had a very old-world, traditional sense of education. Having been denied the opportunity to continue theirs, they established expectations for their children. I would be the first to live up to those norms. The first educational decision my parents took was to move out of New York. My father believed that a good education required several provisions: a good community, united expectations, accessible parents, and determination. Because my parents had already established the latter three, they now searched for a better community; they packed me up and went west. We ended up in Chicago.

I entered school at the age of five—bilingual, biliterate, and reading at a second grade level—while the teacher was teaching phonemic sounds and blends. Little did I know that this would set the foundation for my career in education. I try to flashback to those early days, try to pinpoint when my parents transitioned from being monolingual Spanish speakers to bilingual—I have not been successful in that quest.

My years as a student passed quickly and easily, as I was a curious child who loved learning. Reading became my passport and I soon became the "teacher" for any of my siblings who struggled through school. High school brought me honors, advanced placement courses, and scholarships for college. In college, I struggled a bit; I was commuting on public transportation, working two jobs, and helping my then high-school-aged brothers. I double majored in psychology and criminal justice and would soon apply for a federal position with the DEA, AFT, FBI, or CIA; forensic criminology was what I wanted to do.

Then I took an unexpected turn from my path, marrying almost immediately after college. While looking for a job to help pay for my last semester of college, I was given the opportunity to teach. The state board evaluated my resume and transcripts and granted me credentials to teach adult education. This surprising turn of events (only possible because of my bilingual status) would change my life forever. Upon being handed the dry erase markers and a curriculum, I realized that teaching was my calling. That was the beginning of three years in adult education. One job was teaching secretarial science and workplace English; the other was a one-room storefront schoolhouse where I grew the GED, ESL, Spanish literacy, and citizenship classes for our community. Then in early December 1989, I received yet another life changing opportunity.

One of our neighbors was an entrepreneur and his wife was a teacher assistant. She approached me one day and told me that the school where she worked was looking for a teacher, one who spoke English and Spanish. I remembered my own elementary experience of encountering only one teacher who spoke Spanish … right before I transferred schools. She told me to interview and, to my great disbelief, I was hired on the spot to lead a class of 7th and 8th grade students. I became a substitute with a permanent classroom. The following year, a new administrator came on board. She began searching for a master's degree program for me to obtain my full credentials. I was blessed with a fully funded program; when I completed my degree, my five-month-old son attended my graduation (with a little help!).

My initial experience in the classroom showed me that I had a natural instinct in curriculum development and mapping, use of authentic instructional practices, and integration of community and parents into the students' learning experience. Whenever I felt stuck, I would close my eyes and think back to the teachers that kept me engaged and excited about learning: Mrs. Lyons (2nd grade), Mrs. Hampton (HS World History), and most intently Mrs. Wilson my 6th grade teacher. These women helped shape my love for learning; they never killed my spirit and they encouraged my curiosity and exploration. In honor of those who taught me, I continue my quest to be the best teacher and leader I can be.

Lorraine Cruz is the Curriculum Coordinator and Leadership Coach at Youth Connection Charter School Network. She is a certified leadership coach through the National Association of Elementary School Principals and has a 100% passing rate of her students becoming principals or assistant principals. In the last three years, she has been on two design teams, Chicago and Atlanta, helping to design and develop a charter school in each city, both of which will be presented to their respective boards of education in 2018. Lorraine has developed various dual language programs across several schools to support bilingualism and biliteracy for all children.

The Little Red Schoolhouse

John Roberts

When discussing educational leadership, I find it hard not to think back to my elementary school days. These were the days that formed me as an academic and, later, as an adult in various walks of life. Those were different times, of course, when most of the principles of effective school leadership as we know them today were undefined. Yet despite the nearly primitive academic conditions I found myself in, everything I became is due to the skills of my elementary teacher.

In the 1950's, I attended a one-room red brick country school-house, the kind that you see on television's *Little House on the Prairie*. There were eight grades in one room, 16 students in the entire school, one teacher, and one wood-burning stove in the middle of the room to give us all the heat we needed during the cold eight winters I spent in the school.

Our teacher's name was Mildred Collop—Mrs. Collop (who in his or her right mind would dare to use her first name). She was all of five feet tall, and to the students she looked ancient with her white hair and slightly wrinkled features; she was likely all of 40 years old. Mrs. Collop was married to a local farmer, had a teen-aged daughter named Marjorie who attended another school (we were never told where that school was located), and doubtless Mrs. Collop never saw the inside of a teacher's college.

We sat at long desks that were intended for two students. Usually two students in the same grade were paired up, but if there was only one person in the grade, you were out of luck, and could be paired up with someone quite a bit younger or older than you. Boys sat on one side of the room, and girls on the other, and unless you wanted to start a rumour, if you were a boy, that you had a "girlfriend," you didn't even glance at the girls' side of the room.

A student could skip a grade (advance from Grade 4 to Grade 6, for example), if the teacher thought that student was ready for "higher" education. I was never favoured in this way; Mrs. Collop thought that I was too "nervous," but what she considered to be nervousness was actually boredom. By the time I got to Grade 4, I was bored silly. I not only had to sit through Grade 4 lessons, but also listened to repeats of Grades 1–3, and then listen to what was being taught to Grades 5–8. By the time I reached Grade 8, I had heard the Grade 8 lessons eight times. Remember, we were all in one room.

I don't know how Mrs. Collop did it. Eight grades at one time. I've been teaching over 30 years and still have enough trouble with one CLASS in one grade.

But she was tough. She and the strap (perfectly legal in those days) ruled the classroom. Disobey at your peril. Even the mildest of infractions was reported to your parents, and punishment for your sins at school was reinforced at home.

My father thought that mathematical skills were the only academic area that mattered. He had won a medal for mathematics in Grade 10. Unfortunately, the Depression kept him from going any farther. He lived vicariously through his son, having the teacher give me extra math tests to make sure that I was "keeping up." I was a major disappointment to him; I didn't have a brain in my head for mathematics.

I did, however, have other academic strengths which were encouraged by Mrs. Collop. I wrote well; I was likely the best writer in the school (which isn't saying much), and she continually informed by father of my progress. He wasn't impressed.

But what does this have to do with educational leadership? It's a nostalgic tale of education in another time, when learning by rote, penmanship, poetry, and writing shills. (I still remember working from *Phonics Fun*). I haven't discussed leadership styles that Mrs. Collop may have exhibited, or whether she showed any of the qualities of successful school leaders— focus, clarity, creativity and compassion. Her main leadership quality consisted in the fact that she wanted ever one of her students to have an equal chance at life, it was her responsibility to offer these chances.

The most significant thing she did was to point down the gravel road in front of the school and tell us to follow that road away from where we were. We could achieve success by taking advantage of the opportunities that education gave us.

Very few of us followed that advice. Most students were from farming or fishing families, and wanted only to complete their compulsory education and then work on the farm or fishing boats with their fathers. In fact, only two of us in my class went on to finish high school, myself and another boy who became an electrical engineer.

So, Mrs. Collop's success ratio wasn't too good, but she showed us the way to find a better life through education. The showed me that a good grasp of the language and the ability to communicate were my personal foundations for success. She showed me that the ability to read and write well was crucial to whatever I tried to achieve in the future.

It worked for me.

Dr. John Roberts is a Metis who has been active in Indigenous affairs in Canada for over 26 years. John was the founder and President for 11 years of the Canadian Metis Council, a national Metis organization that has over 10,000 members. He was also Director of Education and Governor, region 9, for the Ontario Coalition of Indigenous People. John retired from Mohawk College as a Professor of Language Studies and Manager of the Aboriginal Education program at the college. Since his retirement, he has worked as an occasional teacher with the Hamilton Board of Education. Dr. Roberts has written or contributed to 30 text books in the fields of communications, law enforcement, and Aboriginal education, along with numerous journal articles.

Pen Pals in Cross-Cultural Understanding

Banu Yaman Ortaş

In many aspects of life, I have seen that the educational system must be strengthened in its efforts to teach co-existence and mutual respect, especially in multicultural societies with major sociological diversities. As I have witnessed how badly we are being parsed out, isolated, and alienated based on different features, languages, or backgrounds, I have also noticed that we are interconnected just like a perfect lace pattern, yet we are not aware of it.

My interest in multilingual, multicultural families and their children has directed my academic life and my teaching. In 1998, I was assigned to teach 3rd grade in a primary school in an Arabic village in the region of Adana, Turkey. My students were simply beautiful and my profession was fun. The majority of my students, however, had socio-economic insufficiencies.

One day I noticed one of my students carrying the schoolbag of a classmate. When I asked why, my student replied, "Teacher, his father is a laborer on our farm. My father is his Agha. Of course he will carry my schoolbag." I began to understand that socioeconomic differences formed the foundation of discrimination amongst kids. I hoped that such perspectives could possibly be changed by getting the kids to play local games together. I conferred on them the responsibilities that would allow them to support each other's learning based on collaboration. I organized drama sessions to allow the kids to comprehend the importance of helping, valuing, and respecting each other.

I also visited their parents. During such visits, I realized that most of them had insufficient Turkish language skills. In fact, some of my students were trying to interpret between their families and me. I began seeking new ways to improve the language skills of my students.

Meanwhile, a friend of mine was teaching 3rd grade students of Kurdish descent in a village in Eastern Anatolia. We regularly exchanged letters and shared our professional experiences, discussing what to do to improve the language skills of our students. One day I came up with an idea and suggested it to her: "How about making our students pen pals?" She agreed and we started to match up our willing students by drawing lots. Each letter was going to be about a particular subject such as "where I live," "who I am," or "our holiday celebrations." We read their letters and then had them correct their mistakes. We did not allow them to use offensive expressions in their letters and we sent the letters at our own expense. Our students started writing to each other about their dreams. There were students who had never seen the sea, a movie theater, or a city, yet they were extremely curious about all of them. After two years, they began sending each other little presents.

Our pen pal initiative then inspired a beautiful project that excited the attention of various institutions. Students from various schools, cultural groups, and ages throughout the country started to host each other. The students finally realized some of the modest dreams—visiting the sea, going to a movie theater, visiting cities they had never seen. They finally had the chance to expand their horizons and make their dreams come true. I started working at the university, but I kept following the project through the national press. The project continued for a while but ended due to financial reasons.

The beautiful effects of the pen pal project that my friend and I started together include remaining in contact with some of my students many years later. I also share this experience with my prospective teacher students, emphasizing to them the importance of education in fostering a multicultural society. I do my best to get my students to realize that education requires hard work, just as creating fine lace does. We discuss the necessity of taking advantage of alternative teaching methods in order to get our students to learn the importance of respecting and valuing each other without alienating others. Throughout my professional life, I have done my best to lead the way to action on the idea that our society will be strengthened by getting to know each other in personal ways. Only then can we understand that the "other" is actually part of "us."

Banu Yaman Ortaş, Ph.D., completed undergraduate studies in Classroom Education and master's and doctoral studies in the Educational Programs and Teaching division of the Educational Sciences Department at University of Çukurova in Turkey. Dr. Yaman Ortaş has taught multilingual and multicultural primary education classes. Her master's thesis was on the CIRC technique of learning based on collaboration; her doctoral thesis was based on using the Drama method (a scenario-based learning approach) with multilingual students. Dr. Yaman Ortaş is currently carrying on her research with the Faculty of Education of Trakya University as well as international research on multiculturality in collaboration with the Social Justice Education Department of the University of Toronto under the supervision of Prof. Dr. John Portelli.

No Drowning in the Desert

Kaitlin Jackson

When you exchange pleasantries at the beginning of an interview for a leadership position, it is recommended to respond to "How are you?" with a simple "I'm doing well, thank you." Not me. In my interview, I was eight months pregnant and replied, "Just getting bigger every day."

The rest of the interview was not as much of a disaster as my intro, and I found myself returning from maternity leave as a lead teacher. I was 26, enrolled in a PhD program full-time, and struggling to balance my professional life with taking nursing breaks and raising a new baby. However, I quickly learned that leadership does not have to be scary; you can succeed as a leader even if you have a million and one things going on outside of school. It worked for me. I share my story with you in the hope that you may believe what I now know to be true—there is no drowning in the desert.

I have been a teacher for six years; three of those years were devoted to children with special needs. It had always been my desire to shift the paradigm from "disabled" to "differently abled," and working in this field has only fueled my passion for an inclusive education model. Sounds great, right? Well, of course, if you have the people power to make it happen.

In my new position, I supervised five teachers in a preschool classroom in a school for children with autism. We had one goal in mind: get all the kids out. Not because we did not love them—we did, a whole lot—but because they had reached such high levels of independence and academic skills that they were ready to go to a typical school. With a background in special education, I felt ready, excited even, to take on this task.

The school year began with the hamster wheel inside my head spinning and spinning, and spinning some more, and I was gushing ideas to the teachers left and right. I had updates every day and new ideas every week. I was lucky enough to have teachers who loved our students as much as I did, so they listened readily and jumped on my hamster wheel.

I was working 15 hours a day—on either work or homework for my PhD classes—on top of taking care of my son. My loving husband, though happy to see me passionate about my work, encouraged me every night to stop working and take a much-needed break. I had so many things on my never-ending to-do list that I just would not allow myself to stop. Then, almost overnight, I began waking up in the middle of the night in a panic that someone lost a student, or none of our kids made it to a typical school, or I was fired unexpectedly. I had indeed taken on far too much, and I had learned the lesson that every leader must learn: delegate or drown.

I began to rely on my veteran teachers more, started giving out more tasks, and started to say no when I knew I needed to do home-work instead. I used down time at work to do reading or writing for my classes, and I gave out responsibilities to my teachers like donuts at a coffee shop. Soon enough, a few months went by without doing any work at home, and instead I was able to focus on my classes and my family. Through the months of caffeinated chaos, I learned a hard but important lesson: either you can drown in work or you can earn the title you hold as a leader.

No one is a lost cause—even you, on your hardest day—and if you feel like you're drowning in work, delegate and decide what needs to be done right now, and what can wait until tomorrow. Even on your most hectic days at school, when it feels like every student needs you and you are pulled in every single direction other than your computer or desk, no one is helpless. You can always get better, and your teachers can always get better. There is no drowning; everyone can be better. A student with significantly challenging behaviors can learn to tell you what they want; a teacher with no experience in special education can learn to adapt curriculum. A leader running on five hours of sleep a night can learn to delegate tasks and focus more on what really matters.

However, you can only get better, and your teachers can only get better, if they are buying what you are selling. I once bought a case of kombucha without trying it (kombucha is gross) only because the salesperson was so passionate about its nutritional benefits. People who sell used cars make a living by convincing strangers they should drop thousands of dollars on someone else's car. Your teachers will jump on your hamster wheel if they believe in where you are going—it's your job to get them to believe in you and join your team. Get to know them, what they care about, and what makes their hamster wheel turn—then find the common ground and focus on a mutual goal. Utilize their strengths and capitalize on what they bring to the table.

During the rest of the school year, I spent more of my weekends with my impossibly adorable son and more of my weeknights completing homework for my PhD classes. I strengthened relationships with my teachers by entrusting them increasingly with things to do, and I salvaged my passion and love for special education by learning to stop myself from drowning.

I may still drink a lot of coffee, but I am a better leader because of my struggle. Be kind, be honest, be humble, be respectful, and be human, but most importantly, get your wheels spinning in the same direction. You will be well on your way to swimming upstream.

Kaitlin M. Jackson is a Lead Teacher at the New England Center for Children, Abu Dhabi, United Arab Emirates, where she resides with her husband, son Marley, and two dogs. She is originally from San Jose, California, and attended the University of California, Irvine for her Bachelor Degree and Louisiana State University for her Master's Degree. She is finishing her Ph.D. coursework at the University of Kentucky in the Department of Educational Leadership Studies.

Wicked Problems

Steve Dobo

I turned 60 this summer and it got me thinking; I decided to get away for a few days to reflect on what that meant to me. I went with the intention of dealing with whatever came up during that time. I traveled with journals, colored pens, and an assortment of books on topics including spirituality, business, and design thinking.

While away, I started to reflect on the work that I had not yet been able to get to in my first 60 years, and started to examine the intersection of international development, low literacy rates, endangered species, and refugees. I wondered if these important issues for me intersected somewhere in the world. A quick search brought me to the Democratic Republic of Congo (DRC), where centuries of colonialism, tribal wars, and rebel violence are now threatening the existence of both local villagers and the endangered mountain gorilla. I knew I had found my intersection.

In a sense, I was looking for my wicked problem—the mystery that I most wanted to solve in the world. Throughout my career, I have jumped into one black hole after another to try to crack tough issues that I cared about. Inevitably, most of these issues revolved around education and our most under-resourced and most vulnerable young people. I have created multiple organizations, dozens of alternative schools and programs, and helped thousands of students either stay in or return to school.

My belief is that true leaders dive into black holes that others are reluctant to jump into—being a leader means that you lead. That means leading in your field of interest and expertise. It means taking on the most intractable problems in your field, because you might be the most qualified person to do so, even though you might very well feel unequipped. Wicked problems are called wicked for a reason—issues like poverty and illicit drug use, which many people have tried to address unsuccessfully, even to the point of attacking them with czars and wars.

Diving into a mystery involves a certain set of approaches that I have gleaned over the years, providing different lenses to look at issues. The first I've found helpful is design thinking. Roger Martin wrote a book called *The Design of Business* in which he talks about a knowledge funnel to drive toward a solution from mystery to heuristic. A heuristic is a guiding principle you come up with from looking at an issue in depth. It is the first inkling of what might be a part of the solution. In this case, the plight of the mountain gorilla is integrally tied to the plight of forest villagers living on the slopes of the volcano with them, the city of Goma (two million people) just 25 miles away, and the tribal warfare that has caused a mass exodus of refugees out of the DRC.

The second tool is systems thinking; everything is a system, so to solve a problem you have to deal with the whole and not just one part. Solutions are often separated in time and space from where symptoms appear. A systemic solution in the DRC involves figuring out how to satisfy the needs of an encroaching population without further destroying the habitat of the mountain gorilla. Fixes involve educating the forest villagers to understand that their survival depends on the survival of the mountain gorilla and then coming up with economically sustainable businesses—like eco-tourism or urban farming—that meet the needs of the people without destroying gorilla habitat. It might also involve utilizing new technology like satellite imagery to help monitor the well-being of gorillas.

Finally, ethnographic research is essential to understand the issue well enough to come up with a workable solution. This research goes beyond traditional focus groups and walking in the shoes of the people you want to help. On the ground research means getting close enough to really understand the needs and desires of the people you are trying to impact. It is refraining from imposing a solution from afar, and learning to come alongside to help people realize their greatest aspirations. This research unearths local solutions, like a Congolese refugee building an adult school in the DRC to repatriate Congolese back to Congo. Expanding this approach to create a school for local villagers would be a way to teach people about protecting mountain gorillas and their habitat.

Wicked problems are not easy. Life is short and the time to make a difference is even shorter. True leaders take on the difficult work. For my life, it has made all the difference.

Steve Dobo, Founder and CEO of Zero Dropouts, is a system thinker and serial entrepreneur creating organizations and programs to tackle the most complex social and educational problems in the world. He has consulted with school districts across the United States, helping them serve the most difficult students better. Steve resides in Denver, Colorado, and is always looking for partners around the globe to create collaborative projects. Get in touch with Steve at steve.dobo@comcast.net.

Assessing Education

Henk Frenken

When we talk about education, we are really thinking about the purpose of education. For me the key question to ask is: Why are we working in education? The reason must be meaningful; it says so much about your task as a member of the teaching staff.

As a head of school, you are the centre of a web of relationships, responsible for the vision of education at your school together with your teachers, parents, and students. You work with all these community members and with the young people themselves for their future but also for our future. So what kind of teacher do you want to be? How do you want students to remember you 20 years from now? What are the life lessons that will help them? What are the lasting impacts you can have?

In today's education system, you must step off the major roads and explore some paths less travelled. You must think differently, otherwise, as Einstein said, you are trying to solve problems with the old knowledge that created those problems in the first place.

All of these issues are worth discussing at staff meetings from time to time in order to make sure we are all on the right track. In the busy hustle and bustle of the day-to-day operations of school, however, we usually take less time to talk about these major matters than we do to solve such minor issues as how to alert the office to a shortage of photocopy paper. We are too busy trying to keep up with all the quotidian demands to focus on results and, in so doing, we forget the main task of education—to help young people to develop their own gifts and skills, to teach them critical thinking and then watch them come up with creative solutions to the problems of the world.

At our school, the meeting for assessing ourselves and the education we provide to our students lasts for only three hours. In fact, this time is too short. You can fill a whole day, a whole week, talking about the purpose of education. In the Netherlands, our vision of education is based on the Jenaplan ideas of Peter Petersen, conceived almost a hundred years ago. In this way of thinking, social-emotional development and self-directed learning are the most important skills for students to develop in order to succeed.

As a leader in this way of thinking, you must learn to give responsibility to the teaching staff and trust them instead of trying to control their work. You must shift your thinking to be bottom up rather than top down. In this way, staff will "own" their work, thus feeling competent in doing their daily jobs. The head of the school may create the framework, but within this frame the teaching staff create educational activities and experiences. In turn, the teachers expect the same from their students—that they be involved in and responsible for their own work, know why they are doing this work, and know what they want to achieve.

Social-emotional learning is the basis of all learning. You can't learn if your wellbeing is not taken care of, if your stomach is empty, if no one listens to your opinions. Social-emotional behaviour means having respect, independence, responsibility, cooperation, and communication. We focus on these matters in education instead of "machine" thinking; we focus on the processes of learning rather than the products.

In order to uphold a vision of education, the school must have a common goal that everyone knows and is involved in. The following scheme from Scotland offers a good outline of the Jenaplan view of education:

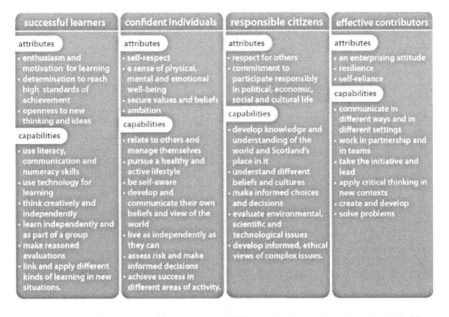

successful learners	confident individuals	responsible citizens	effective contributors
attributes	**attributes**	**attributes**	**attributes**
• enthusiasm and motivation for learning • determination to reach high standards of achievement • openness to new thinking and ideas	• self-respect • a sense of physical, mental and emotional well-being • secure values and beliefs • ambition	• respect for others • commitment to participate responsibly in political, economic, social and cultural life	• an enterprising attitude • resilience • self-reliance
capabilities	**capabilities**	**capabilities**	**capabilities**
• use literacy, communication and numeracy skills • use technology for learning • think creatively and independently • learn independently and as part of a group • make reasoned evaluations • link and apply different kinds of learning in new situations.	• relate to others and manage themselves • pursue a healthy and active lifestyle • be self-aware • develop and communicate their own beliefs and view of the world • live as independently as they can • assess risk and make informed decisions • achieve success in different areas of activity.	• develop knowledge and understanding of the world and Scotland's place in it • understand different beliefs and cultures • make informed choices and decisions • evaluate environmental, scientific and technological issues • develop informed, ethical views of complex issues.	• communicate in different ways and in different settings • work in partnership and in teams • take the initiative and lead • apply critical thinking in new contexts • create and develop • solve problems

Dr. Henk Frenken is Head of the public Jenaplan school de Dukdalf in Leiden, Netherlands. His research interests include the purpose of education and international relations. He spends his educational work life searching for innovative ways to transform education for students by transforming ordinary or failing schools into successful schools using creative and innovative techniques to "mind-shift" the teaching staff. Frenken can be reached via email at h.frenken@dukdalf-leiden.nl. You can see his website here: www.dukdalf-leiden.nl.

Monday Morning Inspirationals

Thomas Seaton

I was at my wits' end, trying to figure out a way to have my messages understood by the staff. I consider myself a skilled communicator, and I have been told that I can turn a phrase and inspire with words. However, what I thought was *urgency* was interpreted as *incompetence*. There is nothing worse than having misunderstanding serve as the roadblock to progress in high-stakes endeavors. Mercifully, the school year ended, and we all went off to our respective corners.

Having spent six years in a seminary, I embarked upon a self-imposed "retreat" during my summer break. I read all I could to try to understand what was going on … in me. Leaders typically believe that everything is their responsibility, and surely staff were not understanding me because of something I was, or wasn't doing. Sound familiar?

This time it *was* appropriate to look inward. What I came to see is that I was so afraid of not being able to move the school forward, that I projected that concern onto the staff. My ultimate fear was that our kids would not have access to the opportunities they deserved if we didn't close achievement gaps. For those of us hard-wired to carry the weight of the world on our shoulders, the desperation of being misunderstood was excruciating.

I have always believed that a large part of discontent in the workplace comes from our desire to be free. We yearn to control our lives, but the very act of setting the alarm clock reminds us that we are never completely free. I chalk up a lot of "daily crabbiness" to this perceived lack of freedom and move on.

I came across a book called *The Untethered Soul* by Michael A. Singer. He helped me identify what I now call the subordinate's twin: fear. Gather a group of people who do not feel free and don't understand the one who controls their freedom, and you have a recipe for misunderstanding.

I began to own my fears, to pinpoint the leadership issues about which I was fearful. I gave them space and let them breathe. A spiritual director under whom I studied as a seminarian used to tell me that the cure is in the wound. I let myself be vulnerable to my fears of not being understood, not knowing how and when to push and pull, and ensuring that our kids would realize success. My fears became my confidants.

Staff returned for another school year, and at our opening in-service, I shared my summer experience with them. I talked about my fears candidly. I cited examples from my summer readings, and asked them to identify what their fears were, and then to decide which things were not worth the surrender of their happiness.

Then I began to write an inspirational staff email each Monday morning. The more I spoke about my fears, the more staff began to open up to me. I saw this infancy of trust most tangibly through the evaluation process. I changed my approach. I realized that the real objective is to coach staff through their instructional fears. I hadn't done that before. I gave staff a safe place to fail during a formal observation, with one caveat: be able to reflect on where the lesson fell apart, and what you would do differently if teaching this lesson again.

I began to use Monday Morning Inspirationals to tap into low- and high-energy times, or fearful events like parent–teacher conferences or benchmarking periods. One can't provide enough encouragement for staff members who work in high poverty schools, so I continued to reiterate the importance of our mission and the contribution that teachers make to kids.

It was very different for me to communicate to the group via technology, so I was unsure at first of the effectiveness of my emails. One Monday morning I had a dental appointment before school, so I did not send a message to begin the week. By the lunch hour, several staff members asked if I was upset with them because I did not send a note of encouragement. The seed had taken root!

When we returned from spring break, I wrote an email about the home stretch, saying we needed to pour on the effort until the finish line. The note was forwarded to my superintendent, who shared it with the entire district.

I retired a little over a month ago. My most cherished retirement gift? A bound copy of my Monday Morning Inspirationals, given to me by my supervisor. Facing fear invites freedom. Curing the wound promotes health. Understanding this dynamic enables kids to flourish as fearless explorers who learn to liberate themselves for life.

Dr. Thomas Seaton recently retired from a 21-year commitment to the principalship. Seaton served in Catholic and public schools in Chicago and in surrounding suburban communities. He applied his dissertation topic on Transformational Leadership (2007), to turnaround efforts he led in the high-poverty ELL schools in which he served. He has begun to write about various aspects of transformation and turnaround and their impact on veteran leaders.

A Gordian Knot

Michelle Eriksen

As in most international schools, our enrolment fluctuates. One year, we had planned for one classroom each of grades 1 and 2. Then, at orientation on the Friday before school started, more children showed up than expected, though not enough to convince the board to hire an additional teacher for each grade. Time was now of the essence, as Monday was the first day of school.

We wanted to keep our classes to a maximum of twenty students, and my teachers suggested a combined grade one/two section. I knew a teacher available for immediate hire and we had an empty classroom, so playing for time, I brought her in as a sub to set up. I met with our parent liaisons to brief them on enrolment and on our proposal. I spent the weekend writing a rationale for the board.

On the second day of school, with board approval, I hired the teacher, assigning her to grade 2. A current member of staff would teach the combination class. The grade 1 teacher would stay put. We met with support services to discuss student needs, tentative class lists, communication with parents, a plan for transition, and scheduling.

On Wednesday, at our welcome coffee for parents of grades 1 and 2 students, I shared the increase in enrolment and our proposal for adding a combined grade 1/2 class. We stressed that smaller groups would allow for better differentiation of instruction and explained that all students would probably be in a mixed grade-level group at some point. Grades 1 and 2 would be a community of learners with three teachers. Following the meeting, I emailed parents with further details, inviting them to contact me with any questions or concerns.

The new class lists were sent home on Thursday. These were carefully designed to consider grade levels, new students, friendships, EAL students, academic performance, behavior, and special needs. Gender balance was a particular challenge: there were only six girls in second grade, of which the combination class received three, plus four girls from first grade, and four boys each from first and second.

Despite our structured change-management process for parents and students, at 8:30 the next day, the parents of a second grade girl in the combination class appeared in my office. They had not slept. They wanted their daughter moved immediately, saying, "I don't care what you need to do. Make it happen." They refused to share their reasons, did not want a discussion, and did not want to hear any arguments. They threatened to remove both of their children from the school unless I moved their daughter. Then they walked out. That afternoon the parents of another second grade girl, a friend of the first, visited to convey a similar message. They, too, did not want to listen to rationale or research and demanded a move or they would be leaving the school. What surprised me most about both encounters was how adamant the parents were; I thought I had had positive, trusting relationships with both.

I reviewed my options. If I acquiesced and moved the two girls, then we would have only one second-grade girl left in the combination class. I would have no choice but to move her too. That would leave only four second graders, all boys. It would no longer be a balanced group. On the other hand, if the families left, we would lose children, with the same result. Even calling their bluff would not yield a positive outcome, and for many reasons, swapping the girls was also not an option. It was a Gordian knot.

And so it was that on the eve before the smaller classes were to start, they were doomed to fail. All the careful planning to best meet our students' needs was for nought. Though I was saddened by this turn of events, I reached out to the two families, and the following week we devised a plan to undo what we had created, returning to one class each of grades 1 and 2. Both were large—twenty-two students—and second grade had sixteen boys! On the plus side, we had gained an additional teacher, though she could not be in two places at once, leaving both classes with no additional support at times. I emailed the parents, explaining that we were strategically scheduling our staff to allow for differentiation, which was our original intent.

Exhausted, I attended the PTSA barbecue. Chatting with parents, I felt better. Some were disappointed, though they appreciated the extra teacher. The two sets of parents made a point to find me and shake hands. We moved on.

I have been an elementary school principal for over twenty years. Every week is different, bringing change, intriguing challenges, exciting opportunities, and sometimes, unexpected predicaments. Along the way, I have learned that students come first. Be approachable. Listen. Think creatively. Be resilient. And, if the situation calls for reversing a decision, be flexible enough to do so.

Michelle Eriksen is a lower school principal at ACS Hillingdon International School, England. A certified Principal Mentor by the National Association of Elementary School Principals, Eriksen is committed to high expectations and the success of all students. Her students have earned five International Student Awards from the Council of International Schools for promoting of global citizenship. In 2016, the school was recognised as an Apple Distinguished School for creating unique learning experiences that enhance student collaboration, communication, critical thinking, and creativity.

Tell Me Your Story

David Stegall

"Tell me your story, young man." The comment caught me off guard. I had just finished helping an elderly stranger open up a condiment packet as he sat alone in a booth at a fast food restaurant late one dreary evening a while back. I couldn't bear to see his weathered arthritic hands labor to open the slippery little package. I was having dinner with my family, stopping to eat on our way home after another busy day of shuttling children from school to practice and back home to finish the masses of homework consuming the waning hours of day before bed. The question seemed strange, and I pondered how I might politely share a few moments with the friendly stranger before hurrying back to my busy life.

Admittedly, I'm a natural performer and storyteller so I had no problem opening up to this inviting gentleman with the calming presence. I shared a short bit about where I was from and how I ended up where I am today. I shared my love for children and how it led me to become an educator. By now my wife, sensing my engagement with the stranger, brought my food to me as Mr. Johnson and I sat in the booth. We were a contradiction in every way. He was African-American, likely in his early 80s, humbly dressed, with years of hard work weathered on his face and hands. I was a young white man wearing a suit; obviously I had never seen the struggles and hardships of my counterpart. As the time passed, he shared his amazing life story with me.

Having grown up in an era where his race limited his educational and work opportunities, Mr. Johnson washed local storefront windows in town for nickels. One day, a bank manager whose window he had just finished cleaning asked him if he would like a job in the bank, cleaning and maintaining the boiler. His eyes sparkled as he told me how that offer ended up changing his life. Mr. Johnson took great pride in his work, using his earnings to buy his own home—something his parents had never owned. The bank manager took Mr. Johnson under his wing and helped him purchase stock in the bank. Through the years, the job at the bank, and the money invested in stock, helped Mr. Johnson put all three of his children, as well as two grandchildren, through college. In his words, he had lived the "American Dream."

The power of his words pierced my heart as he shared how life's twists and turns had led him to where he is today—a proud father and grandfather who had worked hard, sacrificed much, and guarded the well-being of his family. After sharing our meals, we parted ways, but his story never left me.

The act of one leader—the bank manager—had changed his life path. As educational leaders, it's nearly impossible to measure the number of lives our words and actions impact. We have the opportunity to cultivate the success of students every day. Our actions have ripple effects on lives many years down the road.

Each new school year brings with it the excitement of possibility; for some, the possibility of continued success; for others, the prospect of change and improvement. Giving students opportunities and authentic experiences means that educators help students carve the path that leads to *their story*. Today more than ever, we must desire increased opportunities, greater advancements, and clearer pathways for student success, for which we are collectively responsible. Students have opportunities today that many of us never had. We must hold students to a high standard while building a strong support system under them. We don't know what kind of future today's students will encounter as adults; however, without a strong educational foundation, their "American Dream" will be much less attainable.

Part of our own story is not only how we live our lives, but also how we help improve the lives of others—especially children. When the job of school leader seems overwhelming, be assured that your work is critical to helping students gain the knowledge and experience they need to cultivate their own story.

Dr. David Stegall is the superintendent of Newton-Conover City Schools, named a national "Superintendent to Watch" in 2016 and North Carolina Region 7 Superintendent of the Year for 2017. He was also named Outstanding Young Educator for North Carolina (2012) and was a National Finalist for the ASCD (Association for Supervision and Curriculum Development) Outstanding Young Educator Award. Dr. Stegall has presented at the state, national, and international levels on professional learning communities and teacher empowerment. He has a B.Ed. from the University of North Carolina at Charlotte, an M.Ed. from Gardner-Webb University, an education specialist degree in education administration, and a doctorate in educational leadership both from Appalachian State University.

Ask for Help Rather Than Hiding Your Weaknesses

Adam Brown

I became a principal at the age of 28. I had served as a classroom teacher for four years before moving into this position. This rapid movement up provided me with a false sense of confidence as I took on a leadership role. In my first year as an administrator, I sought to prove that I was capable of being followed by the teachers in our building. This approach led to many mistakes.

First, I was afraid of highlighting my weaknesses and lack of knowledge in various areas. In professional development, instructional feedback, and overall leadership capabilities, I covered up my lack of knowledge by doubling down on decisions I felt were appropriate at the time. My lack of confidence led to a lack of growth in our building and in myself.

Second, I was focused on leading through never-ending support and serving those in my building. While servant leadership can be an effective model, I felt that I enabled the teachers in my first year. They were extremely effective at their jobs; however, my failure to provide them with effective feedback and push them towards their own growth was a disservice to the students. My failures as a first-year administrator forced me to reflect on what type of leader I needed to become.

In my fifth year as an administrator, I feel more comfortable in how I lead. First, I consistently read and collaborate with other educational leaders. I seek their guidance by asking questions and soliciting their feedback on my current practices. I readily admit my weaknesses to those I lead. I seek to learn from both novice and veteran teachers. I embrace learning more about what I do not know. This type of mindset allows me to expand and strengthen my current abilities as a leader. Second, I read constantly. Whether it is articles on Twitter, books checked out of the library, or audiobooks, I read and reflect on the words of others.

My abilities as a leader have not grown over the years; they were always there. However, my ability to lead has grown tremendously. I allow myself to be the type of leader that is vulnerable, reflective, and willing to do what is necessary to impact the students we serve. For any young administrator, I offer the following advice:

- **Read**. The most important activity you can embark upon as a leader is to consistently challenge and reflect upon your beliefs and your practice. I could recommend hundreds of books; however, I suggest you browse various leadership titles and read what captures your interest. (This book is a great start!)
- **Embrace what you do not know**. Do not be concerned about how this will affect the perception of your leadership. This perception will only change through your daily actions and decisions. Whenever you are challenged with making a difficult decision, seek the guidance of those you lead, determine what is best for students, and then decide.
- **Have fun**. Being a leader in education can be extremely challenging. You are in charge of various moving parts and do not have the luxury of unilateral control. Without finding balance and embracing the fun side of your work, your days of being a leader will be limited. Be sure to incorporate fun into every day.

Everyone is a leader, but it is important to find out what type of leader you are. This cannot be accomplished without being reflective and transparent about your growth. Whether in your first year as a principal or nearing retirement, you should always strive to grow. The moment when you no longer seek growth is the point when you need to re-evaluate your passion for education.

Adam Brown, Ed.D., is a principal in Virginia. His research and writings have focused on the motivation and burnout of novice and veteran teachers, reaching "at risk" students, and working with those who have experienced trauma. Connect with Adam Brown on Twitter: @AdamBrownEDU.

Fostering Leadership at
Lambert High School

Gary Davison

A cool, brisk October morning wakes the sleepy neighborhoods in Forsyth County, Georgia. As staff, students, and teachers arrive, a young man says, "Hey, are you guys always this happy?" "You bet!" I say as I attend to morning duty. Three thousand students arrive every morning and each is greeted with a smile and a warm start to the day. This short exchange is the cornerstone of the culture at Lambert High School. Being attentive and responsive to the students and staff at Lambert is the hallmark of our interactions.

Lambert High School—with 3,058 students and 186 teachers—is one of five high schools in Forsyth county. Many of the staff have come from outside of the state, including Hawaii, California, New York, Indiana, Florida, Missouri, Alabama, Wisconsin, Michigan, and Connecticut, as well as from Forsyth County itself. Experience ranges from first-year teachers to veterans with 30 years' experience. This demographic could easily represent any school in the United States. What sets this school apart from others primarily is a feeling of shared leadership among the staff. "Leveled" leadership means that all members of our organization are given equal abilities to share and develop together. The typical top-down hierarchy that is the norm in many schools is used here only in extreme times. When planning for and reflecting on events, programs, and areas of student interest, leveled leadership allows for interaction among students, staff, and community, giving weight to the opinions of all.

Leadership is shared at Lambert. Teachers are not only encouraged to take on leadership roles, but are expected to. The leadership team is primarily responsible for working on the school improvement plan, the staff development plan, day-to-day operational issues, school-wide events, and the participation and leadership of their respective departments. Within that structure, they train in facilitation and conflict resolution strategies to allow full participation in team meetings where we do common assessments, share consistent planning, work on curricular maps, and discuss issues relevant to the "Trinity" at Lambert: curriculum, instruction, and assessment.

One of my primary responsibilities as principal is to grow leaders. I am aware that my administrative team and teacher leadership will directly translate into top-notch instruction and collegiality, thus leading to an atmosphere of high expectations and quality instruction. The legacy of quality and caring is evident on the faces of our staff and students. They work hard every day to ensure that students receive the very best, making instructional and managerial decisions aligned with our mission of meeting community needs. Our constant adherence to the inclusion of all members allows for the continual growth of the leaders. We seek the participation of all members ... not just the happy ones. Leveled leadership means being prepared to navigate conflict and opposition to lead the team to a stronger resolution—this is a real skill. My job is to show this in my own leadership and teach my team to be adept at this skill. As these leaders grow, their abilities enable them to achieve higher leadership goals. To date, an amazing 19 leaders have come from our school to become building principals or superintendents.

At Lambert this year we are facing a tremendous obstacle. We are in the midst of a contentious redistricting effort within the school system, with many families being asked to rezone to another high school, accompanied with a changing staff dynamic. While change is difficult for all involved, we are facing this challenge as an opportunity to lead in an intentionality-positive, leveled approach.

Our advice? Make intentional efforts to be positive with students, staff, and the community. Apathy is the enemy of a positive, caring culture. Fight negativism with the most effective means possible—leadership. Being a thoughtful leader means taking the time to develop these skills in others, ensuring your success as an organization and their success as future leaders. After all, isn't that what we are charged with?

Dr. Gary Davison has been a school administrator for 21 years at multiple levels in two different states. In that time, he has focused on developing leadership skills among staff. He is currently the Principal of Lambert High School in Forsyth County, Georgia. He has spoken at many conferences, including the Association for Supervision and Curriculum Development (ASCD) and the Tim Elmore Leadership Conference. Gary earned his Ph.D. at the University of Georgia with many great colleagues who were instrumental in developing his leadership. In his time as a principal, he has mentored over 19 colleagues who became principals or associate superintendents. He works to create mechanisms, opportunities, and feedback strategies to aid all staff to effortlessly exhibit their best leadership attributes. Dr. Davison may be reached at gdavison@forsyth.k12.ga.us.

The Trust Factor

Nicholas Henkle

I clearly remember the phone call offering me my first principalship—the feeling of absolute elation, followed immediately by the overwhelming weight of responsibility. I knew enough to know that I was not ready, but I remained calm. "After all," I thought to myself, "is any new principal ever really ready to lead a school?"

I quickly discovered that I had much to learn. I was a 26 year-old with an idealist's mindset. My limited experience would be offset by my enthusiasm, knowledge, and ability to lead others, inspiring the team and propelling the school to new heights. In hindsight, I am sure my zealous approach in those first years was more irritating than inspiring.

I came in with a foolproof entry plan, or so I thought. The plan was designed to ask the typical questions and then step back and listen. Two ears and one mouth, right? "What can I learn from the previous principal? What are the school's deficiencies? Who are the key leaders in the school? What are the priorities? What does the data say about student attainment and student growth?" My plan consisted of checking these boxes and moving on. In doing so, I rushed through each question without ever considering the process or the response.

What is worse, I started looking to become a problem-solver rather than a relationship-builder or a strengths-finder. I took satisfaction in coming into a difficult situation where I could make an immediate impact. I picked the low-hanging fruit. By identifying needs and providing a quick remedy to the problem, I thought of myself as a bonafide leader. However, this made everyone happy but me. Doing the "principal's job" by managing the school and extinguishing fires meant driving myself towards burnout. Moreover, while I identified numerous capable leaders within the school who could support my growth, I did not have the credibility or comfort level to ask them to come by my side.

Fortunately, the team was mature enough to look beyond my inexperience and recognize my strengths. Not only did they provide grace in my weakness, but they also helped me develop into someone who now understands authentic leadership amounts to one thing: *trust*. Trust is earned only in the authentic development of a personal relationship with another human being. These incredible people took the time to know *me*—not just my "philosophy of education." They asked about my family, my interests, and my beliefs. Over time, I learned each person's strengths and interests, and we developed mutual respect and genuine concern for one another. Moreover, when we made promises to one another, we kept them. We all put in the work every single day, taking pride in our school and what we could achieve together.

Despite my shortcomings in those first two years, our team made a tremendous impact on student learning—and on my learning as well. It was all about trust. Rather than burning out, I found I was energized. I learned that *authentic leadership is not positional*. Yes, my assignment as principal provided me with authority and additional responsibility, but the title did not make me a genuine leader. While I merely talked about what it meant to lead, this team was demonstrating true leadership.

Through this experience, I rejected the idea of a fixed mindset. To be successful I knew that we must continue to grow. Over the next six years, I worked to develop trust with every student, every educator, every parent, and every stakeholder in that school district. This trust developed slowly and intentionally and has become the cornerstone of my leadership.

Now, ten years later, I am honored to serve as superintendent in a remarkable school district in a southwest suburb of Chicago. What I learned from my experience has helped me in this role. Trust is saying what you mean and meaning what you say. Trust is knowing your team and caring for their well-being. Trust is putting the needs of others ahead of your own. Trust is showing up, putting in the work, and getting better each day. If you want to be a leader, build trust and never forget that trust is a prerequisite to credibility.

Sometimes, we "don't know what we don't know." Assessing your own "trust factor" by speaking with a colleague you trust and asking for their honest feedback. More importantly, prepare your heart and mind to receive that feedback. We may do things to enhance or diminish trust in each other's eyes, so reassess regularly. *Trust me*; you'll be glad you did!

Nicholas Henkle, Ed.D., is the Superintendent of Channahon School District 17, a suburban PK–8 School District located approximately 45 miles southwest of Chicago, Illinois. Nick received his doctoral degree at Illinois State University in Normal, Illinois. His interests include leadership, future-ready schools/innovation, personalization, and culturally responsive teaching. Nick is a co-founder of the Illinois Association of Christian Administrators (ILACA). He is an active member of the Illinois Association of School Administrators (IASA), the American Association of School Administrators (AASA), the Suburban School Superintendents' Association (SSA), and the Rotary Club.

The Least Among Us Can Lead

Frank Gaines

Twenty-seven years in public education as a teacher, coach, assistant principal, and principal at eleven public and charter middle and high schools has allowed me to influence the lives of 10,000+ students so far. Many consider these schools disenfranchised, but I don't; these are "neighborhood schools" that provide students with their best hope for opportunity. If not the school, then who?

Coaches will tell you that they do it for the kids, but the empowerment, admiration, and respect that goes with coaching also feeds their egos. As a coach, I also felt this. Administrators are simply coaches who take themselves seriously—maybe too seriously—and who are expected to win. The best of us learn, however, from those we serve, not those to whom we report. In the communities I've served, winning is not measured as it is in affluent communities. Schools offer one thing—opportunity—but opportunities differ depending on the resources available.

My schools are urban/suburban hybrids that I call semi-urban. They are not dilapidated, crumbling, or under-resourced for all students. Nevertheless, there are disparities in the "opportunities" afforded to students based on socioeconomics. In spite of the degrees I've earned, the laboratory of my life will always be the urban high school. My Ph.D. program was simply a forum for me to reflect, organize, cultivate, and validate the lessons I learned there.

Despite any disparities, however, I have seen that the least among us can lead, teach, and inspire. A young man (let's call him Alexander) came to my attention because he was alleged to be a petty thief. Alexander was one of 2,500 students I supervised over a five-year period at this particular high school. In our initial encounters, I did not "convict" Alexander as a petty "thief"; instead, I listened to him and tried to guide him positively. I would later learn that although these encounters weren't noteworthy for me, they were for Alexander, and they would one day have significance for many at the school.

As an African-American male and a former math teacher with a Ph.D., I was the exception as an administrator. My focus was to direct juniors and seniors to attend college. As a high school sophomore, Alexander had not garnered any substantive focus from me yet, except for discipline. As my departure from the school became imminent, however, students who identified with me were displeased, but Alexander was traumatized. One day, he stopped me in the hallway, ushered me into my office, sat me down, and announced that I could not leave the school. Who would listen to Black students like him as I always had? He said I listened, respected them, and wouldn't judge them, even when I knew they were lying to my face. He made me realize something I spoke about, practiced, and preached, but had never reflected upon—the power of letting go of any negative experiences with students and letting the next day be new. We're the adults; we have the education, background, and world experience, but we are quick to judge disenfranchised students without considering their perspectives.

Alexander's proposed response to my departure was to protest and disrupt school. In his mind, school could not continue without me because Black students would lose their voice. I advised him to channel his energy positively by having a discussion with the principal instead. He wanted me to be part of that meeting, but I told him I was moving on and this was his story, not mine. I wanted Alexander to reach his turning point, his defining moment, and he did. He sought that audience with the principal, who agreed to a forum to discuss my replacement and to improve staff demographics, which at the time were a 15% minority serving a 55% minority student population.

The next year, faculty and staff demographics did change in favor of students of color, in part because of Alexander's dialog with the principal. He furthered his cause by distinguishing himself as a potential student ambassador for the local NAACP. Alexander started out as perhaps one of the least among my students because I didn't see him as a spiritual, emotional, or intellectual force to champion change in the school or the community. My focus had been on the middle 50% of students ignored by the American high school system in favor of the top 25%, who are disproportionately white. But I'd done the same thing within that demographic by marginalizing Alexander; he too was part of my middle 50%.

Alexander continued to mature, but has since run into trouble, causing me to return to my former school to continue my work with Alexander and to overcome one of my regrets in education—the pain of leaving behind the students who hope that we will not abandon them, which is the norm in their daily lives. Alexander led, taught, and inspired me, the principal, and many others, showing us all that the least among us can lead.

Dr. Frank Gaines is the principal of an alternative charter high school that uses a blended learning model. His public education experience includes two years as a charter high school principal, 14 years as a middle and high school assistant principal, and 11 years as a middle and high school mathematics teacher. Dr. Gaines holds a Ph.D. in School Leadership. He is an advocate for student self-sufficiency and maintains a professional, lifelong commitment to correcting the inequitable distribution of educational, social, political, and economic opportunities for students facing challenges.

We Are Stronger Together

Trisha Clement-Montgomery

As I remember it, lessons on leadership were always part of my education, usually examples of women and men from different ethnic backgrounds, socioeconomic status, and sexual orientation who achieved greatness. As a result, before entering the workforce I defined leadership as an individual effort. Most of my friends too would define leadership the same way: the heroic efforts of one individual possessing the ability to inspire and motivate others. One model I don't recall learning about was "collaborative leadership." Maybe I wasn't paying attention or perhaps I missed that class about the collective efforts of a group of people working together to achieve a common goal, but if I had learned that lesson early on, I could have saved a ton of time when I entered a career in higher education.

My first job after receiving my bachelor's degree was as a college counselor in New York City. I had a caseload of 345 high school students, and my job was to help them make informed decisions about their college careers. I worked with students, parents, and postsecondary faculty and staff to ensure that students would at least consider a college degree as one of their goals after high school. In many respects, I was successful; many of my students went to either college, community college, or technical school. But many of them returned home for the holiday break in December and decided not to go back, each for different reasons. Some couldn't afford it; others felt like they didn't belong. Regardless of the reasoning, it was still heartbreaking for me. I knew that a college degree would change their lives just as it had changed mine. After a few years of watching countless students return from college never to go back, I decided to make a career change. I not only wanted to get students into college, I wanted help keep them there.

Eventually I switched to a career in higher education and learned that they too (administrators and faculty) were all interested in increasing retention rates in postsecondary institutions. I was part of countless meetings focusing on how we as an institution could provide students with a holistic, well-rounded education including a curricular and co-curricular educational experience to prepare our students to be world "leaders." As I sat in on these discussions for several years, and later researched this topic in my doctoral program, I realized that one person is not going to move that retention needle. Individual leadership will not motivate a cohort of students to persist, complete their degree, and become lifelong learners and change agents.

Instead, I have learned that it takes collective wisdom and the abilities of several leaders to address the needs of undergraduate students. Collaborative leadership means that leadership, power, and decision making is distributed amongst a group of individuals working to achieve a common goal. Typically I need the help of my colleagues in advising, financial aid, students affairs, faculty, undergraduate research, and high-level administration. However, postsecondary institutions are not structured to embrace collaborative leadership effectively. Departmental silos, scarce resources, and budget cuts hinder our ability to work together. The more I learn about collaborative leadership, the more I suspect that it may have been excluded from lessons on leadership because of its complexity. What does collaborative leadership look like? Who coordinates the group? How do you achieve collaborative leadership with individuals with different credentials, experiences, power differentials, and so on? These are all tricky questions that have no definitive answers. I am not sure they could even be properly addressed in a textbook, let alone facilitated in a postsecondary environment.

Yet it may provide the key to what leadership in higher education is missing. The more I learn about collaborative leadership in working for the student experience, the more I learn how difficult it is to do well. Perhaps leadership really is meant to be an individual pursuit, or so I think on the most difficult days. Not only do I really believe that leadership should be tackled collaboratively, I also believe that administrators, teachers, and mentors should model collaborative leadership for our students. Do they understand the value of working with individuals with different talents? Do they respect the contributions of others or do they believe they are responsible for handling it all? Imagine the amount of time we could all save if collaborative leadership was part of the curriculum after all.

Trisha Clement-Montgomery *has spent the past 15 years working to create environments that promote undergraduate student success. She has seen first-hand the benefits of collaborative leadership, particularly between student affairs and academic units. She currently oversees 13 Living Learning programs at the University of Kentucky, striving to transform the undergraduate learning environment with the aid of all stakeholders. Clement-Montgomery may be reached via email at tclem224@gmail.com.*

"I'm a Dog. I Ate It."
What if Everything Needs to Change?

Dennis Darling

While working as a consultant in the Yukon Department of Education after a 30-year career as a teacher and administrator, I accepted a four-month temporary principalship in Teslin, a small community on the Alaska Highway, two hours outside of Whitehorse. Teslin's school population, prekindergarten to grade 9, is almost entirely Indigenous in its composition. Most students and their families are citizens of the Teslin Tlingit Council First Nation, a self-governing First Nation with a guaranteed partnership with the Yukon government in the operation of the school.

The day before school started, I received a phone call from the janitor informing me that almost all of the school's windows had been broken, but that he was going to work as long as necessary to ensure that school could begin on time. I walked into a very dark building the next morning, windows covered with plywood, but all the broken glass swept away.

The physical state of the building turned out to be the least of its problems. There seemed, after the initial welcoming assembly, to be a lack of order or mutual respect. There were students shouting in the hallways, and adults shouting back. At one point, a chair flew down the main hallway, propelled by a very angry young student. I told the superintendent that I had seen all of these behaviours before in other schools, but never on the first day. The school was in crisis.

The day's highlight was the fourth-grade student crawling down the hallway towards me, making barking and growling noises, followed closely by an obviously upset teacher. I intervened, suggesting that the teacher return to the classroom to look after the students there while I took care of the hallway situation. I asked the student to accompany me to the office; I walked away, and he crawled after me. I asked him what was going on. He told me that he had been sent to the office with a note from his teacher. I asked him where the note was, and he gave me a look that suggested I was not the smartest principal he had ever met. "I'm a dog. I ate it," he said. I had to turn away to cover my laughter.

A middle grade teacher found me at recess to ask when I was going to open the detention room. I asked, "What's that?" and she said that the principal stayed in the library at recess with students who had been given detentions by their teachers. I asked what they would do in the library with that time, and the teacher replied that they usually wrote lines. I asked how long they had been trying this system, and the teacher replied, "Years." Luckily she was able to appreciate my humour when I drew her attention to the disorder in the hallways and asked, "Would you say it has been working well?" I told her we would need to try another way.

At assembly the next day, I announced to the student body that there would be no more recess detentions, as they needed their break. I also told them that I was encouraging their teachers to give them extra time after school to help them get to know each other better, and to make daily reports to parents about how well their children were doing.

One Saturday early in September, I had the honour of attending a potlatch, invited by our school's First Nation education support worker, a member of the sponsoring clan. The experience gave me tremendous insight into what was happening, or not happening, at the school. I reported at the next staff meeting that I had been in a hall with all of our students and their families, and that I had seen no disrespect or inappropriate behaviour. Our students were able to sit for hours listening to speeches by their elders. I suggested that we had no real connection with our kids; the school was not real in the eyes of the students because we were not their family. We would direct our efforts towards building those connections and relationships. Our goal would be to become part of our students' family.

As a school team, we moved from a system of punishment to a system of restorative practices that preserved the dignity of all and led to real changes in attitude and behaviour. We also made academic assessment a priority, ensuring that every student was learning what he or she needed to learn, and we increased opportunities for after-school activities. We brought Indigenous ways of celebration and ceremony into our daily routine, along with the use of the Tlingit language, and, yes, the school changed.

I ended my career in Teslin School, retiring after six years of tremendously rewarding work with my "extended family." At the end of the year, the staff and students presented me with a ceremonial blanket, decorated with student art. Prominently displayed was a square painted by my now graduating student, which read "I'm a dog. I ate it."

Dennis Darling completed a 40-year career in northern Canada, teaching high school sciences, elementary classrooms, special education, counseling, and French. He also worked as an educational consultant for the Yukon Department of Education, as a school principal, and as an education manager for the Teslin Tlingit Council First Nation. He was nominated as one of Canada's Outstanding Principals in 2012 for leading his staff to create positive change for an Indigenous school in the Yukon Territory. A letter of commendation from a parent states that Dennis is known for his passionate support of students and his "quiet warrior ways." Dennis is interested in helping others learn more about the relationship-building process that leads to school achievement. He can be reached at dennisdarling2014@gmail.com.

Movin' and Groovin'

Charles Williams

Education is the key that unlocks many doors ... I relied on this guiding principle growing up, and it has become my mantra. Without the education I received at various colleges, I would not be able to influence the teachers and students I do today. Oddly enough, it was right after I earned my doctorate degree that I faced my greatest challenge. I've now marked my seventeenth year in education, my eighth as an administrator, and it has been a roller coaster ride with opportunities to keep movin' and groovin' at several schools. From elementary to college, Title I to economically-advantaged, graduate assistant to administrator, and from New York to the Florida Keys. No matter where I landed, the message I preached to students was "take hold of your education," and "you are responsible for your learning." I also share with young people the importance of resiliency.

Now that I've been an administrator for eight years, I've learned some very important lessons along the way. Some I garnered from district administrators, other educators, parents, community members, pastors, but the best came—and still comes—from the students. Moreover, many would have quit the world of education, and the business of mentoring young folks, after a first year of teaching like the one I experienced. How I made it through teaching at two different schools, with multiple preps, and multiple classroom management issues, I cannot tell you. Well actually, I do remember; I had the best mentor in the universe, who always told me, "Whatever you do, do it for the kids." This teacher was about to retire, but chose to keep it movin' and groovin' when he certainly could of packed it in that year.

Realistically, looking back, it was the students who kept me from quitting. Every day they taught me resiliency, the need to build relationships, and the need to set goals. I took those lessons with me, and those propelled me into administration. The road has not been easy, and even after my administrator told me, "You should think about something else besides education," I have stayed the course ever since. Subsequently, those words have motivated me to help faculty, staff, and students to reach their goals and strive for excellence. It is amazing the things that will provoke us to develop laser-like focus, and when it comes to the students I work with now, they deserve, and get my best.

Movin' and groovin' is more than a saying or even a song, it is a lifestyle. It signifies perpetual motion, activation, problem solving, building relationships and resiliency, along with humble servitude. It is paramount that, as educators, we take on this mindset daily and find the passion to fuel it. Many people throughout my life have told me that I could not do something I knew I could. Most of you reading this know exactly what I am talking about.

Specifically, my current administrative assignment came with loads of advice from a variety of educators. The majority gave me advice on how to survive at a "tough" school, and some said, "You should try to go somewhere else…" which really means they didn't think I would last. The best advice, though, was still that of my old mentor: "Whatever you do, do it for the kids." It didn't take long to realize that the students needed my guidance just as much as the faculty and staff did. This was their second year as an F-rated school, and, in the state of Florida, that means many different people get to tell you what to do, even if it is not "what is best for the students." This was the first F school I had worked at. Prior to this assignment, I helped a high school rise from a D to a B, and a middle school from a C to a B. Building relationships with the faculty, staff, students, and community was at the forefront of my efforts, so everyone expected an increase in student achievement. Truth be told, it felt a lot like two jobs: running the school *and* catering to the higher-ups, who were pacified when we implemented anything new … as if we were an experimental school. The basic approach was "doing things with the students' interests in mind," such as classroom visits to talk to students and see their work, detailed feedback to teachers to help them sharpen their instructional skills, and celebrations that highlighted teachers, staff, and students who were constantly striving for excellence.

The best advice I can give anyone in the field of education—or about to join the field—is simple: "Whatever you do, do it for the kids." When you base your decisions on your students, it speaks volumes and it pays big dividends in the end. My goal is to continue to prepare more and more students for college, career, and to be productive citizens in an ever-changing world. The only way to accomplish that ... keep it movin' and groovin'!

Charles Williams Jr., Ed.D., is Assistant Principal for Lake County Schools, Florida. His research and teaching interests include educational and instructional leadership, closing the achievement gaps, the impact of scheduling on high school students, and music theory and composition. His motivation is his faith, his wife Betsy, and his three daughters Elyn, Emma, and Ella. More information available at https://www.lake.k12.fl.us/Page/26751.

The Highly Expectant School Leader

Arthurlyn Morgan

A lthough the pressure of high-stakes testing is rigorous, student achievement is still the primary focus of school. The time I spent as a teacher afforded me the opportunity to work under three amazing school leaders. Each one was unique, yet each worked diligently towards ensuring their individual campuses reflected a culture of high expectations for students as well as teachers. Whether your role is that of a principal or teacher, others' expectations can influence how you perform. Shared beliefs, coupled with behaviors aligned to those shared beliefs, makes achievement more attainable.

Who is responsible for establishing high expectations? And how does one foster a culture where high expectations are the norm? One might say that establishing high expectations of students starts with the teacher. Others may argue that parents are the primary establishers of high expectations for their children. Over the course of my journey as an educator, and now campus leader, I have begun to view setting high expectations as a shared responsibility for campus leaders and classroom teachers. I am hesitant to include parents; however, I do believe that having a supportive family network produces better outcomes for students.

As a teacher, I put a tremendous amount of work into planning and preparing engaging lessons for my students. I learned that the work of a classroom teacher went beyond a Monday to Friday workweek. Most of my teaching experience was at large in schools located in high poverty areas; however, my students' socioeconomic status did not determine what I believed about them or alter my teaching behaviors.

I expected each of them to achieve to their maximum potential. As a school community, we set the expectations that learning was essential and our classroom practices aligned with what we said we believed about our students and their success. The culture we established as a campus was to do all that we could for our students while we had them, as we knew many would leave our nurturing environment and return to somewhat hectic home lives. I often remember speaking with grandparents who were the primary caregivers of many of my students. The increase in grandparents taking on parental roles also caused me to take on an additional role. I was responsible for setting high expectations for students as well as standing in place of a parent when necessary. I continued this journey for approximately ten years.

For the next eight years after that, I no longer taught in a high poverty area; I was an assistant principal in a school that was more affluent. It was quite easy to establish a culture of high expectations, as most of our parents collectively shared the same beliefs. Additionally, we modeled behavior that aligned with our beliefs. After 23 years in education—and fifth so far as a campus principal—I continue to set high expectations for students, and expect teachers to do so as well.

Each year during the first week back to school, I meet with the entire staff to revise our policies and procedures, review our campus data, and revisit our vision. At the beginning of the 2017–2018 school year, I gave each staff member a salt shaker to represent our standards of excellence that we collaboratively developed with our students. Our goal was to keep our salt shakers in the center at all times. If anyone moved or attempted to move our salt shaker, we gently reminded them about our standards of excellence and the behaviors we modeled to produce the desired results.

As the world continues to evolve, teaching practices should evolve to ensure that students are learning. School leaders are instrumental in leading the change that fosters a culture of high expectations. Our behavior and practices must be clear and align with what we say we believe about our students. Before we can begin setting high expectations for students, we should honestly reflect on our internal beliefs about students and student achievement. Reflection is important for any leader, but in the case of school leaders who set high expectations, we must continuously reflect on *why* we do this every day. My hope is that your answer is student achievement. In order for that achievement to occur, we must ensure each of our campuses fosters a culture of high expectations, led by highly expectant school leaders.

Arthurlyn Morgan, *Ed.D., is an elementary school principal in North Texas. Her research and teaching interests include the role of spirituality in African-American female principals, the importance of work–life balance, and building positive campus cultures within constraints.*

Reach Out

Lisa Clarke

L eadership is often described as a lonely endeavor. Nowhere is this more accurate than in the private educational system. Nineteen years ago, I began my teaching career as the teaching principal of a private Christian school in a small rural town. Eagerly anticipating September and the arrival of my 16 students in grades 1–8, I diligently planned and organized my first year. I had communicated with the previous teacher, set up my classroom, and met with the other part-time teacher who would be working with me. In the arrogance of youth, I was sure I was prepared.

Later, as I reflected upon that first September, I realized the truth in the phrase "No plan survives contact with the enemy." While I would never consider my students or fellow staff members to be the enemy, my diligent planning did not prepare me for the obligations and complexities of being a teaching principal. I was definitely in over my head. Fortunately, my small Christian school was part of a larger network of schools across North America. Needing help, I reached out to a fellow principal in another city. She took me under her wing as I embarked on my teaching and ultimately my leadership career.

Throughout my leadership journey, I have done my best to honour her memory and legacy. Determined to give back to my profession and my fellow administrators, I sought out neighbouring principals to offer peer support and collaboration. While these informal communities of practice were helpful, additional opportunities to collaborate with other principals were needed. The fact that our schools were located so far apart proved problematic for collaboration. We needed to find creative ways to connect principals.

After several years of trying to utilize phone conferencing and face-to-face opportunities, a possible solution revealed itself through our online school. As the new principal, I was invited to a meeting held using videoconferencing software that allowed all the participants to see, speak, and share their screens. Finally, we had access to software that would provide a cost-effective way for principals to meet virtually. Technology shrunk the distance between the schools and enhanced our ability to work together. In addition to the virtual meetings, we had a site where principals could ask questions and share resources. While the online virtual meetings worked well, the sharing platform was a complete failure.

Unfortunately, not all the principals shared my enthusiasm for new ways to share ideas. While I was so excited to finally have an opportunity to share with other principals on a larger, more collaborative platform, they were not as willing to share. After posting a few websites and other resources, I waited for the others to post or respond. I waited one week. I waited two weeks. No one posted. After the third week, I experienced my first a small victory when one principal finally posted. Thrilled that someone else was starting to use the community, I quickly responded and encouraged the principal to keep posting. As the only two posting, it became clear that my collaboration plan wasn't working.

Disheartened, I decided to bring it up at the next face-to-face meeting. One of the principals admitted that he gave up trying to access the community because of his lack of technological knowledge. Another principal found searching the site difficult and was annoyed by all the notifications every time a post was made. In my zeal to reach out, I had not considered the needs of my fellow principals. I had set up the community for me and not for the group.

As leaders, we can have the greatest ideas and concepts but forget our target audience. This experience taught me how essential it is that we reach out to people in a way that is relevant and useful to them if we want them to participate. After listening to the needs and concerns of my fellow principals, we simplified our collaborative endeavours and the community began to grow. Today, more principals are reaching out to support each other. Our community of practice not only supports each other as leaders, but also in learning how to use technology to collaborate, share files, and exchange ideas. As we continue to work together, I have faith that this community will grow and build a knowledge and support network that will reach out to all the principals in our system.

Lisa Clarke, Ed.D., is an associate superintendent of the British Columbia Conference of Seventh-day Adventists. She has worked in the private education system for 19 years. During that time, she completed a Master's Degree in Curriculum and Instruction from LaSierra University (Riverside, California) and a Doctorate in Educational Leadership from Western University (London, Ontario). She has published two novel-study daily lesson guides for teachers and has presented at international private school conferences on education. Her passions include educational change, personalized learning, and technology.

Cultural Management

J Lail

I went to one of my teacher's classrooms for a walkthrough, as I am wont to do, not very long ago. She is a wonderful teacher—a model to others. I didn't get to see her leading a lesson that day, though. She had a student teacher who was leading a lesson. Knowing that one of our teachers would not be returning next year, I took this as a serendipitous opportunity to scout some new talent. The lesson went well; students were engaged in a rigorous task; the student teacher knew her content well; formative assessments used through and after the lesson proved that the students understood the material. I was impressed.

We offered the young woman an interview and it went extremely well. The committee loved her ideas and enthusiasm and we were taken by her professionalism and content knowledge. She got the job.

School resumed in August and, as always, we had our sights set on engaging students in learning. Within the first week of school, I began my informal walkthroughs. I always enjoy the honeymoon period with students getting to know teachers and vice-versa, everyone in new clothes with fresh supplies sitting quietly and attentively, listening to teachers talk about school expectations, the inevitable segue into content.

Within two weeks, I began my formal walkthroughs. I wanted to start with my new teachers so we could begin the work of honing their skills. I went to our newest teacher—the one who had impressed us so much in student teaching and the interview. Utter chaos! Students were talking over the teacher; the teacher was yelling and being ignored; desks were scattered around the room; students were using mobile devices for texting and various other non-related activities. Think of everything you would *not* want to see happening in a classroom … whatever just leapt to your mind was happening in that room.

I stepped in and helped her gain control of the classroom and stayed for the remainder of the period—not too difficult a task. Students tend to check their behaviors when a principal walks in. Students were quiet and devices were away, but they were clearly not engaged in the lesson and obviously had no interest in what my new teacher was saying. Luckily, her planning period was the next hour, so I stayed until after the students left and closed the door behind them—we needed to talk immediately … to debrief.

Through our conversation, we uncovered the issue. She didn't build the cultural foundation for learning in the first days of school because, quite frankly, she didn't know how. The current methods by which many pre-service students are learning about classroom management are, at best, misleading. Student teaching and collaborative student teaching practical experiences each have their merits, but learning how to establish a culture for learning and manage a classroom are not numbered among them. In both cases, student teachers are placed with seasoned veterans who possess excellent management skills and a wealth of content knowledge and strategies (as it should be). The problem then becomes that the student teacher never gets the chance to manage the room, whether alone or collaboratively, because the students know the expectations the mentor teacher has implemented on the first day. Student teachers are given a false sense of their own abilities in these instances because they aren't managing anything—they are experiencing a culture that has already been built, adhered to by all, and maintained with fidelity by a veteran teacher. The critical learning that student teachers need to take away from these experiences is the steps necessary in building such a culture, not the ideal they observe during clinical experience. The tragedy then becomes a new teacher will expect such a culture without proper preparation and planning.

When my new teacher stepped into her own classroom, she expected the kids to have the same desire to learn and drive to succeed she experienced while student teaching. She hadn't taken the time to begin to form relationships with students. She didn't set a cultural expectation from day one. Most importantly, she didn't have a principal who sat with her, and other new teachers, at the beginning of the year to put such a plan and model in place. Since that time, I have put in place a New Teacher Institute—a safe meeting place for administrators, veteran teachers, and new teachers to work together, supporting one another in creating and sustaining a positive classroom climate and culture.

As for my new teacher—she worked diligently for the rest of the year and tried to turn things around. She succeeded with a few, but had lost most of the students in those first crucial days of school, just as I, unfortunately, lost her.

*J **Lail** has worked diligently for nearly two decades to grow as an educator and a leader. Lail has studied at Northern Kentucky University, Xavier University, and the University of Kentucky, where he is pursuing doctoral studies in educational leadership. He takes pride in his personal academic accomplishments, but finds the support these endeavors have enabled him to give others in the field of education even more rewarding. Lail is optimistic for the field of education, not only as it is now, but also as it could be with a shared vision and dedicated leadership.*

The True Focus for
First-Year Principals

Kyle Lee and Jeremy Watts

B oth the successes and failures of that pressing first year as a principal remain freshly ingrained in memory. Many individuals enter the principalship feeling both prepared for and confused about how to do the job. Those formal Interstate School Leaders Licensure Consortium (ISLLC) standards, accompanied by state law and budgeting policies, probably summarize many principal preparation programs, but cannot fully prepare you for the actual role. After all, the principal's job is to ensure quality instruction is leading to student growth, stakeholder groups we serve are happy, and individuals are excited about learning.

Since many principal preparation programs emphasize instructional leadership, most new principals feel the need to start with instruction first. Although it is important to ensure quality instruction occurs in each classroom, it should not actually be a new principal's top priority. Effective principals participate in shaping a vision for academic success, creating a climate hospitable to education, cultivating leadership in others, improving instruction, and managing people, data, and processes to foster school improvement (Wallace Foundation, 2013). Although these practices serve as wonderful goals for all school leaders, new principals should not attempt all of them within their first year.

It is impossible for a first-year principal to successfully fulfill each of these functions at an effective level. Instead, early-career principals should focus on 1) the cultivation of a positive school culture and 2) the management of people, processes, and resources.

It is important for early-career principals to be aware of the role that school culture plays since it has the potential to influence all other factors related to learning. The concept of school culture may be perplexing to grasp, but its influence on what happens in school on a day-to-day basis is remarkable. Increasing awareness of school culture is one of the most important things you can do as a principal. A positive school culture is a predictor for both teacher retention and student achievement.

Principals must take steps to create a school culture that promotes collaborative leadership where school employees, including the principal, share personal values while remaining dedicated to improving the lives of the students they serve. Through promoting opportunities for personal and professional relationships among colleagues, you will positively influence your school culture. These connections between your colleagues are critical to overall success. But do not assume that they occur naturally—they must be nurtured.

Principals must be intentional about providing direct support to their teachers. Retaining quality teachers who effectively enhance student learning is one of the most important aspects of the job. Support means that the principal must encourage and display a positive attitude as a member of the team, specifically through nurturing personal relationships. School colleagues are like a family and work best together when they express concern for and share joy with one another.

New principals also cannot ignore their job as the organizational manager of people, processes, and resources. With principal preparation programs focusing on instructional leadership, however, it is easy to forget the other human resource responsibilities the principal must undertake. Hiring, evaluating, and supporting staff is actually crucial in serving students.

Principals are also profoundly responsible for ensuring that the school utilizes its resources effectively in order to meet the varying needs of the students it serves. This means that transparency in management is essential to allow teachers to focus on instruction. After all, instructional planning should drive how principals use their budgets. Teachers, staff, students, and parents deserve to understand how money and resources are utilized in the school, and how those decisions are made. Monitoring the effectiveness of how resource use influences student achievement, and making adjustments where necessary, completes this particular management circle.

Instructional leadership is indeed important to a successful school; however, new principals must place some intentional time and energy into the areas discussed above. Facilitating a positive school culture and managing people, processes, and resources responsibly means that new principals will begin to gain the trust and confidence of their teachers. And that is the real first step on the path of instructional change.

Reference

Wallace Foundation. (2013). *The school principal as leader: Guiding schools to better teaching and learning.* New York: The Wallace Foundation.

Kyle Lee, EdD, *serves as both the Academic Standards Coordinator and Principal Partnership Program Consultant at the Kentucky Department of Education. Prior to his current appointment, Dr. Lee served as a school principal in Frankfort, Kentucky. He also teaches part-time for the College of Education at the University of Kentucky. Dr. Lee's research agenda focuses on school leadership and teacher efficacy. Dr. Lee resides in Versailles, Kentucky, with his wife and four children.*

Jeremy Watts, PhD, *is the Division Chairman of Teacher Education in the School of Education at Bob Jones University, where he teaches undergraduate and graduate courses with a focus on literacy instruction for young children. His research agenda focuses on school leadership and teacher retention in rural school districts. He has taught elementary, middle, and high school students throughout Kentucky, West Virginia, and South Carolina, as well as served on school leadership. Dr. Watts resides in Greenville, South Carolina, with his wife and daughter.*

PART VIII

Journey's Beginning, Journey's End

Every leader experiences a unique career trajectory. Some careers follow a pre-determined plan while others have elements of serendipity. Do you remember the first, or next, day of your chosen career? Do you remember the first time a well-respected colleague, or even a relative stranger for that matter, approached you and asked whether you have considered leadership? The first time someone saw something in you that you did not see in yourself? Leaders experience multiple successes and disappointments over the course of a career. Not achieving promotion. Watching someone you have mentored climb to great heights. Mishandling a situation, getting knocked down, getting back up, dusting off, and learning from the set-back? As retirement approaches, the internal dialogue shifts to next life stage while still honoring a deep commitment to those individuals and communities who have placed their faith in your leadership. Close your eyes and imagine those conversations with someone who helped to make you a better person, a better leader. Leaders learn to lead from the front, the side, and from behind depending on contextually specific situations. The leadership journey never really ends, but it always leads to life's next journey.

Retirement vs. Revitalization

Chuck Reid

Board reports, community challenges, school closures, union issues, school visits, and ministry demands filled my working day while my mind focused on "freedom 55." After 33 years, I was finally free of timelines, uncontrollable demands, and small "p" and big "P" politics. I was finally living my retirement dream in a home on Lake Huron. "Mac," our beloved bulldog, and I could quietly walk the beach. Like me, our family companion was showing his age. We often joked that "Mac" needed to snooze through the day to be well rested for his evening sleep. Old "Mac" represented the welcome lifestyle towards which both my wife Suzanne and I thought we were evolving. Time would prove us wrong.

Like so many educators in Ontario, retirement came in stages. After leaving the school board, I moved into ministry and board contract work. Providing guest-speaking engagements at a few of our local universities also helped fill the time. Suzanne worked part-time as a special education instructor at a local university. The walks on the beach were not a disappointment. I am grateful that I was one of the few who were able to realize their dream. After three weeks, I came to realize that retirement was much more than an extended vacation. I began to feel guilty that I was not appreciating the life destination that we worked so hard to make a reality. Restlessness was constantly present. Contract work and volunteer work with the local Rotary Club was not filling the void. As the days passed into weeks, it became ever apparent that I needed a new challenge—one last project that I could invest in and feel a sense of accomplishment about.

In January 2012, I left the lake to visit our son in Toronto. Tobin is a graphic artist and at the time living a bohemian lifestyle. Staying in a hotel rather than sleeping on his spare mattress was my preferred choice. There was an international educational conference taking place in the city, so I booked a room where the conference was located. I believe Suzanne was happy just to get me out from underfoot for a couple of days. She certainly was shocked to receive my phone call the following Saturday evening when I made the pitch to move to Cairo for a one-year contract for 2012–2013. Part of the agreement was that Suzanne would be dusting off her secondary school principal's hat. She would lead the high school while I would become a founding school director. Suzanne agreed, with some reservations. We have now completed our sixth year on this project. I will never regret or forget this experience.

Arriving in Cairo was a revelation. The blanket of heat that met us was beyond what we had ever experienced in a Canadian summer. Once in the car, we were struck by the never-ending landscape of sand and rock. The desert is harsh, endless, and yet has unique beauty. The car ride to our apartment became the metaphor for what we would soon experience in our daily work. The traffic was unregulated. The five-lane highway was often jammed with cars six or seven abreast. Those who had SUVs would attempt to avoid the traffic jam by driving off the highway and navigating the desert before angling back into traffic. We inched past a cart with a man dressed in a brown work galabeya. He and his donkey were waiting patiently in the centre lane for the traffic to move. It was very evident we were no longer traveling down Ontario's highway 401.

The following day, we entered the school that quickly became our passion. The foyer was composed of marble floors and pillars. A large circular granite staircase rose three floors with the grandeur of an expensive hotel lobby. We soon came to understand that "show" was important in Egypt. The school employed well-educated staff as exemplified by our science department composed of medical doctors. Most teachers had completed a Master's degree in the subject they were teaching. A surprising number had trained in European or North American universities. Everyone was fluent in English and most spoke three languages. However, like the ride to our apartment, we soon discovered a very different work environment to what we were accustomed.

In a number of ways, the workplace we entered mirrored the social and political operations of the country. During our first staff meeting, we observed that communication was one way. We came to realize that staff compliance to the leader was absolute but demanded a great deal of supervision. For our employees, completing individual expectations was often more important than meeting system goals. This was primarily due to performance being measured by how well individual expectations were met rather than the organizational goals. In this organizational culture, good teachers met timelines, and had clean rooms and disciplined students. Increasing student performance, therefore, was not a measure of success.

Operationally this mindset often interfered with school improvement. For example, in the past when the photocopy centre ran out of paper, no one would inform purchasing. Purchasing would only order paper on fifteenth and last day of the month. If a lack of paper took place during exams, exam papers were not copied because there was no paper. Some teachers were fined for not getting their exams in on time while others worked around the timeline by hoarding paper. No one was at fault because everyone was following the expectations as outlined in their job description. This was a small example of the pervasive challenge we experienced. Building leadership capacity and focusing on common goals became the objective of our work. Radically changing the workplace culture became a necessary outcome.

Change began by creating school-wide interdisciplinary teams responsible for aspects of the school plan. Professional development support was secured by collaborating with Sir Wilfrid Laurier University's Faculty of Education in Canada. Staff were trained on how to use school data to make informed decisions. Staff also interacted in activities such as group work, jigsaws, and the five-minute consultant. These activities resulted in employees having increased collective ownership of the annual strategic plan. In addition, individuals gained greater understanding of how each person's work was connected. Weekly administrative meetings began by reaffirming term objectives. Agendas were built collaboratively, and actions were based on consensus. The leadership capacity throughout the school grew and individuals contributed to school-wide goals. Staff members continue to respect the boundaries of their individual job expectations but no longer at the expense of achieving common goals. An individual's impact in addressing system goals has become a predominate measure in staff performance reviews. Currently, if the photocopy centre runs out of paper, we order more. Staff will problem solve and work collaboratively to ensure schoolwork supports school goals. Shared ownership has been key in our improvement journey.

The cultural shift has begun but is still far from complete. Suzanne and I still need new learning, patience, and understanding. The key to successfully implementing change in our international school, we have learned, requires mutual understanding, joint ownership, and regularly monitoring expectations while being sensitive to local cultural mores. Our journey continues.

Chuck Reid is the Director of Dover American International School in Cairo, Egypt. He has been a passionate advocate for equity in education for the past 35 years. His first eight years in the profession were devoted to teaching in "core" schools with five of these years in special education classrooms. He spent nine years as an administrator in multicultural schools that suffered from the challenges of low socioeconomic status. During this time, he collaborated with local groups to help empower parents to support their children. As a Superintendent and Director of Education, he continued to advocate for the diverse community, establishing ESL, culture awareness, and academic programs of choice. In "retirement," he has followed his passion for supporting diverse populations in an international education setting.

From State to Profit Making

Tracy Lloyd

I have been in education for over 30 years, eighteen of those as a primary school principal. In 2016, I took up my first position as an elementary principal in a family-owned for-profit international school.

My first principalship was at a primary school with around 300 students; my next school had around 500 students. I led these two schools for eight and nine years respectively. The focus for me at both of these schools was to improve student achievement and develop the 'whole child'. During my time at both schools it was critical to help staff 'navel gaze' and see what their strengths and weaknesses might be, and to inquire into their teaching practice so that they would also improve. Therefore, it was very important to get the 'change process' correct. The process that I used was the 'Stewart and Prebble Model for School Development'.

These were not 'turn-around' schools, but had been coasting for a while, so expectations were not that high. We emphasised reviewing our 'culture' and 'climate', and to establishing our beliefs in 'teaching and learning'. Once this was clarified with all stakeholders, we were able to set a vision and strategic direction for the school. With at least 10% of funding going towards staff professional learning and development, which focused on 'whole school' involvement, we were able to share teaching practices and lift student achievement. This, however, does not happen in one year. It took three to five years to embed this new culture of a learning community. As a leader, I had the autonomy to drive the educational direction of these schools as I saw fit (using data) and I worked on encouraging the staff to have as much 'ownership' in the decision making and actions needed as possible, so that we could become an even better school. Over those 17 years in state schools, reports from the governing authorities (in this case the Education Review Office) were excellent.

In my first 'profit-making international' school, I stayed only 12 months. Most frustrating was that there appeared to be no autonomy for me as a leader and that the owner's decisions were based on financial matters, rather than on the educational needs of the students! My philosophies and beliefs were challenged day by day, and it slowly became apparent that this institution was not the right fit for me.

Making decisions that valued staff, kept good staff welfare, and created opportunities for staff ownership in the school's direction, including implementing schoolwide assessment practices and a common curriculum with relevant resources, was always being questioned. As for professional learning, that seemed very piecemeal; however, the whole elementary school was involved in a daylong International Baccalaureate workshop, which was excellent. Lifting student achievement is always at the top of any leader's list. This was a core belief in the staff and the school as well; however, without an investment in teacher support, staff really struggled. In my opinion, too many decisions were based on financial gain for the owners rather than educational gains for the staff and students.

So, what was the difference between the two state schools and the international school? Essentially what was abundant in the former and missing in the latter was the commitment to education as a public good. The businessperson invests in the school, but the state invests in the students and their teachers. The bottom line for the state could be measured in dollars but is more accurately measured in success, achievement, and competence.

My year at the international school was not lost, however, as I was able to take away some positive learnings:

- Staff want the best education for the students they teach
- Staff are professional, work hard, and collaborate no matter what type of school they teach in
- Students want to improve and achieve no matter what type of school they learn in

Working in a for-profit school with a single owner challenged my philosophies and beliefs, but the experience gave me a far greater appreciation for state-run systems of education. A system with one shareholder versus a system where we are all stakeholders … there's just no comparison really. In the end, I felt rather like Dorothy in the Emerald City—it looked all shiny and new from a distance, but when you arrive, you see it's all smoke and mirrors with an ordinary man behind the curtain pulling all the strings. For this state-raised boy turned principal, there really is no place like home.

Tracy Lloyd has spent over 30 years in primary school education, 17 years as principal in two New Zealand primary schools and one year in Europe. His teaching interests lie in the areas of enhancing culture and climate and promoting ownership to improve teaching and learning and lift student achievement.

Keep Going!

Doris Pfingstner

The year 2017 was a high-flying one for my school, the Modulare Mittelstufe Aspern. First, we were promoted as a "lighthouse school" by the national ministry of education—a school with outstanding performance in terms of innovation. A few months later, we received the MINT Award for our commitment to Mathematics, IT, and Science. Finally, my staff nominated me for an award for my supporting my team in varied ways. It had been a long and rocky path to this success, however, with moments of desperation and self-doubt along the way.

When I first came to my school as a principal, I thought I was prepared for the tough job. The reputation of my school was poor, violence amongst students was common, teachers were attacked verbally and sometimes even physically by students, vandalism showed throughout the school, and the popularity of the school was very low. I knew all this before I started, but what did surprise me was that my teachers weren't able to see the causes of the situation. They were fully convinced that they were victims of the system and that their supervisor had let them down. They found all sorts of explanations for the disaster—except their own part in it.

When I applied for the job, I had a clear vision of how my school should "feel": students spend nine hours or more in school every day, so they must feel welcome. On the other hand, my school should be achievement-oriented to prepare students for a successful life. Moreover, I felt the strong obligation to provide a good working atmosphere for my staff. What I found was none of that, but a team of teachers who couldn't see what was going wrong. So what could I do?

What I did was to do everything differently, leaving no stone unturned:

- Establish team structures for each grade and for each subject with clear responsibilities
- Introduce annual appraisals to review the performance of the year in progress, discuss goals for the following year, and examine how each teacher could contribute toward reaching these goals
- Establish a professional development plan to improve teaching skills
- Implement new communications structures with regular conferences, team meetings, a school development team, a PR team, and a school climate team
- Deal with "problem pupils" and their parents not as trouble makers, but rather find out the motives for their behaviour and make them feel welcome
- Convince the local authorities to give me the budget to renovate the building, to establish meeting areas for students, and to decorate the public spaces and classrooms
- Set up a culture where a complaint was no longer perceived as an outrageous criticism but instead a chance to discover blind spots in our organisation
- Proactively look for new teachers with outstanding qualifications and experience outside the education system
- Set up a coaching system for new teachers in order to facilitate their entry and train them in the way we work
- Cooperate with partners both inside and outside the educational sector to support our students
- Innovate as a team to create an attractive "product"—after two years of development, we launched the "Modulare Mittelstufe Aspern"—so that students can choose some of their subjects depending on their abilities and interests

This all seems great at the first glance, but how did my teachers react to all these changes? First, teachers do not like change, which causes uncertainty and worry. Moreover, they felt I wasn't happy with the way they worked. So, what did they do? They started revolting behind my back; the unions began interfering and questioning my new management style.

Believe me, these were lonely times, sitting in my office, doubting whether my vision would ever come true, feeling misunderstood and discouraged. But I got up the next day, went back to work, and got on with the work—despite the many setbacks. I encouraged and supported those teachers who worked professionally and confronted "problem teachers" who weren't doing their job properly. I made it clear that I expect a high level of professionalism from my teachers. After about four years, all those changes have started to show positive results. The school climate has changed, students are proud to attend our school, parents recommend our school to their friends, and my staff is, without a doubt, the most committed team of teachers in the world.

What did I learn in nine years of leadership? I realised that leadership follows the Gaussian distribution—it is all about the top 10% and the bottom 10%. The way I treated these two sections had a dramatic effect on the remaining 80%. They started to orient themselves towards the top teachers, to imitate their behaviour, and to share their values. *My* vision finally became *our* vision, so I encourage other leaders not to lose sight of *your* vision. Keep going!

Doris Pfingstner *is the school principal of "Modulare Mittelstufe Aspern" and a lecturer in school management and public relations for schools at the University College of Pedagogy in Vienna, Austria. She has degrees in Economics and Pedagogy and she has also worked in various marketing and project management positions for international companies.*

Taking the Road Less Travelled

Christopher Bezzina

I would like to share with you the leadership that has made a difference to me as a person. It is not an easy journey. On the contrary, it has been, is, and will remain a challenging one. It is one that focuses on values, character, formation, presence, and connections. It is one that celebrates different views, lifts up voices, and engages people. I have always tried to, as they say, walk the talk, to live a life based on a set of values that determine my thoughts and practices.

This perspective presents us with continuous new challenges given that we are living in an uncertain, turbulent world, a world where issues of corruption, injustice, migration, poverty, acts of terrorism, and more affect many communities, many nations. As we witness such events, they may make us feel helpless, vulnerable, or else we remain detached, oblivious of the realities that surround us. Too many of the conversations we engage in about such events are reductionist or rhetorical in nature. We should be challenging the dynamics and the language used of much educational/social discourse. We are being called to question what we took for granted, to question the unquestionable, to take a stand, to deliberate and engage with issues that affect us and future generations.

To complicate matters further, we can all notice a pattern in modern societies, a pattern in my life. I am packing too much into one day; running after meetings, schedules, events. A life dictated by emails and social media. A certain restlessness, unease permeates our lives. We seem to have less time to focus on our needs, those of our family, our community/society. We need to ask ourselves: Is this really our calling? Is this really us? What sort of life are we living? Are we leaving an impact on others, and if so, what type of impact?

I do believe that in the midst of all this we can lose sight of our calling, for to lead, at whatever level, is not a job, but a journey of giving for a greater cause. I encourage you to occasionally stop and reflect and engage with the question "Who am I?" Is your immediate response to define yourself by your official title, your role, specific characteristics, affiliation, beliefs, achievements, titles? Are you the labels that others have attached to you? What parts combine to be you? Who do you see when you observe yourself?

If you do not know yourself, how can you be true to self? "When one is out of touch with oneself, one cannot touch others," argues Anne Morrow Lindbergh. Being needs to precede doing. Often this does not happen, as we are focused on getting things done. We are more task-oriented than people-oriented.

This is why values are cardinal to the life we lead. The questions we need to ask ourselves are these: "What are the values we espouse? What are the values our organisation promotes? How are these being manifested?" My contention is that leaders and organisations need to establish an appropriate set of values which are then externalised in our attitudes and which attitudes then determine the actions we take. This is where our leadership—at whatever level we are working in—has to be nurtured, for everyone has a leadership role to play.

This belief very much determines the way I view and manifest leadership, that of positive leadership. Positive leadership (PL) is based on positive psychology. PL is seen as a choice, an act of the mind and the will. It is a continual commitment that individuals make to themselves, repeatedly; one that necessitates that organisations, and those within the organisation, have values, ideals, standards and integrity. Evidence shows that positivity makes a difference. If you are a leader, you have a direct effect on the lives of others at a surprisingly powerful level. We all have a direct effect on others—in both positive and/or negative ways. I am sure that we can all relate to the positive side of transformational or distributed forms of leadership. PL builds on what is already working well. It appreciates people for their unique contributions. It is trusting people so that they will engage in different ways. It means acknowledging good things and actions. It includes leadership that enables, that connects with people, that expresses kindness, being authentic and honest, offering a positive outlook/perspective to life.

Therefore, it is important to reflect on what we convey to colleagues, co-workers, or clients. Confidence? Arrogance? Humility? Enthusiasm? Authenticity? Does everyone like what they get from you? For as Marcella Bremer asks, "Dare we be authentic?" For being fully human includes doubts and indecision, learning, making mistakes, which lead to insecurities; it includes shame, fear, anger, grief, guilt, discouragement... Being authentic inspires, encourages, expresses kindness, support, optimism. How do we approach people, our work? What are the challenges that affect our lives?

At the end of the day, what is it that really matters? In my opinion, to quote a line from the play *War Horse*, ultimately we are "*only remembered for what we have done.*" Hence, our acts, our deeds will live beyond our stay in any group/organisation/community. Developing authenticity is work we must do ourselves in communion with others. We can choose our legacy.

We need to ensure that we reframe our current views about the things that matter—the way we look at our colleagues, at decision making, at what determines our actions, at the things that happen but we are ignoring. We need to create more opportunities for people to share their views and opinions about things. This leads to the second fundamental issue in reframing views, and that is character formation.

In the schools I work with, I emphasise character building. We need to nurture communities where learning takes place as a natural way of life, where we challenge issues that are relevant to our vision, questions that engage us passionately, that challenge us. As the leadership expert, speaker, and author John Maxwell points out, "Good character is not given to us. We have to build it piece by piece—by thought, choice, courage and determination. This will only be accomplished with a disciplined lifestyle." This will help us to develop communities of practice in the true sense of the term where thoughts, emotions, and behaviour are interlinked. This is the leadership that must take us forward, and we have to make sure that we start with our children when they are young.

We need to review our practices in this domain. What are we doing to engage our students in the world around them? Are students engaged in any community work? And, what happens once they join the workforce? Are such engagements encouraged? Do we take on the example of some who are constantly looking for ways to support the community, to be of service to others? We need to be not only thinkers and orators, but also doers.

I know that I have raised quite a number of questions and one can raise even more. My intention has not been to dissuade you from engaging with leadership, but to help you realise how interlinked the leader is with the person within you and the leadership acts that follow. Indeed, my intention has been to challenge you to take the road less travelled.

I leave you with the words of Paul Wellstone for you to mull over: "Never separate the life you lead from the words you speak."

Christopher Bezzina is a professor in the Department of Leadership for Learning and Innovation, Faculty of Education, University of Malta, and in the Department of Education, Uppsala University, Sweden. His research and teaching interests include leadership, the professional development and learning of teachers and school leaders, and turning schools into professional learning communities. He can be reached at christopher.bezzina@um.edu.mt.

Policy, Procedure, Protocol, and the Three Percent Principle

John Forbeck

Throughout almost four decades in various roles in education, I've come to understand the significance and importance of policy, procedure, protocol, and knowing when to use the three percent principle in decision-making. For consistency within a large, complex organization, successful leaders must know these three tools:

1. **Policy**: clear, concise statements of organizational commitments and direction
2. **Procedure**: rules and directives with respect to the administrative and operational functions to put policy into action
3. **Protocol**: a formal agreement between two or more parties on a common response to specified issues, events, or circumstances

It is impossible to create a policy, procedure, or protocol for every possible scenario. To address the gap, there's the "three percent principle." Simply stated, in three percent of situations, policies, procedures, and protocols can't help you at all.

One grade 7 student I was suspending asked me, "What gives you the power to suspend?" Without hesitation, I showed her the Ontario Education Act, a large document filled with regulations governing education in the province. Weeks later, when I needed to refer to my copy of the Education Act, I couldn't find it. On a hunch, I called the girl's mother who confirmed that my copy was in her daughter's bedroom. The discipline policy outlines the potential consequences for theft, however, in this case what would the most appropriate consequence be? Her ingenuity and bravado were clearly beyond the reach of policy. Instead of suspending her again, we had a long chat.

Later in my career as a Superintendent of Human Resources, a staff member and union leader appealed to me to extend an employee's paid sick leave. In this case, the staff member needed just a bit more time to heal. Months before, she had arrived home from work one day to find her child had committed suicide in the backyard. Clearly, the three percent principle could apply here. A compassionate solution outside of the policy, procedure, and protocol was required.

While serving at an inner-city school, I was shown some graffiti written by a student on the underside of a built-in bookcase shelf. The inscription said "Mr. K–greatest teacher ever." This often-challenging student artist had even signed and dated it. Policy required a consequence, of which restitution, detention, suspension, were possible options. Since it could not be seen and indeed was a nice message, I ignored it. Was this one of those three percent situations when I needed to think differently? I'm still not sure. Years later, however, in my role as superintendent in charge of closing schools, I asked the contractors to cut the shelf with the inscription out of the built-in cupboard before the school was demolished. I presented it to "Mr. K," who had retired years earlier.

We were all horrified on December 14, 2012, to hear about the shootings at Sandy Hook Elementary School in Connecticut. As a Director of Education, I was responsible for the flag protocol, which is outlined in an Administrative Memorandum. In this case, lowering the flags did not fit any of the criteria outlined in the protocol; however, I issued the directive to lower school flags to half-mast. Some trustees told me that my decision was beyond the intent of the protocol, even though I had discretionary power within the protocol. As events unfolded in the hours and days following the event, school boards and other organizations united in sadness for the students and families of our southern neighbours. Applying the three percent principle to show our visible expression of sympathy for students everywhere was definitely the right decision.

How can we recognize *when* to use the three percent principle? If a leader truly knows the students, staff, colleagues, parents, and community then it will become clear. In short, educators need to think about the people affected by a decision and not force a policy, procedure, or protocol onto a situation that requires compassion and good judgement instead.

As an educator, I challenge you to reflect on your own practice. Is there a time when you should have used the three percent principle? How can you signal to yourself that thinking differently is necessary for the decision at hand? Recognizing and reacting appropriately that three percent of the time when the rules don't fit can make a principled leadership difference.

John Forbeck retired as a Director of Education with the Grand Erie District School Board in 2015. John began his career as a special education teacher and served as a school administrator in both at the elementary and secondary level. Forbeck was Superintendent of Education for the Hamilton-Wentworth District School Board where he held a variety of portfolios, including responsibility for families of elementary and secondary schools, compensatory education, human resources, board operations, as well as staff and community engagement. Throughout his career in public education Forbeck remained strong in his advocacy for what is right for students. His success can be attributed to his belief that all decisions are made with the child's best interests in mind. John continues to serve the educational community in his retirement.

It's Not About You

Jack Durkan

On 1 September 1999, I started my first day as principal of 320 students at an all-boys primary school in the southern suburbs of Cork City, Ireland.

Having qualified in 1980 as a primary teacher and having spent the following 19 years in a primary school classroom teaching four to twelve year olds, I launched into the world of school leadership and all that entailed until my 'retirement' in November 2016. I then took up a position on the leadership support team of our own professional leadership organisation, the Irish Primary Principals' Network (IPPN).

Do I miss it? I am surprised how much I miss the people, both big and little. Well, most of them anyway! The job? No, I do not miss it at all. Yard duty? No again, though as an administrative principal, yard duty was one of the few chances you had to interact with the kids on a day-to-day basis.

Truth is, I was very fond of my people, the staff. Even when we disagreed, they knew that no matter how much we argued, our relationship was more important to me than anything that divided us. Perhaps this sounds naïve, but it worked, mostly, because I meant it and tried to work at it.

While studying for a Master's degree in School Leadership and Management, the concept of "values-driven leadership" came to the fore as did the idea that your school is "as good as what is happening in the classrooms," not what is going on in the principal's office, or anywhere else. My realisation that the values of the leader 'become' the values of the organisation—good, bad, or ugly!—was actually scary.

This forced me to examine more closely what "really mattered" in our school. The tricky bit is, everyone else has their own set of values too. This is the nature of a variety of people thrown together, not always in a structured way, working within the four walls of their own individual classroom and school.

Thankfully, my default leadership style was to avoid micromanaging people, based on the belief that my job was really to spend time getting the 'right' people and letting them get on with it. This way of working can be fine on paper but can also be tricky because it depends wholly on trust. As a rule, I saw my job as a learning support, alongside the other support teachers, i.e., supporting the teacher in the classroom, who had the toughest 'gig' in town.

I never lost a chance to meet with parents, who are the primary educators (school is secondary). Mostly I tried to listen while they spoke about some concern related to their child. There were a few 'dodgy' ones over the years, but most parents do the very best they can for their kids. They may not always see things the same way as the school, but that's okay. They are not necessarily meant to. It is my job to do that! It is theirs to see it from their own and their child's perspective.

In the beginning, my staff told me that perhaps I was "spending too much time listening to parents," believing, understandably, that I was listening to complaints about teachers. Over time, they came to understand that often I was engaged in taking the heat from the said parent! Parents have a duty and a right to come to their child's school and to confer about how their child is progressing. It is of course well documented and well researched that the closer parents and schools align their efforts, the better the outcome for the child.

I regard my present role as a member of our principals' leadership support team as a privilege. Strange word perhaps, but it fits the idea that everyone outside of the classroom supports the work within. And everyone outside of the school does the same. Sometimes, in these days of increasing focus on the quality of leadership in schools, we must take care to ensure that we do what we do for that one child, that one pupil who needs us most.

We know that you cannot have an effective school without an effective leader. However, leadership is not a person—it can emanate from the strangest of sources. The "sacred space" in schools is not the principal's office; it is the classroom, in that interface of privilege between teacher and student.

Therefore, it is teachers who "captivate and inspire our children every day; instil a love of learning in young minds; nurture the students' dreams and build ladders to reach them, and have the power to transform lives."

We need to thank, every day, all teachers everywhere—thank you!

Jack Durkan, A.D.A.E.S., M.ED., was principal at Togher Boys' Primary School until he retired to take up a position with the Irish Primary Principals' Network (IPPN) on the leadership support team. Durkan has a B.Ed. from Mary Immaculate College, Limerick, and a Master's degree in School Leadership and School Management. He is a lecturer and tutor in the Future Leaders Programme at Maynooth University in Kildare. As well, Jack is a trained Relationship Counsellor, a qualified Executive Coach and Mentor, and an associate of Ireland's Centre for School Leadership.

Barely Above Water

Jason B. Allen

I began my career in education 12 years ago. On July 1, 2017, I became the Dean of School Culture/Assistant Principal at Latin College Prep in East Point, Georgia. I left a district that I not only matriculated through, but also served tirelessly for years. Moving from one school system to the next, from one leadership position to another was a huge deal. In fact, for weeks afterwards, I felt like I was *barely above water.*

Unknowingly, I was still mentally in my previous school district while trying to learn how to make my new school great again. As educators, we are confounded with many day-to-day challenges that become roadblocks to the success we seek for our scholars and ourselves. In my transition, I felt like I was not effectively making a difference. I found myself doing old things in a new place. Although the old things worked before, nothing seemed to work in the new school. Culture takes time to rebuild and change in a place conditioned to doing things a certain way.

Working under three different superintendents in my former school district, it took a year for a new leader to get things settled and adjust to the systems in place. Within the first 60 days, of course, there was a lot of resistance to the changes our leadership sought to implement. Change is hard for everyone to adjust to, regardless of your level of leadership. For change to go over smoothly, stakeholders must be engaged, team players must buy into the vision, and everyone must be willing to implement change to meet the goals.

Stakeholders must be engaged in the change! When I began at my new school, many of the stakeholders had been promised things they never received, believing that changes were going to help their children excel academically and they failed. So as new administration and leadership came on board to implement change, the stakeholders were naturally resistant. It is hard to get scholars to follow directions and vision that faculty, staff, and families have no connection to. The entire team must drive any vision to reach success. Nothing I did was good enough or seemed effective until I listened to the words and saw the actions of our scholars, faculty, staff, parents, and supporters. This allowed me to connect with our stakeholders in a different way that made them feel a part of the change.

If those on the team do not buy into the vision, then you will find yourself wasting time. I had to learn that if the faculty and staff were not fully on board with the changes leadership has designed, then we are all wasting our time. We had a few returning teachers, but many new ones coming from different places. Everyone walked into an atmosphere where the disciplinary, academic, and operational systems were changing. It can be overwhelming for the teachers charged with closing the achievement gap, learning new systems, planning lessons, and implementing interventions while all the while managing students. So, it was hard to get the faculty and staff on board with the basic vision never mind the lack of development and passion, poor classroom management, lack of usage of best practices, personality conflicts, and egos that come with the territory.

On this new journey, I have learned that it is tireless work engaging adults, persuading them to change to best practices, and most importantly getting them to buy into a new vision. It is hard! I felt like I was failing, that I could barely keep my head above water just simply keeping the chaos and daily confusion down within the school. But then a statement that I made to our faculty and staff stuck with me after 60 days on the job, *"Our scholars have to see us at human first before they can receive what we have to give them!"*

One of the challenges of being a school leader is managing adults. I get it! We are already set in our ways. Depending on where we are in life, we are either very open and go with the flow or basically resistant to change. But children are constantly changing. There is no black and white in education. Education is colorful—at least one different color for each child. Our work is to ensure that each child finds a pattern of success in the picture of life. We must help them to get there, even if we are *barely above water.*

Jason B. Allen *has served students, families, and communities for 13 years as an educator. His main goal is to help others along his life's journey. Throughout his academic career, he has mentored many young African-American males through his national mentoring program, Black Men with Initiative (BMWI). He speaks at conferences and he blogs for EdLanta on education topics. As an advocate for single-gender education, he serves as the Board Chairman for Ivy Preparatory Academies All Girls Charter Network. Allen also serves as the Dean of School Culture/Assistant Principal of Latin College Prep Academy. Jason can be reached at professorjba@gmail.com.*

Building a Collaborative Framework for Effective School Leadership

Selena Mell

Beginning my administrative journey in British Columbia, Canada, I was eager to start a professional quest for leading change, believing my contributions would allow for advancements in teaching and learning. Approaching three decades of varied educational roles in North America, South America, the Middle East, and Europe, this conviction remains, though admittedly, time has made me less ostentatious than in my earlier career. Aware that my decisions directly affect my school and staff, I feel it is necessary to seek out alternate perspectives. I define my educational leadership role by building collaborative initiatives and using every effort to harness and promote the talents within my team.

We all experience moments when our leadership role feels isolating. Despite enthusiasm, professional training, and experience, I've realized that improving outcomes is best accomplished by instilling ownership, creating opportunities, and enlisting help from others. Research reveals that school climate affects student achievement but that creating these positive environments is not arbitrarily achieved. The onus on a school leader to build a trusting environment to allow for growth and future success is paramount. Change is within our reach, but it takes time, team effort, and dedication to create initiatives that move us forward to realize our goals.

I have had the opportunity and privilege to work in both the private and public sectors, in rural, urban, multilingual, and multicultural settings. Based on this, I have tried to summarize key elements that have helped to define my own learning and growth as an educational leader:

1. **Visibility**: Undoubtedly, there are times as a school leader where I have wanted to hide from challenging issues. However, I've learned that visibility remains a key aspect of my role. Creating a presence in the school helps sustain my professional awareness and builds relationships. It sends a powerful message to all stakeholders and shows my alignment with the adage *inspect what you expect*. Walkthroughs assists in revealing what might have otherwise been left unseen. Effective leadership relies on my ability have a presence but also to build an understanding of the people within the learning community. I still continuously strive to improve in this area.

2. **Distributive Leadership**: When I first began, I believed it was my responsibility to take charge of all areas, but soon realized that this created overdependence. I grew into a greater understanding of my role and embedded myself into the multifaceted landscape. Experiencing the school firsthand, I could learn about the needs, the staff expectations, and their professional goals. Armed with greater insight, I help staff members foster their skills, which can later be shared. By allowing others to showcase their talents or lead initiatives, we all benefit by creating a stronger team. The distributive model is equally important to staff morale, demonstrating that each is valued for their expertise. However, even with the benefits of molding the environment for sharing responsibilities, this process requires ongoing training and coaching.

3. **Supportive Foundation**: A leader needs to ensure the environment is a safe and supportive for learning and growth. Although schools focus on academic achievement, a targeted focus on the social, emotional, and behavioral components is more important to student well-being and future success. Establishing positive support services for students both inside and outside of

the classroom, as well as providing mentors for teachers, helps create trust and improves the learning environment for all.

4. **Communication**: When identifying key initiatives to help lead school improvement, I connect to stakeholder groups so that all voices and varied opinions are represented. Promoting our school goals and convincing others to embrace these priorities requires a plan for sharing information and collecting ideas and feedback data. Strategic plans can only be implemented successfully if we continue giving them a voice in every message, evoking a shared team goal. Beyond what we say, it is equally important to instill values as you *walk the talk*. We communicate not only through our words but also with our everyday actions.

5. **Reflection**: Our leadership responsibilities are defined differently in varied contexts. I've learned that no one can advise you on best leadership methods as your environment is unique. For this reason, it is important to self-diagnose and reflect on practice. Self-assessment should be part of an honest journey of reviewing strengths and identifying needs.

Contemplating your unique leadership path, I would advise maintaining high expectations while pursuing your vision. Identify obstacles as opportunities instead of barriers. Don't lose your humility or sense of humour. Look past the paperwork and policies to discover and inspire the unique talents and professional resources that surround you. Most importantly, build partnerships and inclusive environments so that the journey is shared and enjoyed.

Selena Mell (B.A., B.Ed., M.Ed.) is from Lachute, Quebec (Canada), and has been involved in the field of education, in a range of positions from kindergarten to adult education, since 1989. She has worked as a principal for multiple K–7 schools in Quesnel, British Columbia (Canada), and in senior leadership positions in Chile and Abu Dhabi. Selena worked for Vanderbilt University and the Abu Dhabi Educational Council (ADEC) as an instructional leadership coach for K–12 school leaders before moving to Berlin in 2015 to begin her position as a head of primary.

Knowing What to Do as a Leader

Greg Morgan

As a young teacher, I always marvelled at the confidence of senior teachers carrying out their work. Whereas I doubted myself on lesson preparation, behaviour management, and pedagogy, my senior colleagues seemed to navigate, intuitively and smoothly, through serious incidents involving students, aggressive parents, ineffective colleagues, and curriculum development.

Over several years, my own leadership ability developed gradually along a tortuous path of trial and error. On one occasion as assistant principal, I found myself trying to break a pattern of behaviour in which 15-year-old Jack was stuck. Jack had a good heart, but the four walls of a classroom were not for him. He was regularly referred to me for disruptive behaviour and was sent each time, as per school policy, to in-school suspension. Jack found the close supervision of internal suspension tougher than a regular classroom and inevitably ended up suspended externally in a frustrating, repeating pattern—a situation that Jack, his mother, and I all agreed was unsatisfactory. Before long, Jack's mother railed against the futility of the external suspensions. At the same time, I had a principal and teachers expecting me to adhere to established protocols. As Jack's mother became increasingly intransigent during the conversation I said, "We both want Jack to learn more effective ways of responding when someone wants him to do something he would rather not do."

"I agree, but this approach is not working. We both know what's going to happen every time he goes to internal suspension," she said.

"That's true. However, other students learn to cope, to save themselves a whole lot of extra trouble."

Jack's mother glared at me for a moment before firing back. "Well Jack is not 'other students'. He's *my* boy and what you are doing is making things worse for him!" And I realised she was right.

This event was one of many that helped me learn that knowing what to do as a leader has less to do with rules and more to do with navigating the nuances to find the desired outcomes. During my last decade as a principal, amongst the continuing trial and error, I learned to be guided by my personal vision of the leader I yearned to be, and by my deepest core values. These are the values that have formed like diamonds, hardened by ongoing, honest reflection through the heat of those years of trial and error. Amongst the white noise of district guidelines, school policies, established precedent, and staff and parent expectations, my core values carry me through.

One day, a distressed teacher summoned me from my office at 3:57 p.m. As we rushed out, I heard that 14-year-old Tim refused to leave a school bus after the driver insisted that he must for abusing him. Tim would not leave at the teacher's request either, even after the other students were evacuated. As I approached, 30 students were milling around outside the bus, with the driver and other teachers hovering near the door. I could see Tim on the bus, sitting up near the front.

As I approached, I wondered how I would diffuse the situation. Time was an issue, as the bus was already late leaving. I asked a teacher to remove the other students from sight. As I walked past the group of adults near the bus door, one of the teachers called out to Tim, "You're in for it now!" I frowned at him. None of them realised that they had formed an adult barrier through which Tim could not pass. I leaned towards them, "Could you all just step around to the other side of the bus please? Thank you."

I entered the bus and sat across from Tim, one seat behind. "Tough day, Tim?" From side-on I could see his eyes welling up. "Looks to me, Tim, like this has all blown up from nowhere. That right?" No response. "Looks like you've found yourself down a deep hole and don't know how to climb out." Still nothing. "Tell you what—how about I help you up out of that hole?" Nothing for a moment and then Tim turned towards me, weighing whether to trust me or not. "Tim, I know you're worried about how you'll get home. I'll sort that out for you and I'm sure we can easily sort all this out too. This is big for you, but we'll sort it out together." I stood in the aisle behind him and gestured for him to stand. As he stood I said, "Well done, Tim. I'll let you go ahead to my office. I'll be there shortly." The bus was on its way within a few short minutes.

The intuition of an experienced leader can seem a mystery to others. My career has taught me that it is not a mystery but rather the result of rigorous reflection on *what is unfolding and what is important*. These are the clues to how I address it and what I learn from it, and all from within a well-honed set of explicit, personal guiding values.

Greg Morgan has led schools of varying sizes during his 30 years as a teacher and administrator in public education, with students as young as three and as old as 70+. While a school principal, Morgan completed a Ph.D. in Leadership and believes that wise leaders are rich in narrative intelligence, giving them the capacity to "rewrite" the narratives they hold about them- selves and others. He has been recognised by state and national bodies for his contribution as an educator and to the professional learning of his prin- cipal colleagues. Morgan now offers his consulting services in personalised, action-oriented leadership development to a range of clients in the corporate and education sectors. You can email him at greg@allora.org.au and see his website: https://www.allora.org.au.

In Touch with Society

Joachim Broecher

As school principal, consultant, and professor in teacher education, I always felt responsible to address the challenge of social cohesion, and still do so. To bring my message out, I tell teachers and university students a particular story, from my early years as teacher.

With the Atlantic to the west and the Wadden Sea to the east, the island of Sylt with its thatch-roofed houses, boasts Germany's highest-priced real estate. The boutiques in Kampen offer women's handbags that would cost an elementary school teacher her month's salary.

However, there is another side to Sylt. Several former military barracks located on the southern part of the island were converted into hostels after World War II. This made it possible for large numbers of youth to come to Sylt, including a group of nine-year-old boys from a specialized school for children with behavioral difficulties. They were ten in number, but it was like handling 30 children when it came to rendering necessary supervision and care.

We took over several adjoining train compartments. Naturally, there was no way of keeping the boys in there for long. Some ran into the neighboring cars and my colleague and I went to corral them again. The social educator held down the fort outside the compartments. I hurried through the corridors. Before I reached the front of the train, it had started to slow down. The doors opened and out ran some of the boys down the train platform.

People began to notice me. I made my way along the platform toward the engine and then systematically combed back through the train. I happened straight onto a melee. One of the boys had jostled a woman having coffee. A man was cursing at him. I apologized for the boy's behavior, pressed some Euros into the woman's hand for getting her dress cleaned, and pushed the little group out of that car.

It seemed by now that the entire train was aware of our ruckus-causing presence. I could not expect this well-to-do crowd, heading for their snug vacation houses, to put up with this. I read it in their faces: *How could you travel with these children to this destination?* But, weren't we all responsible for this young generation that, in some respects, had *gone off the rails*? I longed for this day to end and wished to find solace in conversation with Mrs. Moll, a colleague from Cologne, over a cold Frisian beer. She traveled to Sylt with her classes every year.

By now all boys were seated again. With the glass doors shut, my colleagues and I stood in the corridor and assessed the situation. I had treated the boys to a round of Cokes. In one of the compartments, they had pulled down the sunshade. What I had failed to notice was that the window behind the shade had also been opened as wide as it would go. Meanwhile, the train was hurtling along at top speed. Suddenly, the sunshade was torn out the window, flapping wildly, and its metal rod smashed from outside back in through the windowpanes doubled-up one behind the other. The rod remained stuck in the splintering glass.

I tore open the door. A warm blast of wind hit my face. Small glass fragments threatened to come loose from the fracture. I pushed the boys out, locked the door, and went to find the conductor. He phoned the chief conductor who decided to uncouple the car with the damaged window at the Hamburg train station. The voices by the exits sounded angry and furious looks came my way as people heaved their suitcases about.

Thirty minutes behind schedule, the train resumed its journey north. We had our hands full trying to calm the boys down. Then a man rushed up to me claiming damages for the train delay, which caused him to miss an important business appointment that, supposedly, involved millions. Sweat broke out on my forehead ... The other passengers listened intently. I didn't know how to react. Snorting with rage, the man repeated his demand.

Suddenly, a group of women standing in the aisle went after the man: "Can't you see what kind of work these young people are doing here? How would you like to be the one to do it? What's this nonsense about millions?" Irritated he went away. The women also gave us practical help by talking with the boys, and being considerate to them during the last part of the journey, which took another three hours.

Late that evening I told Mrs. Moll the whole story. "That is why I always take the train with my classes," she said, "because it gets me in touch with society."

Joachim Broecher is a professor and the Director of the Department for Teaching Students with Emotional, Social, and Behavioral Difficulties, University of Flensburg, Germany. Before moving fulltime into higher education, he worked as a teacher and ultimately as a school principal. His research and teaching interests include participative and critical pedagogy, school culture development, and schools as learning organizations. More information is available from www.broecher-research.de.

Unity in Diversity

Sumona Roy

...let us unite, not in spite of our differences, but through them. For differences can never be wiped away, and life would be so much the poorer without them. Let all human races keep their own personalities, and yet come together, not in a uniformity that is dead, but in a unity that is living.
—Rabindranath Tagore

As a child, when I first started school I was shy and quiet. The demographics at my school made me one of a handful of racialized students. This didn't bother me, and I didn't really think about my cultural identity. I made friends with everyone without difficulty. I was fortunate to have an amazing teacher, Mrs. Jones, who brought me out of my shell and gave me a variety of leadership tasks in the classroom and the school. I didn't display any outward emotion, but I was secretly excited and loved doing these tasks. This was just the beginning of what Mrs. Jones did for me and partly why I have become the leader I am today.

Mrs. Jones fostered my identity as a person, as a Canadian-born Indian student whose parents were first generation East Indian immigrants. She encouraged me to share my cultural background of wearing a sari, but also to share my talents as a pianist and ballet dancer with the class. She nurtured me to speak up for myself and find my voice. The teacher who pronounced my name with the correct Indian pronunciation and encouraged me to let other people know when they weren't pronouncing it correctly. She let me teach her Bengali words and new games that I learned from cousins in India when I went to visit.

As I moved on to the next phase of my educational path, I ended up skipping Grade 1. Grade 2 was a very different experience and I was a different child. I had learned to socialize more with all the children and was confident in answering questions, contributing regularly, and volunteering for different jobs. I was very curious and completed my work very quickly. I would finish tasks and ask the teacher for more or I would go and visit my friends in the class to "help" them finish their tasks faster so they could play with me in the quiet corner. After some time, my teacher would send me to the Grade 3 class, the library, the office, or other rooms to help the other teachers.

This teacher was a very different personality from Mrs. Jones. My name, Sumona, is pronounced with a "Sh" sound ("Shumona"). She would always pronounce my name with an "S" sound instead. I corrected her many times, repeating my name to her, but she would ignore me and keep on saying it incorrectly. Once she corrected my friend with the incorrect pronunciation and announced to the entire class that it confused everyone and that everyone was to pronounce it the incorrect way. I spoke up and said, "No. Mrs. S., it isn't wrong. My name is 'Shumona,' just like 'Shugar,' spelled S-U-G-A-R. See, Sumona and Sugar have the same 'S' sound both have SU in them."

These contrasting experiences in the first three years of my schooling had a deep effect on me as a leader later in life. Leadership can take on many forms at different times in our lives, and sometimes when we are in the midst of it we don't even realize that we are being leaders.

An important aspect to leadership is to build our own leadership identity. You need to know who you are as a leader or who you want to be. We all have diverse personalities and experiences; we all have our own stories and ideas. We need to learn to look at things from different perspectives, be open to learning from everyone, even a child, to try to break down assumptions and to be true to ourselves. It all starts with us, as individuals. We need to believe and be comfortable with our own identities. Once we are comfortable with ourselves, we will be able to clearly see the greatness in others, embrace new learnings, and reflect on them. We need to open ourselves to other personalities and embrace the differences we bring to the table both as learners and as leaders. Remember, we are all human. The key is to acknowledge the unity in diversity that connects our world.

Sumona Roy is a vice-principal in the Halton District School Board. She is a Ph.D. student at the Ontario Institute for Studies in Education (OISE, University of Toronto) in the Department of Leadership, Higher and Adult Education, specializing in collaborative, international and developmental education (CIDE), specifically leadership and policy. Her research interests include international education, Indigenous education, equity and leadership, well-being, and mathematics education. She is a workshop developer, a facilitator in social justice and equity, and she works on integrating curriculum in literacy, numeracy, and technology. Sumona is also an Indian classical and modern dancer and the founder of Shakti Fine Arts.

Losing Focus

Benton M. Brown

I t's a Thursday morning. Over the course of the week, I've managed to create a to-do list that looks like it will take weeks to finish but needs to be completed by tomorrow. I have financial reports to review, drafts of grant applications to edit, website updates to finalize, lunch to eat (important!), and a conference call that I know will last at least 30 minutes longer than it needs to, just to name a few. No distractions; I need to be extremely focused and productive today. Another day in the life. My phone buzzes. Facebook alert: someone has just posted on your wall. Oh come on … as if you don't look at Facebook at work every once in a while. I foolishly open it to see which friend of mine has decided to post an old picture from 15 years ago or a humorous video of a dog. But this time it was different.

Facebook showed a note on my wall from one of my old students from when I taught in the Arkansas Delta with Teach for America. She thanked me for teaching her statistics. She said she was taking a psychology statistics class in university now and it's not so bad since she had already learned most of it from my class. I was humbled, and probably teared up if I'm being honest. I remember her statistics class because it was the first time I had taught the class, and the first time in a while that the school had offered it. They had only offered it because I volunteered to teach it. I also couldn't imagine that anyone in that class had learned or retained anything because I knew it was far, far from perfect. It made me take a step back and think about why we, as so-called "leaders" in education, do what we do. It's for the students who, directly or indirectly, we impact every day. It is too easy to lose that focus, yet we sometimes do.

As educators move up the proverbial ladder, we begin to spend less and less time interacting with students and more and more time interacting with adults. So many times we make decisions focusing on how it is going to affect the adults that we work with in our teams. "Oh my staff won't like it if I make them do an extra school visit," I've thought to myself. For others, it may be school inspectors, parents, governors, or government officials that we think about. In truth, we spend more of our time focusing on the impact our decisions will have on adults and less on children. In every decision we make, we should ask ourselves this question: "Is this the best decision for the students this will affect?" In the end, your staff (or other adults) may not like it at first, but when they see the positive impact it has on students, they will appreciate it. If the decisions you make lead to positive gains for your teachers and in turn for their students, caring adults will praise rather than question. In the end, few will criticise what makes a positive impact on students.

I should be clear; I'm not saying ignore what your staff think nor that we shouldn't concern ourselves with staff feedback or morale. We should strive for a team that enjoys their work and does not feel micromanaged. The way we can all achieve this, though, is to remain constantly student focused. In the end, that is (or should be) what drives us. If we create a culture within our teams that puts student learning at the centre of all that we do, these conflicts will not arise and all our programmes, projects, and policies will be properly focused.

We all live in a world of complicated systems, never-ending bureaucratic processes, and paperwork coming out of our ears. It is far too easy for us to lose focus. Take a moment to remind yourself why you do the job you do. Why are you in education in the first place? It's the joy on a student's face when she finally realises she can divide fractions, conjugate irregular verbs, or balance a chemical equation. It's the student who never thought that education was "for him" but you showed him how it could change his life. And, yes, it's the student whose Facebook post to say thank you was a welcome distraction from your Thursday morning to-do list because it helped you refocus on the real reason you became an educator in the first place.

Benton M. Brown, PhD, *is an educator and researcher who currently serves as Head of Initial Teacher Education at Bath Spa University (UK). He holds a Master's degree in Community and Economic Development and Bachelor's degrees in Political Science and Sociology. He is currently completing his Ph.D. in Public Policy with a specialisation in primary and secondary education. Brown has worked in education internationally, previously serving as the Executive Director of the Arkansas Teacher Corps in the US. He is also a former secondary math teacher and a Teach for America corps member. He can be reached by email at b.brown3@bathspa.ac.uk.*

Knowing Myself as a Leader

Susan Dunlop

The unexamined life is not worth living.—Socrates

Years ago, a course at Brock University had a profound impact on how I think about leadership and my own leadership development. "The Reflective Practitioner," inspired by the Donald A. Schön (1984) book of the same name, was designed so participants could consider tacit elements of their personal lives—including deep-seated beliefs and experiences—and what the impact of these might have on our practice. It opened the door to a career of reflection, self-assessment, and knowledge.

To understand ourselves, we must always begin with our location in the world, including geography, ethnicity, class, gender, and family. When I react to a situation, plan for a learning session, or work with parents and guardians, all that knowledge comes to bear on my decision. Knowing where I come from and what that means in my daily life and in my leadership practice is essential to improvement. What assumptions and biases do I carry with me every day that inform every opinion and decision I make? Uncovering these is the hard work of becoming a better leader.

While much of this work is internal, it cannot be done alone. We need others to challenge our ideas, ask us probing questions, and give us feedback about our leadership. One of the best ways I have found is to engage in conversations with those who do not think like me. It is easy to surround ourselves with people like us—a very human trap that many leaders fall into, me included. If you are looking for a way to disrupt your thinking patterns and create cognitive dissonance that you can learn from, then it's crucial to find contrary opinions. I am using more active listening strategies with these folks who don't think like me and prompts designed to help me listen more, like "Say more about that" or "Can you give me an example?"

Feedback can be scary. We've all had negative feedback, and it does not feel good. I have discovered, with the help of others, that specific questions can elicit useful feedback, and I've used anonymous surveys and suggestion boxes with some success in the quest for feedback. Lately, however, I have been asking for a lot more face-to-face feedback from colleagues and from those who report to me. Shakil Choudhury from Anima Leadership suggests three questions: What I am doing well? What can I improve? What are my next steps for learning? These questions allow me to show vulnerability, a key leadership attribute, as well as a willingness to listen.

Asking for feedback is the first step. And it is not easy. I need to put myself in the right frame of mind so that I am open to hearing however someone else is perceiving my actions or understanding me. This is very powerful. When more than one person gives the same feedback, positive or not, you cannot ignore it. Further, once someone has been courageous enough to offer thoughtful and honest feedback, I need to share what I am going to do about it. It is important to make some realistic and transparent commitments to get better.

Blogging has also become a valuable route to self-knowledge. Many people have written about the usefulness of working ideas into words. I have often taken a thought that was niggling and turned it into a blog post through reflection. My blog has become indispensable to me as a repository of my own learning.

Leadership is a messy journey of successes and setbacks. To replicate successes whether on a project, an initiative, or when coaching individuals, I need to understand how that success happened in the first place. What strengths contributed to it? What did I do or say that inspired others to go further and learn more? What structures and learning were useful? If I cannot answer these questions, that success might have been a fluke, maybe it can be repeated, but most likely not.

The same is true for setbacks. It is common now for people to talk about the value of failure and how much we can learn from it. While I agree, my experiences have taught me to go further: How did I personally contribute to the problem? Was it my interactions with others? Was my way of decision making off? Did I do or say something that jeopardized success? Again, these are not easy questions. Once I resolve them, the next step is not to repeat the actions that led to the setback.

Great leaders are not perfect, and they know it. More important, great leaders know themselves. The only way to improve your leadership in any domain, education included, is through ruthless self-honesty as advocated by Shakil Choudhury. My quest to understand my strengths and weaknesses and how they play out in my work and my personal life is a lifelong pursuit. And oh, so worth it.

Susan Dunlop is the Superintendent of Student Achievement, Learning Services at Hamilton-Wentworth District School Board in Ontario, Canada. Sue works with leaders in schools from kindergarten to grade 12 to improve leadership capacity and student learning. More information is available at www.suedunlop.ca.

Reflections of a Teacher Educator–Researcher

Stephanie Chitpin

As I pause to reflect on the experiences that have facilitated my learning, I wish to acknowledge that reflection begins with self. Thus, I juxtapose different settings in the following narrative to present my life as a student, classroom teacher, and university professor to illustrate how my prior experiences have shaped my teaching in different contexts and how I overcame the tension between conveying subject matter, or the science of teaching, and teaching for understanding. Many of my views about teaching and learning came from the demonstrations of my first teachers, the sisters at the Loreto Convent Primary School in Mauritius. My sense of teaching was born of those teachers in the convent school and university and others I met in the most unlikely places.

After obtaining my teaching certification from the University of Toronto in the late 1990s, I began as a French immersion teacher. On many occasions, I noted the reluctance of my students and the frustration they showed in class. I continued to provide them with more of the same teaching because I felt that was what they needed to learn. I did not have the knowledge or ability to take student needs, learning styles, and personal knowledge into consideration. I thought of myself more as a technician hired to implement the curriculum and policies mandated by the school district.

With my appointment at the University of Ottawa, despite having taught in elementary and secondary public schools, I was quite overwhelmed. I should have expected the same learning curve when I began my university teaching. However, learning to teach is deceptively simple; while I was aware that my experience was typical of a "beginner," I was not aware of the contextual differences between my life as a beginning classroom teacher and my life as a university professor. The university landscape appeared to be like that of any other classroom or school, yet their differences were profound.

My stories of teaching are not isolated. In fact, they are part of the sociocultural and historical contexts. When I began to acknowledge the interconnected nature of my narrative and the institutional histories, only then did I begin to understand the complexities of learning to teach. As Jean Clandinin and Michael Connelly put it, each of us approaches teaching from different places on the "professional knowledge landscape," which is composed of diverse relationships among people, places, things, and events. I had to work together with my colleagues and students in ways that acknowledged the unique contributions and needs of the individuals in different contexts. I needed to understand more deeply the nuances and contexts that shaped what I did. There was no doubt that I brought other important aspects of my background into my classroom. It was equally important for me to acknowledge the uniqueness of individuals, and their learning needs and styles—an aspect I overlooked in the past.

My lessons then were designed based on the adage that if you give people fish, they can eat for a day, but if you teach them to fish, they can eat for a lifetime. Through discussion, I became aware of the tension between teaching for the short-term needs of pre-service teachers and teaching for their long-term needs. Although I wanted pre-service teachers to learn how to fish for themselves, I realized that in the short term they just needed some fish (teaching strategies and materials to use right away). They could not learn how to fish if they were pre-occupied with having no fish. Armed with this knowledge, I now see my dual role: one that teaches them how to fish and one that provides fish.

In January 2009, I received a teaching grant to design an online curriculum course for pre-service teachers. I sought the advice of a trusted colleague. Our conversations forced me to spell out my reasons for doing certain things in my practice. The joint planning sessions acted as a catalyst for examining my personal views, which are influenced by Karl Popper. Through our discussions, I also came to understand that learning to teach is a laborious, time-consuming, reflective process. It is more than acquiring teaching strategies, delivering curricular content, grading papers, and assessing student growth. My life experiences are important, and they influence what and how I teach. This chapter is only a small marker on my professional journey; a place where I stopped to think about where I was in my teaching a few years ago and where I am heading in the future.

Dr. Stephanie Chitpin is an Associate Professor of Leadership at the University of Ottawa, Canada, and the series editor of Educational Leadership and Policy Decision-Making in Neoliberal Times, published by Routledge. Dr. Chitpin is also a member of several editorial boards of education and management journals. Her funded research by the Social Sciences and Humanities Research Council of Canada (SSHRC) looks at principal decision-making as it relates to reducing achievement gaps and investigates dilemmas faced by educational leaders in school and hospital settings.

Lessons in Leadership:
The Process Must be Inclusive and Iterative

David Hile

In the summer of 2015, I entered the Miami University Ed.D. program. Our very first class was a sociology course taught by a legendary Miami professor. In all my formal educational experiences I had never taken a sociology course and had no idea what to expect, but the professor was fascinating, as was the subject matter, and I learned a great deal and really enjoyed the experience. The final project was to write a 20-page paper, applying everything we had learned about basic sociology theory and culture-based leadership theory. This assignment involved an important reflective process, and thus helped me grow as an educational leader.

For the assignment, I chose to reflect on and analyze a specific case that I initiated as the superintendent in the public school district I lead. My research question for the paper was "How do I get teachers to value data, evidence, and research to inform their instructional practice?"

From my perspective, all the data, evidence, and research pointed out the obvious: that we were not achieving our goal of 90% of second graders reading at grade level. I also considered it obvious that if we continued to do what we had been doing for the past five years, we'd get the same results. We had studied, collectively and in depth, a school district that had figured out how to achieve the goal and it was doing so successfully and consistently. Looking at the same data, evidence, and research, the teachers did not reach the same conclusions, and I wanted to understand why because I believed it would make me a better educational leader.

This is where my analysis of this case benefitted from my new learning about sociology. We learned that schools, like most other places of employment, are culture-based because they are made up of people who exist, usually, in a hierarchy, such as the subordinate relationship of teachers to administrators. This creates a "culture of teaching" in which administrators are the "other" and teachers value classroom experience (us) over all non-classroom experience (them). As a result, zones of control develop; the teachers control curricular matters and the classroom, and view the administrators as responsible for all matters external to the classroom such as schedules, buses, budgets, and so on. Within their zone of control, teachers see themselves as the experts on curricular, pedagogical, and classroom matters, and fend off what they see as intrusions into those realms by administrators.

After learning some sociology, I had reason to believe that some insight into my case and research question might also lie in culture-based leadership theory. Schools are shared spaces where distinct groups exist and struggle for recognition and legitimacy. Teachers comprise one of those groups, administrators comprise another, and teachers see administrators as the dominant group with power. Thus, when I, the administrator, pointed out that the teachers had never achieved the 90% reading goal, and that as a result we needed to make pre-determined curricular and pedagogical changes to do so, the teachers felt disrespected and denigrated. Obviously, my leadership in this case was lacking, and provided some insight into why the teachers didn't "value the data, the evidence, and the research." What I should have done was to structure the initial conversation about the goal, the curriculum, and the pedagogy in a way that provided teachers with an opportunity to express their interests and expertise. What I had done instead was to confront them with research, expecting them to see it from my perspective. Essentially, I had denigrated them as professionals and they responded with frustration and anger at the loss of group recognition and legitimacy.

I came to realize that I should have asked myself some important questions before initiating the discussion about the change in reading curriculum and pedagogy: How can I engage our teachers in a conversation about reading curriculum and pedagogy? How do I show them that I respect and value their unique cultural group perspective, their knowledge and experience, their role in our decision-making process, their perspective on our assessment results? How do we productively discuss the data, the evidence, and the research in an effort to improve reading instruction for primary students?

David Hile has been superintendent of the Licking Valley Local Schools in central Ohio for the past 11 years. Before going into the superintendency, David taught history and US government, served as a full-time teacher mentor, a high school assistant principal, and high school principal. He is currently a doctoral candidate in the Department of Educational Leadership at Miami University. The focus of his dissertation is school readiness. David lives in Hanover, Ohio, with his wife Angie and their two teenage sons, Ethan and Hayden.

Upon Retirement:
I Ask for a Field that is Fair

Scott Lowrey

Over the holidays, I had a chance to reconnect with some colleagues. An old friend asked, "What do you miss about being a principal?" My response? "Recess duty." Those gathered were taken aback. I explained that recess duty provided opportunities to foster relationships with pretty much everyone on the playground. I took pride in being present and accessible to children, families, staff, and the community. I have heard rumours of principals, perhaps metaphorically, who never leave their office. Sorry, but I cannot relate.

I did not attend the retirement function offered by my former employer; however, I did attend the retirement celebration offered by my principals' organization. These decisions were purposeful; I do not believe in random. What I share below, is the essence of my retirement farewell speech.

I am a product of Hamilton public schools. Four generations of my family are products of Hamilton public schools. My parents met at a Hamilton public school. My roots are deep. I define character as how individuals behave when no one is watching. It was as a middle school student that I learned that it was possible to influence someone else's life indirectly without even knowing them. Sometimes words do speak louder than actions. My most prized possession is a letter that I received from Ellison Kelly, an inductee to the Canadian Football League (CFL) Hall of Fame in 1992.

Gordon Lightfoot once sang, *"The city where we live might be quite large, but the circle is small."* It turns out that I played football with Ellison

Kelly's son Jerry. I did meet Ellison Kelly later in life, now as an elementary school principal. Somewhere in The Sports Network (TSN) vaults there is a video of Ellison Kelly's visit to Billy Green School. Reading from the letter he had written me when I was a teenager he began, *"Dear God, in the battle that goes on through life, I ask for a field that is fair."* Although I do not profess to be a man of faith, the prayer continues to resonate with me as a profound life lesson. Life's successes and failures must be predicated on the honourable and ethical pursuit of a goal in good faith for the greater good. When combined with character, failure requires that you celebrate the success of another. Personal and professional experience have taught me that the field is not always fair, and that those further up the hierarchy sometimes engage in unethical leadership.

I went on to discuss two individuals who were influential in my development as a leader: Susan Mawson (human resources officer) and Rich McQueen (secondary school vice-principal). Susan thrived in creating successes for others. Occasionally, others, in pursuit of promotion, appeared to take credit for the foundational work that Susan had done. Rich's priority was students, not promotion. I believe that it was Michael Fullan who wrote that one measure of a leader's success is the leadership cultivated in others. Leadership succession and sustainability is driven by the moral purpose of the current generation of leaders. The role of the principal is to nurture the talent of those they supervise, not to make themselves look good through the efforts of others. When I see what counts as leadership in 2018, it makes me sad. We need to do better.

I concluded my reflections with four personal belief statements:

1. School systems exist to serve school communities; school communities do not exist to serve school systems. School systems must first seek to understand and then to serve communities.
2. Events that occur within a system should never be viewed in isolation; rather, they should be viewed as interconnected and interdependent components of complex systems. Ethical hiring decisions honour the greater good, longer term. Unethical

hiring decisions destroy trust. One measure of the health of an organization is the trust that people have in its leaders.

3. The health of a democratic society is sustained by the quality of its public education system. The quality of our education system is a function of competent leadership in the field working directly with school communities to improve student achievement and well-being. In theory, the best teachers become principals. In practice, this is not always the case. In theory, the best principals become supervisory officers. In practice, this also is not always the case. To be fair, we all know exemplary principals whose success is demonstrated by their deep commitment to children, not by pursuing promotion.

4. Vocational schools will rise again.

I end with the words of Ellison Kelly: *"When I was a young lad of ten, an old man who cared for me, gave me this prayer about sports and life. I would like for you to have it. Maybe Mom and Dad will explain it fully."*

Dr. Scott Lowrey *is a former elementary school principal residing in Hamilton, Ontario, Canada. He is also an Assistant Professor (limited duties) at Western University. He received Canada's Outstanding Principal's (COP) recognition in 2005, the inaugural year of the program, for initiatives relating to early literacy and the creation of a multigenerational continuum of community partnerships encompassing society's youngest to most senior. Scott holds a doctorate in Educational Administration from the Ontario Institute for Studies in Education. In 2014, Scott was inducted into McMaster University's Alumni Gallery. In 2018, Scott will receive a Western University Alumni Award of Merit for Professional Achievement.*

Lessons Learned:
The Role of Jargon and Acronyms in Education Training

Wes Armstrong

My former teaching partner, Yuki Matsuo, and I once led a teacher-training session in Kyoto, Japan. Teachers from all over Japan came to observe our class. The majority of the visitors were Japanese, but some were from English-speaking countries. The EFL lessons Ms. Matsuo and I planned for this advanced-level class were highly interactive, fast-paced, and fun. We were vigilant in making sure that students were learning new vocabulary, reading, writing, and speaking in every class.

Ms. Matsuo explained the rationale for our classes in Japanese in the teacher meeting that followed our observed class, and then I explained the rationale in English. My part of the thirty-minute presentation featured a lot of teaching jargon, acronyms, initialisms, and EFL-specific terms. Having never been observed by so many visiting teachers, I worked hard to appear as knowledgeable as I could. I thought I nailed it! Twenty minutes after the presentation, Matsuo-sensei approached my desk.

"Mr. Armstrong, thank you very much for helping me today."

"My pleasure." There was a look of concern on her face.

"Some of the observers have asked me for a written copy of your speech. Actually, I would like one, too. The lesson went well, and the presentation was fine. The only problem is, some of them didn't understand you."

It immediately dawned on me that even the English-speaking teacher observers were asking me to clarify some of the terms in my presentation. Unsurprisingly, there are regional differences in the terms taught at teacher-training programs in Australia, the United Kingdom, and the United States from the ones taught to me in Canada. This was further complicated by the incorporation of English-teaching terms specific to Japan. The result was clearly a mess. This experience caused me to reflect on what it means to be an effective communicator. Additionally, it has caused me to reflect on the role of jargon and acronyms in education training.

Research on groups of science students shows that jargon can inhibit learning (Brown & Ryoo, 2008; McDonnell, Barker, & Wieman, 2016). Control groups were taught the traditional way (with key terms and concepts), and compared with groups of students taught only the concepts. Students taught concepts without jargon could apply their learning more successfully and accurately than students taught in the traditional manner. Many believe this is due to a phenomenon called cognitive load theory (Ibid.). In fact, the acceptance of cognitive load theory has become so widespread that an Australian education department recently published a document outlining suggested classroom practices to counter it (Centre for Education Statistics and Evaluation, 2017). Teachers and educational leaders should reflect on whether to use subject-specific terms when those concepts can be explained by known vocabulary.

Similarly, Elon Musk (the founder of PayPal, Tesla Motors, and SpaceX), singled out the deleterious effects of acronyms on understanding when workers collaborated across departments. In a memo entitled "A.S.S., Acronyms Seriously Suck" (Vance, 2015, p. 238), Musk argued that his engineers were creating too many acronyms in the interest of saving time. Musk continued his point by arguing that people in meetings do not want to appear "dumb" and therefore just pretend to understand what something means, which leads to far greater problems. Musk's idea about limiting acronym usage is salient for schools given the wide variety of professional and academic backgrounds among teaching staff and the specialized terminology and acronyms specific to each discipline.

One could argue that my anecdote, the research with science students, and the Elon Musk story are particular to certain types of teaching/administrative jobs. Have you thought, however, about your staff's level of understanding after you give a presentation? Have you thought about how much a parent understood after a meeting about an IEP or EQAO scores (especially if they speak another language at home)? How much time did you save saying IEP instead of individualized education program? Could you not have called the EQAO a standardized assessment?

It is incumbent on school leaders to communicate their ideas as clearly as possible to ensure understanding. Jargon can lead to cognitive overload and other forms of misunderstanding, and acronyms can be too specialized, hinder understanding, and worst of all, make people feel "dumb." Leading a school is incredibly important work—too important to leave understanding to chance.

Although many educational theorists caution against adopting lessons from the business world for use in schools, Elon Musk's argument for limiting the use of acronyms may have positive benefits for overall school communications. Why not try it?

Further Reading:

Brown, B. A., & Ryoo, K. (2008). Teaching science as a language: A "content-first" approach to science teaching. *Journal of Research in Science Teaching, 45*(5), 529–553.

Centre for Education Statistics and Evaluation (2017). Improving high school engagement, classroom practices and achievement. *Learning Curve, 18.* https://www.cese.nsw.gov.au//images/stories/PDF/2017_engagement_NAPLAN_AA_DN_v4.pdf

McDonnell, L., Barker, M. K., & Wieman, C. (2016). Concepts first, jargon second improves student articulation of understanding. *Biochemistry and Molecular Biology Education, 44*(1), 12–19.

Vance, A. (2015). *Elon Musk: Tesla, SpaceX, and the Quest for a Fantastic Future.* New York: Ecco Press.

*Wes **Armstrong*** *is an Ontario-trained teacher who lives and works in Osaka, Japan. He teaches English as a Second Language classes at Kyoto Seika University. He also tutors businesspeople who work for large multinational Japanese companies in English conversation and writing. Armstrong is also enrolled in the Master's of Professional Education (Educational Leadership) program at Western University.*

Collaborative Accomplishment

Al Gardiner

A s an educational leader, I have been praised for many accomplishments, but I will tell you quite candidly that as time elapsed and as
my leadership skills developed, I came to realize that in the main, those
accomplishments stemmed primarily from collaborative activities. My
participation in a variety of learning communities has led to a greater
involvement with others and, more often than not, the focus of each of
these interactions was developing and pursuing shared goals. Whether
the development of an experiential learning program in our middle
school, the creation of distance French Immersion utilizing video conferencing to share programming among different school divisions, or
participating in the establishment of an Early Years community school,
the achievements were brought to fruition through social interaction.
Ongoing discussion enabled participants to establish shared goals,
learn together, and guide the development of each of the initiatives.
Working together allowed us to overcome obstacles that we faced and
provided opportunities to make changes designed to further enhance
the efficacy of each initiative.

In these collaborative activities, I often did not have the initial idea
for the project nor could I have created these initiatives as well as we
did together. Since input came from all of the participants and direction
was shared, my exercise of leadership, to a significant degree, involved
the coordination of activities. I have learned to appreciate that effective
leadership is best facilitated through collaborative activity grounded
in the good working relationships that exist within a particular learning community. Not surprisingly, collaborative leadership not only has

created good outcomes in the form of worthwhile projects for the participants to pursue but has also created a collaborative culture that can produce unanticipated, positive benefits.

The development of a summer enrichment program for children and youth illustrates this type of collaborative leadership. As Dean of Education at our university college, I was invited to a meeting with superintendents and principals representing school divisions in our region to discuss with representatives of the provincial government possible anti-poverty initiatives for Aboriginal and northern school-aged children. Some options for programming were discussed, and eventually we agreed to initiate a summer enrichment program designed to augment and reinforce the students' previous learning. A regional learning consortium would guide the development of the program and I was given the responsibility of overseeing the daily development and implementation of the program. As Dean of Education and as a link to the learning consortium, I worked with education students and the program coordinator to develop the program's themes, activities, and marketing. Although I was a link to the governing consortium and in constant dialogue with the education students and the program's coordinator, I often felt I was an observer during this collaborative process. These enthusiastic and creative program planners shared amazing ideas about programming and organization as they created the summer enrichment program that still serves over 300 participants in the region at the cost of $20 per week for each student!

The summer enrichment program allowed prospective teachers to participate in collaborative leadership. Education students applied a variety of instructional strategies by providing culture-based and place-based learning activities for elementary students residing in the surrounding area. Education students engaged in the joint planning of lessons and utilized their gifts to share ideas and to define their roles within the program. Program participants and pre-service teachers learned to develop effective relationships for teaching and learning within the context of this learning community. The summer program continues to serve as a living laboratory for education students in taking further steps to develop their teaching skills. These experiences also enable education students to learn more about the value of collaboration and the benefits that can be derived from shared leadership.

While it was nice to be acknowledged for those accomplishments where I have provided some of the leadership, I also feel that these accolades were not wholly deserved. At these times, I often pause to reflect on my role in these collaborative ventures, and am humbled to think about my contributions compared to those of others. Generally, I am in awe of their efforts and glad that I was part of these learning communities. I am still pleasantly surprised that broad and meaningful input, which lies at the heart of collaboration, produces such rich dialogue and an openness to many possibilities. I am optimistic that the accomplishments that stemmed from these working relationships, shared activities, and collaborative leadership projects will continue to make a difference for children and youth.

Al Gardiner has almost forty years of experience in education as a classroom teacher, school counselor, school administrator, superintendent of schools in the Kelsey School Division, and Dean of Education, researcher, and faculty member at University College of the North. He has also held leadership positions in the Kelsey Teachers' Association, Manitoba Association of School Superintendents, and various community organizations. Gardiner has retired from teaching, but remains active researching relational pedagogies, democratic and critical theory, and inclusive educational practices.

Speak Up and Elevate the Discourse

Chizoba Imoka

My decision to switch from the field of economics into education policy was driven by the urgent need I saw to reposition Africa's education system towards humanization, cultural relevance, justice, and the critical engagement of its diverse student population. Being a product of the Nigerian secondary school education system myself and having engaged with thousands of Nigerian youth, the system's damage to the intellect and soul of its citizens is clearly reprehensible and tragic. The Nigerian education system dehumanizes its youth to varying degrees, ill-equipping them to provide culturally relevant, socially responsive, critically inclusive leadership.

In my own experience, schooling objectified and pacified me because knowledge production and dissemination was *always* in one direction—from the teacher to me. My life experiences, my unique personal attributes, or my immediate environment were not validated as sites of knowledge that could be mobilized, engaged, interrogated, and extended towards bigger societal questions and philosophical reflections. Schooling decentered me from my natural indigenous cultural bearing and relocated me to a Eurocentric intellectual and social location where colonizing ways of being and seeing the world became the *only* way of being. To be successful and educated, then, was to be as removed as possible from your indigenous cultural self and instead uphold Eurocentric ways of being. Our school actively rewarded students for proclaiming foreign religions—Christianity or Islam—and for denigrating or being ignorant of indigenous ways.

To be eligible for admission into Nigerian universities, we were assessed on our "Europeanization" and our English, which is a *foreign* language imposed on Nigerians. Students are not required to be versed in their indigenous languages and speaking English with an "Igbo accent" merits humiliation or outright punishment. Even fellow students will call you "razz," meaning uncivilized. School authorities could fine or physically assault you. Put succinctly, indigenous religions, languages, and ways of being had no place in our schools. Instead, the Eurocentric histories, philosophies, and perspectives imposed through slavery, Black genocides, and the violent uprooting of anything indigenous was central to our schooling.

Many young Nigerians have shared similar horrifying experiences with me. For example, a colleague told me how she failed a geography mapping exercise—she was unable to place the colonially imposed African countries on a map. Another colleague, who is blind and from one of the "minority" ethnic groups, told me that he was pushed into the arts because his school could not afford the sciences. Even in the arts, he could not learn about his heritage and was forced to assimilate into one of the three "major" Nigerian ethnic groups. Another student, involved in an anti-colonial youth leadership project I organized through Unveiling Africa, trivialized the importance of learning about her unique origin story because "these cultural ways of being are primitive and the European way is better."

To be clear, these troubling schooling experiences are not unique to Nigerian students. Students from colonized and enslaved histories across the globe—indigenous populations in Canada's own residential schools, non-European immigrants to North America, Black populations in Columbia, Sri Lanka, Ecuador, and Brazil—share similar stories. The legacy of colonialism, the logic of racism, and the architecture of our current Eurocentric socioeconomic systems must be robustly understood, explicated, and implicated in education policy, planning, and leadership. This is the *sine qua non* for reorienting education systems globally towards justice, relevance, and inclusion for all.

As an education researcher, community mobilizer, and education reform advocate, my practice has been shaped by this perspective. This has meant conducting research that reveals the contradictions and shortcomings of the education system in the lives of diverse students. With Unveiling Africa, a non-profit I founded as a 19-year-old undergraduate, I have organized programs that help young people critically reflect on their social conditions, reimagine themselves from pre-colonial times, and actively re-engage in socio-political life. The greatest challenge with this is what I call "intellectual racism"—the intentional (or unintentional) reduction of standards, simplification of education processes, erasure of history and the socioeconomic/sociopolitical context of schooling, or any other Eurocentricity in the education of youth from colonized communities. Meanwhile, in education policy for children of European descent, their complex histories and sociopolitical lives are always considered. Unveiling, calling out, and disrupting intellectual racism is extremely draining, exhausting, and dehumanizing. However, it is a pre-condition for creating a new education system that is humanizing and just; one that unleashes the boundless potential of all students.

Chizoba Imoka *has dedicated her life to unveiling the injustices in our current school system. Through her doctoral research at the Ontario Institute for Studies in Education (OISE, University of Toronto), Imoka is researching the diverse oppressive schooling experiences of Nigerian secondary school students and leading many initiatives for reform. Imoka is also the founder of Unveiling Africa (www.unveilingafrica.org), a non-profit that provides a platform for Nigerian youth to engage in community leadership and civic projects. She has received many awards including the Adrienne Clarkson Public Laureateship, Adel Sedra Distinguished Graduate Student Award, New College Senior Doctoral Fellowship, and Hancock Lecturer, amongst others. Imoka may be reached via email at c.imoka@mail.utoronto.ca.*

From Teacher to Supervisor in a Day:
Leading in Early Childhood Education

Heather Beaudin

A s is the experience of many educators, I have been working with children my whole life (otherwise the sentence reads that many educators would tell us about this author's experience). So when considering next steps after secondary school, it was no surprise that I would be studying education. Several years and several education degrees later, I work as a Registered Early Childhood Educator. Working in this role, I have held informal and formal leadership positions within different early childhood education (ECE) contexts. All of these experiences influenced my practice to varying degrees. However, my first formal leadership position, an assistant supervisor in a non-profit childcare centre, was perhaps one of my most significant experiences. Leadership within the early years profession is still evolving in terms of support systems for leaders, training programs, research, and literature. It falls considerably far behind the world of educational leadership; however, the importance of understanding leadership within this unique sector is emerging. Looking specifically at training, there is little continuity in Canada in terms of how ECE leaders are prepared for their roles and supported once in these roles. In fact, most ECE leaders move directly from working with children to leading the organization, and I was no different.

The day before I became an assistant supervisor, I was working as a preschool teacher, though I was also wearing the hat of informal leader. Reflecting first on this informal role, my leadership within our centre developed organically over time. I was an employee that often took initiative to improve our organization for children, families, and educators. This initiative—combined with an overworked, under-trained supervisor—meant that I did not go unnoticed. As I sought out areas to improve our centre, my supervisor distributed leadership opportunities.

Despite this informal experience, moving into formal leadership was still a steep, nerve-wracking learning curve. The process of moving from teacher to assistant supervisor was as simple as a Tuesday after-noon conversation with my supervisor. I remember her explaining that she was struggling with workload and that an assistant was needed and perhaps I would be interested. I recall being excited for the opportunity to lead our small staff of ten, but also surprised. I had not been in the field for long and had no direct training for this role.

Throughout my time as assistant supervisor, I encountered numer-ous roadblocks, too many to list! One immediate challenge was the new relationship dynamic between colleagues and myself. For some, I was the same person with a new title; for others, I was no longer a friend, co-worker, or equal. I was in a position of power—whether or not I had even started to execute this power was irrelevant. At the time, I struggled with this transition and did not recognize all of the power dynamics at play. A second early challenge was in simultaneously learn-ing to manage and lead. I found managing, because of my informal experience, came more easily. I was able to help balance records and staff timetables but had no idea how to help our team move towards a shared vision. With these two challenges on the forefront, I dove right in to a servant leadership approach. I needed others to see I was still like them and not above daily ECE tasks. Moreover, with little knowledge on leadership, I was more inclined to stick to what I knew—the class-room and child development.

Over time, I learned a great deal about myself and about the larger workings of an ECE organization. First, through formal leader-ship I became acutely aware of my strengths and weaknesses as a team member. For example, when I was unable to calm an irate parent who owed months of childcare fees, I realized I needed to improve my ability to navigate conflict (I still have work to do here!). Moreover, I learned that listening is more important than talking in almost all settings. Over time I learned to hear what others were communicating, which greatly improved my ability to be a supportive leader (again, still working on listening more and talking less—hard for a type A, extrovert!). Finally, I came to see that my teaching philosophy translated almost directly to my leadership philosophy. This insight made leading less intimidating, allowing me to stay grounded in what I believed to be best practices.

I have since transitioned to a new role in a different organization. However, I often reflect on my first formal leadership role. What is most enlightening is how what I initially saw as roadblocks or challenges were actually moments of significant professional learning. An insight that translates beyond leadership to many walks of life!

Heather Beaudin, Ed.D., is a Registered Early Childhood Educator in Ontario, Canada. She holds a Doctorate of Education from the University of Western Ontario and a Master of Education from Wilfrid Laurier University. She researches early educational leadership, specifically how leaders can use a distributed leadership framework to navigate organizational problems.

PART IX

In the Leader's Office:
Do You Have a Minute?

Every leader engages in leadership opportunities through a unique combination of leadership theories, integrated with life-embedded experiences. At the end of the day, middle of the day, and beginning of the day, supervisors and those being supervised rely on leaders to provide guidance and direction balancing emotional intelligence and political intelligence. There are certain questions that have the potential to give an adult pause." "Will you still love me tomorrow?" "How will I know?" "Should I stay or should I go?" "Does anybody really know what time of day it is?" "When will I be loved?" Fortunately, leaders embrace opportunities to exercise their leadership prowess. Leaders laugh in the face of danger! Unfortunately, there is one question that all leaders fear, especially at the end of a stressful week or when they are in a rush to do call it a day and head home. "Do you have a minute?" Narratives of leadership represent all emotions. With this final section, we wish to bring smiles to faces. These are the types of stories that you can't wait to share with colleagues, partners, and friends. Enjoy!

My First Days in My First Job as Principal

Jeanne Surface

M y first administrative job was as a K–12 principal in a district of 500 students. I was elated to begin and looked forward to the opportunity to lead. I stopped by to visit with the superintendent the day before I was supposed to report. He told me that a group of three parents had requested a meeting with me on my first day on the job. Being the positive person that I am, I assumed the problem could be easily solved. I was wrong. Very wrong. The parents were concerned about verbal abuse from the volleyball coaches, one in particular. They had been frustrated with the previous principal because he was a close friend of the coaches and, according to the parents, had done nothing to stop the abusive behavior. I told the parents that I would not allow the abuse to continue. What I didn't realize was that the head coach, the most verbal of the group, was a "hometown hero." He had been a long-time swimming coach and the community had likely overlooked his abusive tendencies because of his successful record.

I talked to him about the parents' concerns and made it clear that this sort of behavior would not be allowed. He responded that the parents were overprotective and those who complained had kids who were not the top athletes on the team. He accused the parents of complaining because their teenagers did not get playing time like the rest of the athletes. School started, the season continued, and so did the abusive behavior. I began documenting what I saw, and the parents continued to share their concerns. I continued to discuss the abuse with the coach and assistant coaches. About three weeks into the school year, the coach left a sticky note on my desk that said, "I resign from all of my coaching responsibilities immediately." I accepted the resignation and the athletic director made the announcement public before the coach could rescind his resignation. I discovered later that he had already resigned numerous times when the pressure was on and then rescinded the resignation after he was encouraged to keep coaching.

The volleyball team lost their match the following night. The assistant coach left the girls unattended on the bus and rode home with the head coach. He told the girls that he was quitting and that they would have to end the season because they didn't have a coach. Looking back, I should have terminated him from all coaching and teaching duties for leaving the students unsupervised. The next morning, a group of girls came into my office and threw their uniforms on my desk. I found out later that they had been told to do this by the coach. I looked at them, said "Okay," and kept on working. I'm sure they thought that their behavior would upset me.

The next day, the superintendent told me that a group of parents would be coming to the next school board meeting to support the coach who resigned. The parents demanded that the coach be reinstated but, fortunately, I had the support of the Board of Education. The parents wanted their daughters to play under an "outstanding" coach, and claimed that no one else could fill his shoes. I was not certain if I had the support of the superintendent; he didn't express his support or non-support. Finding a coach midseason was difficult, but a retired teacher and coach took the position. It was a tough season for the girls; after all, they had signed up for volleyball, not drama.

The coaches who resigned decided to start a competitive club league and the girls who quit the team became a part of that league. Interestingly, the activities of the club league consistently conflicted with school activities, such as our community night, vocal and instrumental concerts, et cetera. Our students were penalized if they missed one of these required activities. On one particularly frustrating evening, the father of one of the girls called me, concerned that his daughter was being penalized for not attending our community night because of a club league volleyball tournament. I thought that we had resolved the issue on the phone, but then he showed up at the school. I spoke to him for a few minutes but had to leave to help with activity. He followed me around the school "airing his anger." I needed to get a ladder from the custodial closet and shut the door behind me. He eventually left and the night continued. His daughter stayed for the activity.

My first principalship, and that first challenge on the first day on the job, was not what I expected. My father used to call this "baptism by fire." I learned that I needed to have a better grasp of school law so that I would have had the confidence to fire the coach who left the students unattended. It was a difficult since I bore the brunt of the anger, from both sides. I learned that I needed to imagine myself wearing a rubber raincoat and letting the anger drip off me, not soak me and weigh me down. I also needed to seek out friends and mentors to support me during tough times. Most importantly, I put the kids first, so I knew that I had made the right decision.

Jeanne L. Surface is an Associate Professor of Educational Leadership at the University of Nebraska Omaha. She has served as a rural principal in Nebraska and most recently as a superintendent in a remote rural school district in northwestern Wyoming, next to Yellowstone National Park. Her research interests are rural education and public school law. Jeanne can be contacted at jsurface@unomaha.edu.

Psychological Martial Arts for the School Administrator

Doug Dunford

A tap at the door. As the teacher entered, I could literally smell the iron tang of fear. As a school VP about 15 years ago, I had already experienced a certain amount of rock and roll, some of it entirely unpredictable. "What's up?"

The letter she showed me was from the parent of a grade 8 student, a lawyer, on his official letterhead challenging the inadequate mark his daughter had received on her science project. He intended to take unspecified legal action to right this situation. After reading the letter, I started to chuckle because of its breathtakingly blustering tone. The teacher, in her probationary year, was becoming increasingly despondent. I asked myself how I could bring her back to her normally level-headed, competent demeanor?

Completing the science project was the girl's first real effort all year. Her project highlighted information sharing only and not a clear scientific hypothesis. Yet, the project showed effort and care, and was actually completed. For encouragement, the teacher assigned a B, a much higher mark than the work merited.

My relationship with the teacher was such that I proposed the following experiment to attempt to lessen her deepening panic. I asked her to pretend that she was the student's father threatening to hit me with a baseball bat instead of a threatening letter. How might someone respond to this situation?

Option 1: We agreed that I could stand there and let her hit me with the bat. We considered how that might play out as a phone call.

"Mr. X, yes I totally agree! What was I thinking? Your daughter's science project showed so much effort and work. I will change the mark to an A.

Besides the obvious pain for the teacher in making this call, the dad might see through this thinly veiled attempt at manipulation, trumpet that the teacher had capriciously changed a mark at the slightest challenge, and phone the superintendent to complain about the lack of academic standards. The father, in this case, would be entirely correct.

Option 2: I could block the bat, which is not as hard as you might think. Once someone starts to swing, they are telegraphing their brief future movement. Stepping forward, blocking the arms holding the bat, including a disabling punch are all very doable. "Mr. X, I am so sorry you did not get the high mark you expected for the work you did on your daughter's science project. Yes we both know that you did most of the work as it was actually completed with care and on time. By the way, the project did not fulfill the clearly stated criteria in the project's assessment rubric. As teachers, we developed the project and its assessment together, including marking samples of each other's class work to ensure consistency. By the way, I have a science degree." While this call would have been, no doubt, more pleasurable to make than the first one, the superintendent would again have been involved.

Yes, there is a third option. The bat is raised and coming down. The attacker's action has a fixed trajectory. At this moment, it is possible to pivot 180 degrees on your front leg, allowing you to stand beside the attacker, as you both watch the bat coming down together. If you don't believe me, Google "yoshinkan aikido"!

Contemporary aikido, based on ancient unarmed tactics employed by the Shogan/Emperor's bodyguards, is the martial art of the Tokyo riot police. Its founder, Ueshiba—the model for Yoda in *Star Wars*—intended aikido, shared after World War II, to be a force for peace in the world. The primary intent is to avoid conflict and, if conflict is unavoidable, to use the least possible force while simultaneously protecting the aggressor. Practising aikido for several decades has taught me much about responding to psychological conflict, a major element of being a school administrator. Working toward a personal habit of continuous relaxed self-control helps set the tone for staff, students, and parents; accepting conflict as natural allows a focus on issues not personalities; and being conversational/appropriately humorous and honest under pressure are all effective de-escalation tactics.

Here is how the third option might play out. We are now standing beside the father seeing his point of view too: "Mr. Jones: I sense your deep frustration with your daughter's lack of achievement this year, and your concern about next year when she goes to high school. I encourage your continued involvement in your daughter's work. She needs the support. I gave the science project the highest mark I could. I will send home the assessment rubric; I suspect she did not share it with you."

By this time, the teacher was laughing, her confidence and courage returning. I asked if she wanted me there when she met with the dad. No need, she said. She could handle it.

Doug Dunford *is presently in his 17th year as a school administrator in the Hamilton–Wentworth District School Board, Ontario, Canada.*

"Did You See the Giant Rabbit?"

Catherine Zeisner

As an administrator, your relationship with your secretary is critical to the success and safety of your school. Never was that more important than when I was the vice-principal of a busy, beautiful, culturally diverse elementary school in London, Ontario. Our secretary was second to none and knew that I was overwhelmed. She worked hard to deflect problems from coming to my desk, but there were days when it took *both* of us to head off problems from affecting the students and the school.

I would know if I was needed to tackle a problem at the front counter by the way she would say my name or code words indicating an injury or upset parent. By the tone of her voice, I would know if I was needed right away, should approach the desk with my happy face, or come prepared for a tough battle.

One morning, she called my name in a way I had never heard before—fear and confusion—so I immediately got up from my desk to approach the counter. There was a man holding a leash. As a person scared of dogs, I had a moment of trepidation until I saw what was on the other end of the leash. I understood why our secretary's tone was new. Up popped a large, furry, long-faced creature I had never seen in real life before. The creature put its very large forearms on the desk and lifted itself up until it was over six feet tall. It took me at least five seconds to realize that the man had brought a kangaroo into the school.

What do you say to a person and their kangaroo? "Hi, can we help you *and* your kangaroo?" The man told us that he had a started a local petting zoo and wondered if we would distribute his promotional items and if he could visit classrooms with his kangaroo. While we didn't mind giving out his flyers, I didn't even know if kangaroos were allowed in school. I knew our school board had a live animal in the classroom procedure, but I was not positive if marsupials were included. I recalled perusing the document earlier in the year when a teacher wanted to keep fish in her room. It clarified the matter: "only relatively small animals which are easily confined, maintained and handled should be kept in the classroom" so a kangaroo was definitely not a suitable visitor as we also could not ensure it was in good health and free of disease.

Just as I was turning around to return to my office to retrieve a copy of the procedure, he dropped the leash, allowing the kangaroo to go free. Disaster! The kangaroo took one look around, saw the open office door, took two huge hops, and was down the hall. We froze! There was a huge, wild Australian animal in the halls of our elementary school. I peered down the hall just in time to see the kangaroo hop around the corner. What was around that corner? The library? The music room? The *students*? The man laughed as I yelled four words I didn't think I would ever say as an administrator—or in the same sentence—"Go get your kangaroo!"

As the man took off down the hall, I could see a kindergarten class walking hand-in-hand towards us. Had they seen the kangaroo? Did the kangaroo kick them? Does the kangaroo have a communicable disease? My career is over. I can see the newspaper headline now, *Macropod Attacks Kindergarteners!*

As I ran up the hall past the kindergarteners, I could see that the man had caught the kangaroo and had picked up the leash again. I assessed the students to see if anyone was hurt, upset, or scared. The man walked past us with the kangaroo and I advised him to leave the building immediately. The class continued to walk down the hall towards their classroom and everyone looked intact. As my heart rate began to slow back down, a little face looked up at me and said, "Mrs. Zeisner, did you see the giant rabbit?" I was caught completely off guard by this little tyke's question. Rabbit? You mean the dangerous, rabid beast that could have killed us all? I took a deep breath, calmed down, and said, "Yes, Ahmed, I saw the giant rabbit."

Returning to the office, I confirmed that the marsupial had left the building. Hugging our secretary, we both sighed with relief knowing the situation could have ended much differently. Seeing the petting zoo van driving away, I picked up the phone and called my husband. "You won't believe *what* came to school today!"

Dr. Catherine Zeisner *completed her Ed.D. at Western University in London, Ontario, Canada. She is an elementary school principal with the Thames Valley District School Board and an adjunct professor with Western's Faculty of Education. She is very passionate about leadership development, using the Ontario Leadership Framework, and providing authentic professional learning for current and future educators. She's afraid of dogs, not rabbits.*

Afterword

There is something very powerful about story. As a genre it rarely disappoints, and this collection of tales—an insightful exposé of what it means to lead—succeeds brilliantly. We have been invited to share vignettes of practice that provide profound insights into the leadership styles of a range of leaders in their everyday lives in a range of organizations. Cleary these stories are very meaningful to the contributors—each episode intended to provide a key message for the reader. This is how we experience the most powerful learning moments from each leader. In choosing what to share, contributors sift through their careers for the most significant leadership moments.

Here are the key lessons as I see them; you may glean different ones. The power of story means that multiple lessons are possible. These stories are real, the level of authenticity underpinning each one is powerful, their core truths are easily discernible. We are invited deep into the leadership world of the contributors—into their hearts and minds. We are asked to share real-life experiences, "warts and all" as they say. One of the strengths of this collection is that contributors didn't choose their most heroic moments to share with us. We didn't get a series of self-congratulatory "what a wonderful leader I am!" testimonials. Instead, we get moments of true insight where each leader learned something from their practice that was worth sharing.

A key achievement of the book is how clearly learners—children and young people—are so central to its core messages. So often in books about school leadership it can difficult to find the child in the narrative. The central message of "whatever you do, do it for the kids" is emphasised in this collection. The power of culturally responsive pedagogy, with students and teachers co-creating rich cross-curricular learning opportunities, posing interesting questions based on students' lived experiences, and celebrating the search for answers is strongly explicated. The collection shares success stories about children's learning, emphasizing the centrality of this as a driver of leadership.

The vignettes recounted here also contain lessons that leaders and aspiring leaders can learn much from about leadership itself, such as the need to engage deeply and personally with the development of one's own leadership identity. There are no readymade solutions for what leaders should do; each leadership path is unique. While training and mentorship are available, each person must work it out for themselves, colouring their own leadership role. This is hard work, and we are reminded that it extends from the first day on the job to the last.

The misunderstandings that can arise and the difficulties that these can cause are very honestly explored in the collection. The well-established leadership imperatives of sharing the mission, building alliances, and making sure that the leadership direction resonates with people are reaffirmed. When things go wrong, it is usually because this reaching out did not go far enough and we are reminded that schools do not exist on their own. In many of the stories, the centrality of relationship-building in the task of leading is strongly supported. There are also moments of isolation that can be painful. And though there are times when leaders might be tempted to say "bring it on, I can always fly a kite," it is not professionally responsible for leaders to walk away from a situation where they have become marginalized. Sometimes only tenacity can resolve the issue.

The many examples of bravery, courage, dedication, and strong leadership that explicate the transformative potential of education on young people's learning and lives are inspiring. When leaders use their power to challenge and reimagine worlds, they in turn are nourished and affirmed and the promise of personal and professional fulfillment is revealed. In facing our fears we invite freedom, and then the task of leadership in education reaches beyond the head to the heart. A leader must be authentic, real, open, and present in the classroom. Rhetoric must align with action because ultimately educators are only remembered for what they do, not what they say.

The achievements in the collection are significantly enhanced by the stories that focus on some of the more ineffable qualities of teaching, learning, and leading, specifically the signs and symbols that provide a powerful added dimension to the school experience for students. Finally, and perhaps most importantly, we get insight into some of the magical moments that are all too often marginalized in a field dogged by neoliberal imperatives. A school is a special place; the leaders in this collection believe this to their core. Children makes things work if we help them to create the circumstances; that is their magic—how else could they so brilliantly turn a kangaroo into a giant rabbit?

Gerry Mac Ruairc,
Cully, Sligo, Ireland

Gerry Mac Ruairc *is the Professor of Education and Head of the School of Education at the National University of Ireland, Galway. Previously to taking up this role Gerry was a teacher, School Inspector and Associate Professor in the School of Education in University College Dublin. He has published widely in the areas of leadership for inclusive schooling, language and social class, literacy as well as in the areas of leadership and school improvement for equity and social justice. He has a strong track record in the area of funded research and leadership development work including projects funded by Atlantic Philanthropies, the World Bank and Erasmus.*

About the Editors

Darrin Griffiths has worked as an educator in urban elementary schools for more than 25 years in the roles of teacher, vice-principal, and principal. He is also a Senior Lecturer at Niagara University and an in-demand conference speaker and session facilitator. Griffiths earned his Doctorate in Education from OISE/University of Toronto with a specific focus on urban school leadership and inclusion. His first book, *The Principals of Inclusion: Practical Strategies to Grow Inclusion in Urban Schools*, is used in many schools and districts as a foundational piece in the quest for genuine inclusion of all students. He has also co-authored and edited several books that relate directly to issues of equity and social justice in education. Griffiths lives with his family in Burlington, Ontario, and he is the principal of an elementary school in the Hamilton-Wentworth District School Board.

Scott Lowrey, EdD, is a former Elementary School Principal residing in Hamilton, Ontario, Canada and currently an Assistant Professor (Limited Duties) at Western University (London, Ontario). He received Canada's Outstanding Principal (COP) recognition in 2005, the inaugural year of the program, for his work on early literacy and the creation of a multigenerational continuum of community partnerships encompassing society's youngest to most senior. Scott is also an annual participant with the COP Academy (COPA) Executive Leadership Development Program (Rotman School of Management, University of Toronto). Scott holds a doctorate in Educational Administration from the Ontario Institute for Studies in Education (OISE), University of Toronto, and was nominated for the Canadian Association for the Study of Educational Administration (CASEA) Thomas B. Greenfield Dissertation Award. To relax, Scott enjoys the Stratford Shakespeare Festival and Canadian music (i.e., Trent Severn, Blue Rodeo, Lee Harvey

Osmond, Whitehorse, Gordon Lightfoot, Ian Thomas, and Kathleen Edwards). He is the co-editor, with Darrin Griffiths, of *The Principal Reader: Narratives of Experience*. Scott was inducted into McMaster University's Alumni Gallery in 2014 and received a Western University Alumni Award of Merit for Professional Achievement in 2018.

Mark Cassar graduated from the Ontario Institute for Studies in Education (OISE), University of Toronto, with his Master in Education in School Leadership. He is a dedicated Elementary Catholic School Principal, currently of St. Alphonsa Catholic Elementary School in Brampton, Ontario, Canada. Having taught various grades for some 13 years, Mark led nine schools as an administrator, the last four in the role of principal. Mark believes in the vocation of his role. He is a staunch promoter, defender, and cheerleader of Catholic Education and infuses the teachings of Jesus into his school culture at all levels. From working with his School Council, to engaging his incredible staff in professional development, to motivating his students to always demonstrate respect and "do as Jesus would do," Mark is on the cutting edge of curriculum practice and school management. Most of all, Mark believes and trusts in the relationships built around him. Collaborative leadership helps Mark to pioneer tremendous movement in the students and people he works with. Mark is known for pushing students and staff out of their comfort zones and engaging them in reflective practice, always cheering them on to be their best. His curriculum passions include helping teachers and students develop a growth mindset and love for math, along with infusing technology into learning opportunities in meaningful ways. His "kids first" approach leaves no doubt where his priorities lie. You can always find students visiting Mark's office to show him their accomplishments. Mark was nominated twice for the *Toronto Star*'s Teacher of the Year Award and he was the recipient of the 2013 Premier's Award for Teaching Excellence. Mark can be reached at <u>mark.cassar21@rogers.com.</u>